A Funny Thing Hapened on My Way Out of Church

JOHN SCHMITZ

to
Geary
Thanks
for a
wonderful
time
John Schmitz

i

All inquiries should be addressed to:

CARITAS COMMUNICATIONS

5526 West Elmhurst Drive

Mequon, WI 53092-2010

262.242.5049…VOICE

262.242.5826…FAX

DGAWLIK@WI.RR.COM…EMAIL

CONTENTS

The papacy of John XXIII and the Vatican Council brought new hope to the Church in the 1960's. Pope John convened an Ecumenical Council for the first time in nearly a century, and only the second such gathering of the bishops of the world since the 16th century when the bishops gathered at Trent to respond to the Reformation.

Pope John spoke of an "aggiornamento" – a renewal, a breath of fresh air to bring the Church in touch with the modern world. There was a great deal of anticipation when the bishops met in Rome with the best theological minds in the world as their advisors. Yet after months of deliberation, all they could agree on was to insert the name of St. Joseph in the "Canon" of the Mass and to meet again in a few years.

The second session of the Council in the 1960's heralded more significant discussions, and the documents of the Council brought expectation of wonderful things to come in the Church of Rome, changes in a Church that had not changed much since the middle ages. Hope would often turn to disappointment in the years that followed.

At the close of the Council, seminaries in this country were filled with nearly forty thousand young men aspiring to the priesthood, and new houses of study were being built. In most dioceses in the US there were adequate priests to meet the needs of the faithful and send missionaries to far off lands. Parochial schools, staffed by nuns, were crowded with children. Churches were filled with the faithful for Mass on Sunday and long lines formed at the confession box on Saturdays.

A mere decade later many of the finest priests had left the active ministry. Few in the Church had the courage to ask why, at least publicly. There was no simple answer, and perhaps the reasons are as varied and complex as the men themselves.

SCHNEIDER RIGHT / SCHMITZ LEFT: The sign to direct callers to separate entrances at the rectory in Wisconsin was accurate, theologically as well as geographically. The Church was again veering toward the conservative while many priests were hoping for a more liberal Church that could respond to the needs of the modern world. Younger and more liberal priests struggled in a Church that had the resources to respond to a modern world but were stifled by the egos and entrenchment of its leadership.

Today the American Church is facing an acute shortage of priests. Parishes are being consolidated or closed because of the shortage of priests to staff them. Seminaries stand empty or have been converted to other uses as the number of men entering the course of studies for the priesthood has plummeted.

There were studies done on the subject in the 80's and 90's, which revealed that most of those who left the active ministry did so not because of marriage, but because they did not like the work they were assigned to do or were unhappy with the conditions under which they were forced to live. They were often called upon to fill roles for which they had no adequate response in their repertoire, or they were frustrated in their efforts by a church and its leaders that were resistant to change.

For another significant group, the reason was one of honesty: their personal convictions differed from the "party line." Many disagreed with Pope Paul VI's encyclical that condemned birth control as seriously sinful, while others could not swallow the statement by the US bishops that a Catholic could not be a conscientious objector to the war in Viet Nam. Others looked at the hypocrisy of Rome's position that a divorced person who remarried lived in sin and could not be admitted to the sacraments, while at the same time "annulments" were given to those who went through the process to have their marriages declared null and void by the Church, often on grounds that were seen as accommodating. A few had personal problems of their own, most notably alcoholism and sexual abuse of parishioners, problems the Church never publicly admitted at the time, but addressed through several "retreats" around the country where a priest could go to dry out, and there were treatment centers for priests who had been found to have sexually abused members of their flock, a dark secret closely guarded. We knew these centers existed because each year around Christmas every priest in the country received an appeal for funds from several of these places and apparently the dioceses supported them financially. It seemed the Church tolerated and covered up the sexual sins of its priests. Some of us were horrified that these cases were kept quiet, often with the civil authorities bowing to Church pressure to keep the matter quiet and let the diocesan authorities deal with it. Nothing happened in most cases. Only one thing seemed to get a priest removed from his position: to fall in love with a woman and have the integrity to grace that love with marriage. At the same time the Church allowed Lutheran and Anglican clergy who converted to Catholicism to become priests and retain their spouses and families but was adamant about excluding married Catholic men from the priesthood.

Many of those who left were among the most talented and dedicated priests, respected leaders not only in the Church, but also in the communities they served. At some point each came to a decision that we could not continue serving a priest in the Church. Most were young, with the expectation of many years of service to the Church. In the single decade when the Church lost some of its finest priests and religious men and women, the numbers of seminarians and young women entering convents dwindled to a trickle and the quality seemed to diminish greatly as well. What happened?

To answer that question is difficult if not impossible. To ask the question provokes thought. We can gain some insight by examining the families and communities that nurtured those men's vocations to the religious life. We can look at the training they received, the jobs they filled, the conditions under which they lived, their goals and frustrations. Each of these men could tell a different story, but with familiar themes.

The men who left the active priesthood faced condemnation by the Church or, at best, with the proper dispensations, grudging tolerance. No one bothered to thank them for years of service. There were no farewell fetes. Most of the time their departure was done quietly, sometimes in secret, leaving parishioners wondering about what might have happened. Some were racked with guilt. Most were lost to any involvement with the institutional Church. Their families often felt betrayed and showed bitter disappointment. Many of these men were not prepared for life without the Roman collar. Their decision was painful and they took the step only when it was more painful to stay than to leave and often the wounds took years to heal, and even then left scars they will carry to their graves.

I am one of those men. What follows here is my story, my journey, lived with some tears and with laughter. My story may provide some insight to help us understand what happened in the lives of those who left the active ministry of the Church in the 60's and 70's.

Chapter One

Betrayal

My meeting with my bishop in the spring of 1970 left bitter memories. I had called his office a few weeks before asking for a personal appointment with him. His secretary called back and told me he would be available for me on a Monday afternoon and I should be at the bishop's home at 2:00 PM. It took a great deal of soul searching to make the phone call for the appointment and the two weeks before the meeting were filled with anxiety. I knew that this was a step that would change my life, and that there was no turning back. Few of the men I knew who had left the active priesthood had ever returned and those who did found their ecclesiastical careers compromised.

By all measures, I had a successful career in the priesthood, known and respected widely for my abilities, leadership, and concern for the people in the communities. I was in a position envied by many: university chaplain with my own private residence, and for the most part my own boss. At the time, many priests sought assignments that took them out of parish work where they lived under often difficult circumstances, were at the beck and call of a pastor whose qualification for the post too often was mere seniority, and their ministry was often limited to ritual functions. Yes, I had a plum position but under the surface I was unhappy. I knew that I could not stand in front of a congregation at Sunday Mass and support the Vatican position that all forms of birth control with the exception of abstinence was sinful. Even more galling was the Vatican's statement that in this matter Catholics were not allowed to follow their own consciences. It was a position that most Catholics of childbearing age mostly ignored but were burdened by guilt. My own integrity forced me to avoid the issue when I spoke publicly and skirt the issue in private discussions. On campus and in other areas of my activity I was called upon to defend the position of the Vatican and the bishops. I could not, other than to state that this was the position of Rome and the bishops. Friends of mine who had disagreed with the Vatican on the subject were harassed or called in to the Chancery office to be chastised.

Another issue was the bishops' meeting in 1969 in which they issued a statement that a Catholic could not be a conscientious objector to the Viet Nam war. It seemed I was trapped in a conservative Church that I could no longer support. It became a question of honesty. If I could not support or agree with the bishops or the Vatican, to continue would erode my personal integrity. It was difficult to come to this decision to leave the priesthood, but it would have been more painful for me to continue.

I arrived at the bishop's 1890's Flemish renaissance mansion donated to the diocese by one of the beer baron families of Milwaukee. The ornate structure has since been restored and is open as a museum today. The building was nearly lost to posterity when the diocese sold it to the Holiday Inn next door and moved the bishop to a new home in a plush suburban, lily-white neighborhood. Preservationists saved the building from the wrecking ball. However the coach house behind the mansion, which at one time housed the chancery office for the diocese, was lost.

I rang the doorbell and was admitted by the secretary to the bishop and told to wait in the entryway furnished with period furniture. I sat there in awe of the ornate carved woodwork of the building. It was a relic of the opulence of the rich nearly a century before, the kind of luxury residence one associated with the wealthy, the politicians, and the bishops who often had the houses donated to them by the wealthy benefactors. I had been in this building on one other occasion, for a meeting with the bishop and the Campus Chaplains association of which I was the president.

I had rehearsed my speech hundreds of times in my mind. I wondered what his reaction would be. Would it be condemnation? Criticism? Would he try to talk me out of it? Would he offer me any assistance? Any sympathy? What would I do afterward? How would I be able to wind down the many programs and activities that I was involved with? I was prepared with a long list of issues that had led me to this moment; the cases of sexual abuse that I was aware of and knew that the bishop was informed and had simply swept them under the sanctuary rug, transferring the priest, in some cases out of the diocese. I knew of a case where a teacher in a parish school brought the matter to the bishop; the result was that the teacher was fired. It was common knowledge among priests that if a priest got in trouble the church would twist the arms of law enforcement and judges and the matter would be hushed up. As University chaplain I was the butt of malicious slander by one of the priests in town, and when I asked the bishop to intervene, he did nothing. Another priest, an alcoholic, was shuffled from one parish to another, a problem all too common with priests. Nothing was being done to get help for his condition, but rather he was put in charge of another parish. My mind was spinning at incredible speed when the secretary came out to show me into the bishop's private office.

This was a bishop I knew well. He had ordained me nearly seven years before and performed all the "minor orders" leading to the priesthood. I had met with him on numerous occasions through programs I was involved with. He had attended my mother's funeral two years before. He always attended the funeral of a parent of one of his priests. A crazy thought entered my mind just as I was taking a seat in his office. I thought of his technique of working a crowd. He'd shake a hand or offer his bishop's ring for the person to kiss, say "hello" to the person, using his name, chat for a bit and then ask "Who's the person standing next to you?" As he moved down the line, he was sure to know the name of the next person in line. People thought he had a marvelous memory for names and faces. Those of us who'd been with him more than once or twice knew his trick. Some of us used to sabotage his ruse by giving him a blank look and tell him we didn't have the foggiest idea of the person standing next to us. We hoped he would never catch on that he'd been had and actually was forced to start a conversation without knowing the person's name. A silly thought that relieved the tension of conversation that was about to take place.

I drew a deep breath and told the bishop that I had come to a decision after long and careful consideration, and would like to resign from the active ministry as of the end of May. I explained that I was involved in a number of programs that would need my attention until that time and I would stay on the job until the end of May to complete projects and programs that would continue until then. I asked him to keep my decision in the strictest confidence for two reasons: one, I did not want to jeopardize the things I was involved with at the time and secondly, I had not yet had the opportunity to talk to my family, particularly my dad, about my decision. He should hear of it from me personally.

I didn't know what reaction to expect. I am sure that it came as a complete surprise to him that I had made this decision. While I had not hesitated to voice my concerns in the past, I had learned long ago to keep my own counsel. No one knew of my feelings or my decision.

I expected some empathy, some offer of assistance, perhaps some discussion to perhaps uncover what led me to this point and the offer of some assistance to keep me in the fold, or at least some assistance in making a transition from the priesthood to another career. What happened next can only be described as bizarre.

"John" his resonant nasal voice was unmistakable, "Each year we have to submit the names of our priests to the Catholic Directory, along with their address and assignment. How do you want them to list your name? Do you want it "leave of absence? Inactive? Or what?"

"Just omit it," I replied. I was numb. I had become nothing more than a line in a directory of priests that no one outside a handful in the Church and perhaps some fund raisers ever looked at. But he wasn't finished.

"If you are thinking of asking for a dispensation from Rome, I would encourage you to get started on that right away. They are currently taking between five and seven years to come through. You can call the chancery office for the forms to complete and they will handle the processing."

In less than fifteen minutes my life had changed irrevocably. The years of preparation in the seminary, seven years as a priest, aspirations for a lifetime of ministry all faded into a dark memory. As I pulled onto the freeway and headed back to Kenosha, my mind raced back to the retreats before ordination and the recurrent thought "What did you do now, John?" But life is a one-way street and there would be no going back. Even if I attempted to withdraw my resignation, I had compromised my future. My conversation with the bishop would be duly recorded for any future consideration. My mind was overwhelmed by the realization of how little I meant to the Church that I had given my adult life in service or preparation for that service.

I wanted to complete a number of projects I had been involved with. I felt at ease, since no one would know of my leaving until it actually happened. Sunday I would visit my dad in Fond du Lac and talk to him about it. I hoped he would understand. I worried about some of my family. But tonight I would gather with a group from one of the High School retreats I had given a few months before. Tuesday I had a two-hour class on Paul's Epistles to religion teachers from various parishes. Wednesday and Thursday I usually spent on campus. I was helping out at one of the parishes on Saturday, and preaching at all the Masses at another on Sunday morning. In between I was writing an article for a catechetical publication on how the concept of faith influenced religious education throughout history and I was working on a slide program for retreats to open a discussion on the meaning of our faith in our lives. It would be a busy week.

I was awakened Thursday morning by a phone call. It was 6:30. Who would call me at this hour of the morning? Who even knew my number?

"John?" I recognized the voice as that of a woman who had worked at St. Mary's in Fond du Lac when I was there. "What's this I hear about you?"

"Hear what?" I was still in a fog and had no idea what to expect.

"The bishop was in town last night for Confirmation, and told the priests that you were leaving the priesthood at the end of May. Is this true?"

I took a deep breath before I could respond. I never was able to analyze my reaction. Was I angry? Very! Did I feel betrayed? Absolutely. I had specifically asked the bishop to keep the matter in strictest confidence until I had time to talk to my family. It hurt. It hurt deeply: the kind of hurt that leaves its scars in one's soul and gets in the way of any respect and leaves a resolve never to be so hurt again.

I admitted that the rumor was true and asked her to keep it secret. I didn't want my family to hear the news on the gossip lines. I just hoped they would not hear the news before I got to see them on Sunday.

It didn't surprise me that the topic of priests would come up at a gathering of priests. In 1970 the topic seemed to be which priests were leaving or had left recently. Today, when there is a gathering of Catholics, the topic turns to the shortage of priests. Parishes are closing, combining and sharing one priest among several churches. Parishes that once had three or four priests. are now served by one, and an increasing number are near or beyond retirement age. Catholics are being asked to finance the building of large churches to house several combined parishes which have been closed for lack of priests to serve them.. What's happening? Why is the Church having problems attracting men to the seminary when other denominations seem to have more than enough to serve their needs?

Conservatives like to think that the problem began with the Vatican Council. While the decline became evident shortly after, there are many other factors, including failure to allow married priests in the Roman Rite. The issue is complex and the causes have roots in demographics, hierarchical structure, the job itself, management practice as well as sociology and theology.

No one thought there were problems in the 1950's when large numbers of boys, fresh out of Catholic grade schools, entered seminaries across the country. In the early 1960's many religious orders maintained a seminary in Wisconsin, along with each diocese, so the number of institutions serving young men studying for the priesthood probably numbered around twenty and enrollment was in the thousands. The Church prided itself in the numbers of seminarians. Seldom, if ever, did they examine the quality or character of the candidates.

These young men faced twelve years of preparation for ordination and some dropout was expected. While the number of priests and semi-narians peaked about the time of the Vatican Council, the number who persisted to ordination showed a marked decline well before the Council. Shortly after, the number of young men who were even willing to start that journey declined, despite the "vocation" efforts at a diocesan level, heavy advertising in newspapers and magazines and even one enterprising vocations director placing ads in Playboy Magazine. I wonder what reader response was or what the Playboy reader's reaction would be when he learned that lifelong celibacy was part of the package? Of course just looking at pictures was not as heterosexual as actual social or physical contact with a woman. He might dream without risk of rejection or commitment.

Where are the answers? In many places, in many issues. One of the first is to look at the demographics of our society. Prior to the 1950's only a handful of professionals had the prestige in the Catholic Community that was afforded the priest. Catholics in general were not the elite of society and were not as well educated as some of their Protestant neighbors. Consider that most seminarians came from small towns, farms or working class neighborhoods where there were only two visible and respected professions: priesthood and medicine. The priest was seen as a visible leader in the community, usually one of the highest educated and respected people in town. He drove a nice car, lived in a nice house at the parish and always had a place of honor at any occasion. And certainly the dream of every Catholic mother was to have a son who was a priest. It seemed that this above all merited her a high place in heaven and gave her bragging rights with her peers. Seminarians were celebrities when they came home for vacations and were paraded around to adoring aunts and uncles. In a word, it was surreal. It could not last.

But the country had changed. People moved from farms to cities and they became more educated, they learned a wider range of opportunity and careers other than serving the Church. Television brought the world into every living room and every child had to attend high school. The sheltered homes that were the incubators of vocations were no more. Working mothers widened their sphere of interest beyond the home, the parish church and parochial school. We began to look more critically at our priests and the institution of the priesthood itself. The job of the priest was no longer as attractive when there were many other roles in life that offered fulfilling careers and prestige without the baggage of lifelong celibacy and commitment to a system that allowed for little personal freedom or rewards. The Church itself changed from the center of an immigrant community to a suburban white Church on the one hand and a socially active urban Church concerned with poverty, racism and moral issues of justice on the other.

The psychological profile of the seminarians might have given a clue long before the decline became evident. For the most part, they came from conservative, sheltered families with traditional, even quaint, values and beliefs. In their homes they often played "church" as children and in the Catholic schools they received a steady dose of religion each day with Mass before school, prayers frequently during the day, and religious stories inserted into the lessons. The reading materials in the home included a share of religious publications replete with ads for various orders of priests, brothers and nuns doing God's work in some exotic mission field. While the brochures and ads featured the "All American Boy" types who were prom kings and stars on every sports team, the reality in many cases was that a number of misfits who were not good at sports, not popular with the girls or fellow students and had a dream of someday being respected and accepted.

Many wonder in retrospect what percentage of vocations were vocations of escape rather than vocations of dedication. Seminarians often came from homes where sex was a taboo subject and even a fleeting sexual thought was deserving of hellfire. Young men who had difficulty coming to grips with their own sexuality and guilt could find an honorable escape in the seminary where they would not have to deal with relating to the other gender. They sought refuge in the seminary and the celibate life as a place where they hoped to control the sexual urges they all too often carried with a heavy load of guilt and little understanding. It is little wonder that a lot of women in the Church suffered greatly at the hands of men who never matured in their ability to relate to women other than to order them around or that sexual abuse of young men not only occurred but was kept secret while the priests were allowed to continue to function. The profile of the sexual predator is often that of a person who never attained the maturity to relate to another adult in a wholesome manner.

As the percentage of children who finished high school and went on to college increased, the pedestal on which the priest stood became shorter and shorter. People now read more than religious magazines and papers. There was more to life they thought and one could gain respect, fulfillment and probably salvation in fields of endeavor other than deciding on 12 lonely years of secluded preparation for the priesthood and celibacy forever. The isolation left many with a view of the world that was at best naïve and at worst pathetically unreal.

The religious environment that gave birth to the "vocations" ought to have been examined carefully. The Church had changed little since the Reformation: the Mass was still in a foreign language that hadn't been spoken by the people for nearly a millennium. Even a large percentage of the priests barely understood it. The cult of the saints expanded to fill the void where liturgy was unintelligible and meaningless. In the major seminary, students of the 1950's and 60's, in the last years of their preparation recited aloud the rosary during Mass, as if what was going on at the altar had little relevance to the people in the pews. It was part of an environment in which the "spiritual world" was somehow not connected to the world in which we lived. Certainly many of the young men had come from parishes where the priest mumbled in some ancient language facing the back wall while the faithful mindlessly fumbled with their rosary beads or read pious prayers from their prayer books and stood, sat or knelt on cue at various parts of the Mass, usually with an acolyte ringing a bell as a signal for the people to stand or kneel or sit, which was about their only response to what was happening at the far end of the building, other than, of course, to put their donation in the basket as it came around.

There was an army of Saints who somehow had the magic way to salvation and carried on an extensive lobbying effort with the Lord. Like the medieval royalty who were surrounded by their courtiers through whom all requests were funneled to the king or lord, a court of Saints was seen as necessary to convey our petitions to the King of Kings, our God. The favorites were those whose prayers and personal devotions were copied in prayer books and printed on holy cards that were used as book markers in the prayer books. Every religious order worked to get their founder declared a Saint. It seemed that everybody came to Mass with a prayer book reciting prayers to one Saint or the other, rather than participating in the celebration of the Mass.

The reforms of the early 20th century to the liturgy were not to modernize but rather to revert back to some doctrinal or liturgical purity of some by-gone era. Pius X's initiative to restore the Mass to its pristine origins led to the reintroduction of Gregorian Chant as the music of choice. Gone were the flowery baroque compositions of Bach, Verdi, and others. Flowing vestments began to replace the brocaded "sandwich boards" and choirs learned to sing parts of the Mass in the music of the Middle Ages. It had immense historical significance and artistic beauty and did a great deal for the publishers of music but very little to validate the sentiments of the congregation.

There was also a heavy dose of left over Victorian Puritanism in the Church. The concept of God as untouchable and transcendent was at the base of the use of intermediary Saints and Mary since poor, sinful man could not possibly obtain a hearing from such a distant God. The teachings of Calvin were not without influence in the Catholic Church, particularly through the theology of Jansen in the late 19th century and there was a "guilt machine" based on the concept of man as basically flawed, born in sin and in need of constant purification and redemption. The idea was not new, having roots in the early ascetics who left the corrupt cities of the Empire and retired to caves in the desert to pray and commune with God. St. Simeon Stylites spent twenty-nine years perched naked atop a stone column in Greece in prayer and contemplation. Many of them preferred the desert to the martyrdom that awaited those who remained in Rome.

The story of Adam and Eve as taught in the schools was one of sin and not of creation. Somewhere along the line theologians forgot the text of Genesis "male and female he created them, and He saw that it was good." They concentrated rather on the fact that once Adam ate of the forbidden fruit he realized he was naked. Not to mention that the people for whom the book was written needed to protect themselves from the climate and that their enemies in Egypt and the South lived in climates where it was not necessary to be clothed, and in particular the Egyptians worshiped idols symbolized by mysterious snakes that seemed to appear without warning from their hiding places.

Somehow the connection between reproductive activity and sin loomed large in Christian theology. Biblical texts honoring the established practice of believing peoples railed against adultery and fornication. We often fail to realize that many of our reproductive practices were intertwined with rights of property and inheritance. It was as much to protect the bloodlines and remove any doubt as to the heir (it was always the oldest son) as it was about anything else. However, when this was transferred to the Greco-Roman world, among writers who were not familiar with the mores of Israel, the property and lineage aspects of the Bible were ignored but the sin connection remained.

The Manichean theology taught that man was inherently evil and sinful. Sound familiar? It was this culture that defined much of our moral doctrine with Augustine and other "Fathers" of the Church. With the rise of the monasteries, celibacy became a substitute for martyrdom as a show of dedication to the faith. There was a new generation of writers whose influence would provide the paradigm for morality in the Church well into the middle of the 20th century.

Was it their avoidance of relationship with women that brought men to join monasteries in that day? Was it escape from the responsibilities of fatherhood? Was it the only place where a medieval man could become educated and have a better life? Was it a refuge of men other than the first born who would never inherit the land or the title? Was it an escape from serfdom? Was it a bit of all of these?

To deny oneself something as basic as the natural inclination to reproduce was elevated to one of the highest virtues. The renunciation of marriage brought with it a disdain of the sexual nature of man, while virginity and chastity were considered the highest form of virtue and the lack thereof considered the most vile and base of all vices. Devotion to the Virgin Mary has been most prominent when the Church was mired in a discussion of sinfulness of anything sexual. Many of the monastics deemed sinful anything sexual that was not for the express purpose of generation of new life, including fleeting thoughts of pleasure. Of course we have ignored their primitive understanding of the physiology of reproduction. They believed that the male sperm was like a "seed" that contained the entire miniature person, which was "planted" in the womb of the woman, much like we would plant garden seeds in a container in the garden.

Most theologians until the modern era believed that the woman made no contribution to the genetics of the newborn but that she was merely the receptacle for his "seed," and thus all rights followed the male of the species since life came from him. Even God in the Christian tradition, was described as male. It is interesting that in most primitive religions the god figures were female.

The Victorian age didn't end in the Church until the 1960's. Women still wore skirts to their ankles and sleeves to their wrists. Nuns wore long, heavy habits with their heads nearly completely covered, showing no hair at all. The church was clearly a man's world and women were second rate. I always wondered why Mary Magdalene, the first person to see Christ risen from the dead and obviously one of his closest follow-ers, was somewhere along the line branded as a prostitute or evil woman who reformed her life, but remained "tainted" nonetheless. Scripture certainly does not support the view that she was a sinful woman. In fact the opposite seems to true: that she was a disciple of the Lord.

It is curious that devotions to Mary were as much a part of the Church in the mid-twentieth century as the Mass itself. Catholics were encouraged to pray their rosary during Mass rather than participate through dialog and singing. Many parishes in the 40's and 50's built grot-tos or shrines of Mary appearing to someone or another, whether to Bernadette at Lourdes or the children at Fatima. There was a grotto next to the church inviting the faithful to pray. The Redemptorist Fathers, who did many of the "parish missions," spread devotion to the "Mother of Perpetual Help" wherever they went, leaving behind an icon of Mary and weekly devotions to the "Mother of Perpetual Help" complete with prayers that dripped with sentimentality and flowery language, and songs that were equally saccharine. One song in particular was "Mother dear o pray for me..." sung to the tune of "It Came Upon a Midnight Clear." Nearly every church in the country had an altar dedicated to the Virgin Mary. At Catholic weddings the bride would place a special bouquet of flowers before the statue of Mary. It remains an irony that the Church, which had such deep devotion to Mary, would treat its own women as second-class citizens.

Publications distributed in Catholic schools touted "Mary-like" fash-ions for women and girls in which skirt lengths had to be sufficient to reach the floor when a girl knelt on the floor in front of a nun who inspected skirts on a regular basis, and sleeves were considered modest only if they reached halfway between the elbows and wrist. Women were required to wear some head coverings whenever they entered the church. The skirt lengths often posed a problem when the girls were going through their growth spurts, and the head covering entered the twilight zone of the ridiculous when a girl would place a hankie, or even a Kleenex on her head with a bobby pin so that the priest or nun would not yell at her for not having her head covered in church. Somehow a citation from St. Paul was used to require women to keep their heads covered.

There were no church buildings in Paul's time and if archeology tells us anything about womanly headgear, he was probably talking about something that resembles the Muslim woman's "burka" headgear of today, a full covering with slits for eyes only.

Paul, to be sure, was not an ardent champion of women. In fact it is a stretch to reconcile Paul's views on women with those of Christ in the gospels. Yet it was Paul who compared the love of man and woman to the bond between Christ and his church, reflecting the views of the Old Testament, especially the Canticle in which the love of God for his people is described in the beautiful intimacy between man and women.

Certainly there is much in the Bible to support that human love is good, beautiful, and indeed a sacred and wonderful thing. The roots of celibacy are many, but hardly scriptural or theological, since much of the theology at its base was at one time deemed heretical.

One wonders if the development of sexual morality would have been different if the theoreticians were involved in a beautiful, intimate sexual relationship rather than by celibate men who from adolescence had disdained any relationship with women as a threat to their own salvation. A side issue is the manner in which theologians and the Church treated women over the centuries of the male celibate priesthood.

The seminary environment before the Vatican Council certainly did little to prepare priests for the demands of their profession. The seminary was a sheltered place and the curriculum largely irrelevant to what they would be called upon to do and career expectations lacked focus at best. In their high school years and into college, the emphasis was on

Latin as preparation for the study of philosophy and theology, as well as the liturgy of the Church, which was still conducted in Latin.

The seminary of the 50's and 60's was pretty much a closed community. From the opening of the school year the men were expected to remain on campus at all times. They needed special permission to leave the grounds and had to check in and out with someone in charge of attendance. Attendance check was taken at every chapel service several times a day to make sure the man was there or he would have to explain his absence. One could understand taking attendance in their early years of formation but as they neared ordination students were in their middle twenties or older in some cases and had nearly twelve years in the seminary before ordination. They were never treated as responsible adults and all too often were mired in the immaturity of pre-adolescence with which they had entered the seminary with years before.

At St. Francis, the diocesan seminary I attended for two years of philosophy and four years of theology, silence was enforced except during recreation periods. The rector in charge considered it magnanimous that he allowed us to talk during meals. Reading material was restricted. We had no daily newspapers, secular magazines in the library were likely to have pictures of women clipped before they appeared on the racks and a particular issue might not make it to the rack at all. Mail was watched carefully so that no offensive materials made it into the sterile confines of the seminary to corrupt the minds of the "holy" seminarians. I remember a young man held back from ordination for six months because a spot check of his room uncovered one of the novels of Henry Miller and a copy of *Human Sexuality* by Havelock Ellis. He was fortunate he was not expelled completely.

Seminarians were required to wear a "cassock," a floor length black robe with rows of small buttons down the front, and a "Roman collar" along with black shoes and socks. This was to be worn at any time the young man was outside his room, with the exception of engaging in sports. It was an odd sight to see the seminarian draping his cassock over his shoulders as he headed for the latrine. For headgear he wore a "biretta," the funny looking relic of the Middle Ages with three "wings" and a tassel in the middle. This was hardly the garb that would identify a person as a male of the 20th century but the "uniform" was intended to mold behavior to what was considered appropriate according to traditions that dated back centuries.

The residence halls were quiet zones. The first night of each school year we were presented with a map of the grounds designating where talking was permitted, where congregating was allowed and where smoking was not banned. Radios, stereos, and television sets were forbidden. Rooms were inspected at the beginning of the year and there were spot checks done while we were in chapel throughout the year. I remember when a portable radio was discovered in a room and the man was expelled. Students were not allowed to visit another room and two men were discovered behind closed doors, it was grounds for expulsion.

On one occasion during the late 50's an inspector of seminaries arrived from Rome. He discovered that, due to crowding, there were two men sharing the same room. He exploded. "Unum aut tres, sed numquam duo in unum cubiculo." You can have one or three but never two men in the same room. Was this an indication that Rome was aware of the level of homosexuality among students for the priesthood? Certainly the discipline and the rules seem to say there was at least serious suspicion, since if two students were seen together frequently someone was sure to mention that such particular friendships could not be tolerated.

Given the societal intolerance at the time for all but the heterosexual lifestyle, religious life was a respectable option and placed the gay man beyond reproach and scrutiny. If a man was not attracted to women or feared such a relationship for any reason, the seminary offered an attractive alternative. He could receive the adulation of his mother and would be spared the horror of trying to relate to a young woman and spared the possibility of rejection or simply because it was not his cup of tea. As a priest he would have the respect and love of the people, something he perhaps could never have acquired from a woman, at least not without risk of rejection and would be afforded a position in society that was given because of his position as a priest, rather than something he would have to earn.

Perhaps one might examine the legalistic culture in the Church in the 20th century, mainly the product of the code of Canon Law promulgated in 1917 which ruled the Church until it was finally revised after the Vatican Council. It was designed to maintain strict discipline and control, regulating every aspect of the lives of people in the Church, particularly those who dedicated their lives to the service of that Church. Priests lived in the parish rectory with the other men assigned to the parish. In most cases it was either attached to the parish church or nearby and often nearly as closed as a cloistered monastery.

The tightly controlled environment of the seminary stunted the process of maturity that men and women experience through adolescence and young adulthood. The grist of relationships, loves won and lost, does a great deal to trim the rough edges of one's personality. This certainly did not happen in the confines of the seminary. Many reached ordination day with their maturity not much more advanced than the day they entered as adolescents many years before. Priests tended to be autocrats who lorded it over their parishes and domineered those who worked with them.

Let's examine the curriculum in the pre-Vatican II seminary. In high school and college the emphasis was on Latin to the detriment of other phases of education, other languages, science, sociology, and other things that we'd expect in a liberal arts education. In fact even mathematics was scorned by many of the students as unimportant because they'd never have to use it. If any subject was not considered "needed" for the priesthood there was no reason to include it. Little attention was given to educating the whole person with arts and sciences.

The last two years of college were devoted to philosophy as a preparation for theology. This was taught in Latin from Latin textbooks in many cases. Not only was the philosophy a rehash of 13th century Aquinas, but the student had to wrestle with translating the text as well. Seminaries espoused the belief that there was little philosophical advance since the time of Aquinas in the thirteenth century. Directives from Rome mandated that philosophy be based on the writings of Aquinas. For some reason this was deemed a pre-requisite for theology. A good liberal education would have been far better.

Our course in psychology was mainly readings of Aquinas who wrote in the 13th century, as if there had not been any progress in the study of the human mind and personality in over 700 years!

I recall Fr. Jack's lecture on the intellectual process of women, which he knew differed greatly from that of men. He emphasized they were considerably inferior to the male in their capacity for higher thinking. He argued that it was impossible for a woman to successfully study philosophy or theology and that their thinking process was far more emotional than logical or rational and they had limited ability for abstract thinking. No wonder many priests had trouble relating to women, particularly intelligent ones.

To be honest, the courses in Greek and Hebrew and archeology were helpful in the study of Scripture. One would have expected if a person was going to study theology, perhaps some study of Scripture and Church history would have been relevant as well, particularly something on the development of religious thought in the Church. There was little.

Theology was a four-year track that could probably have been done in two or less. It included tracks on Canon Law, Scripture, Church History, Dogma and Moral Theology. For the most part these classes were taught from Latin textbooks, which hardly encouraged discussion of contemporary religious thinking and moral problems. However, each class had mimeographed translations of these books though they were not always very accurate. In a couple of cases, the professor used the translation as the basis of his lectures. The sole technique of teaching was the lecture method. Classes tended to be large, with as many as a hundred in a single class. The professors, for the most part, were content to read the text, translating it if they were so disposed, but certainly in most cases not arousing any intellectual inquiry.

I remember reading a moral theology text written in the early 1900's. It was apparent that the text we were using in the 1960's was nearly identical. Were the moral problems the same in the modern world, after two world wars? Had we not progressed in medicine, business, race-relations, social justice?

Was there training for the tasks that a priest would be called on in the parish? Hardly. Part of the problem was that there was only a vague idea of the role of the priest in the parish. There was no training in behavioral psychology, counseling techniques, social issues, or even preparation for teaching, which was one of the major roles of most priests in the parish. A young priest seldom met up with a 4th century heretic, but if he did he would have answers for him, but when it came to dealing with the guilt driven neurosis of the adolescent boy, the young priest often had no clue.

A form of "Internship" for men aspiring to the priesthood would have been helpful, giving them some taste of the ministry before making a life-long commitment, as well as giving them some practical experience under supervised conditions. The Jesuits, whose priests generally worked in education, had used this philosophy for years giving their seminarians practical experience teaching in one of their schools or working on one of their missions before ordination.

Even something as vital to ministry as good public speaking was relegated to the lowliest professor on the pecking order. It generally consisted of class members giving speeches to their classmates, perhaps with a little critique and later sermons on religious topics. It would have been far better if we had received drama coaching and voice training. However, the prevailing thought was that purity of doctrine was important and that the delivery be secondary. It was just part of the Mass which fulfilled the Sunday obligation of the faithful. Each priest in our diocese received a "sermon outline" at the beginning of each year that mandated what the priest should cover in each Sunday sermon.

Upon ordination in the 50's and 60's, few priests were as well educated as graduates of other colleges. Their education was limited to a narrow field that did little to prepare them for effective ministry. Their people skills in all too many cases were sorely lacking. Too often they had not attained the maturity appropriate to their positions.

What were the career expectations of the priest ordained in the 50's and 60's? In most urban dioceses, there was a surplus of priests. Seminarians from larger dioceses would have to wait at least twenty years before they could be considered for a pastorate under the seniority system in place. So the seminarians from larger diocese often transferred to smaller diocese around the country where they could expect to have a pastorate within a few years. Usually they would select a rural or semi-rural diocese where they were not likely to encounter urban social problems as well.

At best, a young priest in a large diocese would spend many years as an assistant to an older pastor, subject in the hierarchy system to every whim and wish of the senior man in charge. In Milwaukee one of the requirements of ordination was a pledge to abstain from alcohol for five years after ordination. Sacramental wine, of course, was excluded but only during Mass. Most of the young priests simply ignored their pledge. It was the diocese response to serious alcohol problems among the priests and it did little to solve them. There was a curfew for assistant pastors set at 11:00 PM, regardless of their age and many of them were in their 40's.

Most parishes had a "live in housekeeper" often a sister or relative of the pastor or a single woman who had been his housekeeper for many years. Some of the women were domineering, protective of the pastor and left little room in their lives for thoughts of other priests living under the same roof. The parish did not compensate these women well and certainly did not provide them with any semblance of job security or retirement. They had to be protective of their jobs and status since they served at the good will of the pastor and in some cases the relationship was more than simple domestic service. Few of them had job skills that would afford them the status or good employment outside the rectory.

One troubling aspect of rectory life was that the young priest really had no place to call his own. He was allotted one or two rooms, usually sharing a bathroom with others and had no place to entertain visitors or friends. At St. Mary's, my first assignment, none of us entertained friends at the rectory other than our fellow priests. The rectory was considered a semi-cloistered area. The arrangement was nearly monastic in most parishes. The house was the domain of the pastor and his housekeeper. Junior associates were tolerated at best. If they were not compliant, they generally were reassigned the next time the deck was shuffled.

This certainly did not sit well with many of the younger priests. Among seminarians the trouble assignments were well known. Priests who had been assigned to a particular parish in prior years talked to friends in the seminary and apprised them of the situation. There were parishes that received a new assistant each year and seldom did one stay there longer than two years. Of course the tyrannical pastor was under the impression that the bishop sent him new priests every year because he was considered outstanding in training the new charges, imparting the discipline needed in the priesthood. In reality he often ruined them for life.

The Assistant Pastor's duties were totally dependent on what the pastor trusted him to do or wanted him to do. In some cases this was limited to celebrating the early Mass every day, two Masses on Sunday, and confessions on Saturday afternoon and evening. Generally the youngest priests were given charge of programs for children and teenagers whether or not they had any talents in dealing with children or adolescents. It was common for pastors to reserve even routine functions to themselves. This preserved control and gave him some aura of importance to his position. For example, he might insist on personally enrolling any new member of the parish or he might reserve to himself setting a date for a wedding. If there were secretarial functions, and few of the parishes had secretaries, the youngest priest was given the task, such as keeping the parish registries for Baptisms or typing and printing the weekly bulletin, answering the doorbell or telephone, counting the Sunday collections and the like.

The result was disillusion of a percentage of priests in the late 60's who had hoped that the Vatican Council would bring about sweeping changes that would bring meaning into their lives, bring some focus to their ministry and give them renewal in their careers. Many saw only emptiness in the mechanical ministry they were asked to perform, they were sort of attendants at the "spiritual filling station" that was the local parish church. There was a growing percentage of Catholics whose attendance at church functions was limited to Baptisms, marriages and funerals.

Change in the Church has often been slow and unpredictable. Vatican II ended and the only thing accomplished in the eyes of many was that the bishops agreed that Catholics could now eat meat on Friday without committing a sin. Since by agreement with Rome centuries before the Spanish speaking countries were not bound by the law, the only notable difference was in the Friday diets of some western Catholics. In the years after the second session of the Council, the changes came slowly and had to be authorized by the bishop in each diocese. The lot of the young priest changed little.

In one of the memorable discussions in the Vatican Council, when the subject of the vernacular for the Mass and religious rites was discussed, the argument was made that the laity could not understand their services since they were in a language none of them understood. Cardinal Bocci, one of the conservatives of the Vatican Curia responded simply "Teach them Latin."

English Masses were celebrated in many dioceses a few years before they were allowed in others. The changes came slowly and unevenly and many of the changes, particularly the early ones in the liturgy, were hardly an improvement. Just mere translation of the words of the Mass from Latin to English didn't quite make it, since in many cases the translations were poor and the music was lacking in artistry when compared with the beauty of the Gregorian chants and the musical lore of great composers. In some cases there were attempts to set English translations to the Gregorian melodies. It didn't work.

While the changes began working their way through the bureaucracy there was a widespread backlash from Rome to the local parish. Rome, noting that thinkers began to challenge long-held beliefs, became threatened. Theologians in the past were free to study and explore as long as they came to the same conclusions that were held by the theologians of the Vatican. Now they began to challenge traditional positions, and many were reprimanded by the watchdogs of the Vatican. In the US, there were the social issues of racial equality and involvement in the Viet Nam War. The "old guard" was for the most part racist and branded any priest who called attention to the injustice of segregation, discrimination and prejudice as a "liberal" or radical. The truth was the conservatives were often afraid to take a position on racial or social issues lest collections from the conservative parish members would drop and the parish might have problems paying its bills, particularly the heavy debt that many of them carried for building schools and churches.

There was little change in the domestic situations of most priests. The pastors still were lords of the manor and the young assistants lived in near poverty with few rights other than a Christian burial, which some of them were not quite confident would be available when their time came. Progress in Milwaukee lagged behind other cities around the country. There were many reasons. The younger priests were eager for change and this was perceived as a challenge to authority and upsetting to the laity. It was a time of social change in the city, with younger priests involved in the civil rights movement, speaking out for racial and social justice. Fr. Groppi in Milwaukee, assigned to an inner city parish, got involved in confronting the city for its segregated housing and led activists and parish members on marches through neighborhoods demanding that the city pass ordinances making discrimination on the basis of race illegal. Many priests (and parishioners) in conservative suburban parishes were vocal in condemnation of the civil rights movement. Our bishops were known to be on the conservative and cautious side and officials on the diocesan level jealously guarded their positions of power. Despite the official pronouncements on social issues, the Catholic Church lagged behind the rest of society in issues of justice, racial equality and freedom.

Impatience with the slow crawl of change was hard to reconcile with a rapidly changing world and pressing demands for action. Impatience soon turned to unhappiness with their priestly roles. Whether consciously or not, there was some reluctance by a young priest to persuade a young man to follow in his footsteps. Despite some feeble efforts on the diocesan level, the enrollment in the seminary dropped dramatically. The role of the young priest had lost its appeal to the idealism of youth.

Another result of the Vatican Council was that the Church was willing to grant dispensation to priests so they would be allowed to leave the active ministry and remain in the good graces of the Church and even marry. Note that the diocesan priests never actually took a vow of celibacy; it was simply a Church law that when a man was ordained to the first of the "major" orders, the sub-diaconate, he came under the Church law of mandatory celibacy for life. Pope John Paul II put an end to this practice of granting individual dispensations for some reason, probably to stem the mass exit. The application process for dispensations was uneven from diocese to diocese. The petition began at a diocesan level, and was forwarded to Rome. Some dioceses were quick to forward the paperwork to Rome and the young men were allowed their dispensations promptly. Other dioceses took the position that they would slow the process down as much as possible to discourage others from following. One could, in one diocese, have it all done within a few months, while a few miles away the process could take years. There were many who did not bother with the dispensation, feeling that if their diocese could arbitrarily delay forwarding it to Rome for years, it certainly could not be a question of one's immortal soul.

One priest I knew was determined to do everything "by the book" and waited seven years before his dispensation was granted. He continued to recite the prayers of the Divine Office according to dictates of Church law until the day his dispensation was received. The cost? The woman he married was now beyond the years when they could consider having a family. It was a steep price to have some bureaucrat in the Church sit on his petition. Another man told me of the inquisition he was subjected to at the diocesan level in which the diocesan official quizzed him on personal aspects of his life, including grilling for considerable length on the frequency and manner in which he masturbated. I wondered if such prurient interest had any theological or biblical basis or merely reflected the twisted mind of the inquisitor. In one of the most bizarre cases, the diocesan authorities offered to put the young priest's love up in a nearby hotel so they could have sex, and then offered a considerable amount of money to the woman to relocate and not see the young priest again.

There were many reasons why men left the active ministry. Marriage is often cited but one has to dig far deeper to get at some of the root problems. One issue seldom discussed is that of loneliness. Loneliness is not simply a question of coping with life without companionship but mainly trying to deal with life's and career challenges without the necessary tools or skills. We all need the support of significant other persons in our lives, to be a sounding board, for encouragement, to take a "life-compass" reading, to authenticate our experiences and fill the gaps between them. Unfortunately for many, these support systems were simply not in place. Few priests were prepared for the changing roles in a changing world. Their education was certainly lacking. There was no help in most rectories and it seemed the more talented, the more socially attuned, the more willing to accept the challenge of leadership, the more lonely the priest became.

Loneliness had been a problem ignored for centuries. It is nothing new. Priests had tried to cope with it in many ways. One strategy was to eventually close off emotions, to become an autocrat who ruled his flock as the lord of the manor. Others took to drink. The problem of alcoholism among priests had been ignored for years, though there were "retreat houses" strategically placed around the country where priests would go to dry out. The percentage of priests with severe drinking problems was much higher than that of the general population. Some estimates placed it at nearly 50%. Drinking was condoned, with the problem priest frequently moving from parish to parish, though most were closet drinkers and not known to many outside the closest circle to be a problem drinker. Another common coping technique was to simply "go along to get along." Don't rock the boat and the Church will take care of you. While these men survived, they were by no means agents of change that the Church desperately needed. They tended to be the followers and not the leaders. A theme often repeated in the seminary was "come weal or woe, our status is quo."

Another reason for priests asking to be relieved of their duties was simply that they had changed, whether through social awareness, education or personal growth, and the church they were called upon to serve did not. Put simply, they no longer fit, much like the person in a marriage who makes significant strides in education or personal growth finds he or she has outgrown a partner who has stagnated, or even regressed. In this category we lost some of the brightest and most charismatic leaders of a generation of priests. I once had a cartoon in my files of an army rushing off over the horizon in a cloud of dust. Way behind came a soldier carrying a banner. The caption was "Wait for me, I'm your leader." This was painfully true of many young priests who saw the world and the Church in a period of growth and change, while the pastors and bishops lagged behind.

For a large percentage the reason was simply that they no longer liked what they were doing or being under control of people they could not respect, and for an almost equal percentage, could no longer tolerate the conditions they were forced to live under in the parish rectories.

The finances of a young priest's life were meager. He was allotted "room and board" as long as he lived and ate at the parish house, so he had no worries about food or housing. During the 50's and 60's, his salary was fixed at $50 per month. He would receive Mass stipends, which for a "Low Mass" was $1 and for a "High Mass" which included some singing it was $5. At best his stipends would amount to something less than a hundred dollars a month. Diocesan priests kidded their counterparts in religious orders who had taken a vow of poverty: "You order priests take a vow of poverty, but we diocesan priests are the ones who keep it." It might have been funny if it were not painfully true.

Stipends or offerings from weddings, funerals, and Baptisms belonged by Canon Law to the pastor of the parish, and most of them did not share with the younger priests even if the younger priest did all the work.

There was a general feeling among priests that the reason they said daily Mass was merely to earn the stipend. In monasteries around the country, there were altars in just about every niche in the church where on a daily basis each priest would say his Mass, often with no one else present for the celebration. At the seminary there were altars placed at various niches near or inside the chapel where the faculty would say their private Mass each day. During the summers the seminary was the site for priests' retreats for a few weeks, and every altar would be used by priests scrambling to say their daily Mass. Party line was that the ritual was for purely religious reasons, but the motivation probably included some financial incentive as well, or simply this was the way things were done and nobody seemed to question it. In reality, given the paltry salaries, they needed every dollar they could get to merely survive.

At one time priests would say several Masses each day merely to receive the stipends, sort of a piece-work incentive. Church law later limited the priest to one Mass per day except on Sundays and Holydays. As a special treat, a priest was allowed to receive three stipends on Christmas if he were to say three Masses. Was this what Christ had in mind when at the Last Supper he bid his disciples to "do this in memory of me"?

Some of the parishes had a tradition of giving cash gifts to their priests at Christmas and in many cases this was all that kept them out of destitution. Of course, more prominent members of the parish were more likely to give a larger amount to the pastor who was more likely to be there beyond the next time priestly assignments were posted. The amount of these gifts depended on the financial status of the parish. Obviously a priest assigned to an affluent parish could expect to receive more than one assigned to a working class neighborhood or an inner city one.

From his meager income, the young priest was expected to provide his own car, clothing, entertainment, books, pay for his health care, and make donations to charity. He was also expected to repay the diocese for his seminary tuition during the four years of theology and to contribute to the priests' retirement fund. Expected contribution to these exceeded our annual incomes.

There was a retirement and disability fund, but it was woefully inadequate. If a priest had health problems he was at the mercy of the local Catholic Hospital and one of the doctors of the parish. The parishes for the most part did not provide health insurance during the 50's and 60's. Most priests who did retire either did so as chaplains of one of the Catholic old age homes or lived with relatives who cared for them. They could never retire on what the Church provided for them. There were no provisions made for priests who left the active ministry after many years of service. Religious organizations are exempt from the pension legislation that protects workers in the secular world. Priests who had served many years left with nothing, in some cases not even receiving their own personal contributions.

When priests read the pronouncements of the popes on justice and a fair wage for a day's work, they were painfully aware that the last bastion of holdouts against a decent wage was the Church itself. Priests were poorly paid and if this is a measure of how they were valued by the diocese and the hierarchy, it certainly showed. The nuns who taught in the schools fared even worse in most cases. They may have lived in a convent that cost a lot of money to build but what they had to spend on their personal needs was indeed abysmal. Most of the small salaries they were paid went to their superiors to be used for support and maintenance of the motherhouse, the elderly and the young nuns in their formative training. They received only a paltry allowance to meet their own expenses. It was simply a law of supply and demand. As long as the supply of new priests and nuns continued, they would be treated and compensated little better than the lowliest of menial servants.

Slightly better were the lay teachers in the schools and other parish employees. The janitor generally was paid more than the lay teachers in the school. While this has changed somewhat, the wages paid by religious institutions severely lag behind what is the normal pay for services rendered. Did someone edit the words of Christ "A laborer is worth his hire"?

Another area that is seldom explored is that the Church's Canon Law, promulgated in 1917, and mainly written by a young aristocratic priest named Pacelli, who later became Pope Pius XII, created a vertical power structure in the Church. Authority emanated from the Vatican, through the local bishops, through the pastors and on down to the lowest ranks of subordinates. By some divine mandate, all one had to do to attain sanctity was to obey the person above on the organizational chart of the Church. In analysis, it was designed to consolidate absolute power in the Vatican. Many young priests could not compromise their values or integrity in the name of obedience.

So the problem has many facets. Sociologically, young men found other careers attractive, particularly since the admission ticket was not bought with lifelong celibacy, which the majority of the laity sensed was not necessary to begin with. Demographically, there was a shift in Catholic population from the working class and farm families to a more middle class and suburban affluent group, which had never been a fertile ground for vocations to the religious life. And with the baby boom winding down, there were fewer of them. Education certainly played a part, as the young were more educated they began to see the shortcomings of their local priests, and had visions of a life that was better than they saw in the rectories. Not the least was the lives of the priests themselves. If the young priests in the parish were unhappy in their lot, it certainly showed, and they would not be convincing in encouraging a young man to begin the journey through the seminary if the priest did not feel his own life was worth the effort.

Certainly the personnel practices of the Church had a great deal to do not only with the number who left the active ministry but also in the decline of candidates who sought to begin their studies. The seniority system that ignored ability was flawed and everybody knew it. People in the parishes tolerated abusive or incompetent pastors much more than they should have. The arbitrary assignment of young priests without consideration to their wishes or talents certainly had to weigh heavily in both retention and attraction. Twelve years of study and another twenty years of internship as an assistant was simply not a strong motivator. During the 60's and early 70's many priests scrambled for positions that took them out of parish work until they had attained enough seniority for a pastoral assignment, whether this was on the faculty of one of the Catholic High Schools, chaplain of an old age home, hospital or any other position that provided escape from the submissive role of the assistant pastor in a parish. Unfortunately when these priests finally were assigned as pastors, they had spent years away from the pastoral ministry of a parish and were seldom effective in parish ministry.

Those who survived to gain the seniority needed for the pastorate often carried with them years of baggage of frustration and often abuse of years serving as assistant to the elder pastor. By this time, their frame of reference and role model for the pastoral practice was distorted by unhappy experience of several decades. Now at long last, he would be on the end giving orders rather than taking them. Many became autocrats themselves, lording it over their younger charges and replicating the pastors they loathed while they served under them.

Finally, the role of priesthood itself as practiced in the 60's was hardly a fulfilling career. Was he the attendant at a "spiritual filling station" where people came to Mass, received Communion? Were the interminable hours in the confessional listening to non-sins helpful in people's lives? Was there some magic that he was missing? Did he really spend all the years in the seminary to be trained to answer the phone and doorbell at the rectory? To coach a grade school basketball team or drive a school bus? Was it the role of the priest to count the Sunday collection? What was it that a priest was ordained to do? Was it to recite the psalms and prayers of the Divine Office each day? That hardly required ordination. Were there any objectives, any goals? Or was it as many cynics quipped, a matter of keeping your mouth shut, your shoes shined and your hair combed. Fortunately, or unfortunately, those who followed that line constitute much of the remnant of the ordination classes of the 60's.

I remember being at a meeting with our archbishop at which the area religious education coordinators asked for some full time personnel to head up the CCD program to implement religious education for children who were not in the parish schools. His first thought was that we were asking for a priest to be assigned to the task, which wasn't the case at all. But the first words out of his mouth were: "John, I'd like to assign somebody to help with that full time but we have a problem with all the priests who have left." Big mouth me, I replied, "Your Excellency, your problem is not with the priests who have left, your problem is with those who have not left. " I remember him taking a deep breath and sighing, "You might have something there, John." I was sure I did.

Since many priests who left the active ministry in the 60's and 70's married, the assumption was that marriage was the main reason for their decision. However, research has debunked this as an over simplification. The reasons are as complex and varied as the priests themselves.

In the early church, celibacy was not required. Some of the Apostles were married. The gospels speak of Peter's mother-in-law. Paul's advice to Timothy, on the qualities of a bishop, mentions that he be married but once. As the Apostles spread the gospel throughout the Greco-Roman world, the local churches established their own traditions. Some of the early popes were married. The "Eastern" churches never required celibacy as a condition for ordination, a tradition held to the present day. The argument can be made that the proscription did not come from the bible or theology, but was an accommodation to the feudal system as a means of keeping church lands in control of the noble families.

The Essenes, among the Jews, practiced celibacy in their time in the desert. But it was never formalized or considered a permanent state. Eunuchs are mentioned in the Bible, and apparently this was the lot of some who served the temples or the harems of the kings. Monasteries in the Middle Ages required celibacy. It was something of a carry over from the monks who went off to live in solitude and pray in the desert in centuries before as well as a practical matter given the living arrangements

The Church in the Middle Ages was an economic force. The monasteries and the cathedrals had Church lands with peasants and serfs attached to the lands. After the prince, the most powerful person in the land was the bishop of the cathedral or the abbot of the monastery in which the monks were bound by their "vow of stability" to serve their masters much like the serfs were attached to the land. With noble families the oldest son inherited the title and the lands while the second son was usually pressed into the service of the Church as the bishop or abbot of the monastery to retain control of church lands and the family would often impose celibacy on the bishop or abbot. Obviously if the bishop married into another noble family the succession and control of Church lands could be in question. The prince wanted to retain the right to name the bishop or the head of the monastery. The issue was control.

The practice of the Eastern Traditions remained unchanged. In the

Roman tradition its acceptance seems to have been less than universal. Certainly there was no great outcry when Martin Luther took a wife and the faithful of England were not scandalized when the bishops under Henry VIII married. But when the bishops met after the Reformation at the city of Trent near the Swiss border their posture was clearly defensive. They met to redefine not only Catholic doctrine, but also to affirm the discipline and authority of Rome. This included a steadfast adherence to the practice of celibacy. Since the main power bases loyal to Rome were the religious orders in Italy, France and Spain whose monks had already espoused celibacy, there was not much discussion. The matter would not be considered for another three hundred years.

Vatican II broke on the scene like the early rays of the sun following a dark and gloomy night of centuries that followed the Council of Trent. For the first time in centuries the bishops gathered in Rome to examine the practice and discipline of the Church and make changes needed to make the Church relevant to modern life. They met a century before at the first Vatican Council but their scope was limited and all they agreed upon was to declare that the Pope is infallible in matters of faith and morals when speaking "ex cathedra" as head of the Church and then they quickly left Rome while the forces of Garibaldi marched on the city. Some historians state that much of the Vatican's motivation for the infallibility issue resulted from Pius IX's declaration that Mary was conceived without sin as an article of faith. Many theologians questioned that decision and the tenuous theological arguments to support it.

Among the issues thought to be under consideration at Vatican II was the practice of celibate only priests in the Roman rite. Along with the change in meatless Friday, Lenten fasts, and the Latin Mass with the priest facing the back wall of the church with his back to the people, many expected the bishops to consider and approve married priests. In this they were disappointed. One wonders what effect this had on the seminarians and young priest who "hung in there" in expectation of a change. One can only imagine what might have happened if the Council had given blanket permission to all current priests to take wives!

It is interesting to note that the Church has welcomed and ordained numerous Protestant ministers and Episcopal priests since the Council, even though they were married and had families, and they are allowed to continue their married state. Rome has been willing to accommodate the married clergy of other persuasions who wish "cross the Tiber" to become Catholic and join the ranks of its priests but clings to a celibate only male priesthood for its own members.

Is there a solid reason for celibacy other than "this is the way we have done it since the 13th century?" Certainly there is no scriptural basis or solid theological basis. Another reason cited is that "without the burden of a family a priest can more fully dedicate himself to the work of the Lord." However the celibate is also without the support and encouragement a loving spouse can provide, ennobling the character rather than diminishing it.

The burden of loneliness is often debilitating. Either because of assignment or the priests he lived with, a priest often found he had no one to share his life, his joys, his fears, and no one to support him in his disappointments or to soften the rough edges of his personality. Spiritual writers advised that he turn to prayer, and so rather than reaching out to the solace of another human being he became more isolated and lonely than before but may have felt he was doing right by praying. Catholics who have known young priests as vivacious and energetic are often surprised to meet them years later and see a broken, sullen man who is more interested in self-preservation than in self-sacrifice.

It is interesting that about the only thing that a man can do that certainly disqualifies him from priesthood in the Roman rite is to fall in love with a woman and have that love solemnized in marriage. There is great theological and biblical support that the love between man and woman is the most noble and sacred of human actions. If so, why does Rome stubbornly cling to the tradition, even in the face of serious shortage of priests to minister to the faithful? One can understand the defensive posture of the Council of Trent after losing the loyalty of much of Europe during the Reformation.

Is there a reason to persist today? Particularly, one wonders how well it is observed throughout the world. Certainly anyone who takes a position to eliminate it would incur severe condemnation from the Vatican. However priests from Europe, as well as those who served in other areas of the globe will admit that it is not uncommon for a priest to have a mistress either discretely or in some cases rather openly. Many cultures do not respect a man who does not have a woman and look with suspicion on any man who is without a woman. Even in America, priests have generally been somewhat discreet about their womanizing, but it is not uncommon, and generally causes little stir.

Sexual abuse of children and adolescents by priests had long been swept under the ecclesiastical carpet. Often the priest was simply transferred to another assignment, or allowed to leave town quietly, and the civil authorities were only too happy to have the problem solved without adverse publicity. Clergy of all faiths were afforded some special immunity by law enforcement. People looked up to them as paragons of virtue, and police and judges were hesitant to punish them for their misdeeds. In the last quarter of the 20th century, this changed dramatically. No longer were civil authorities willing to ignore the problem, and while not admitting there was a problem, the Church paid out millions in out-of-court settlements to men who had been abused by their priests as young lads. In many cases the predators violated dozens of children before finally called to task. Was there any indication this might happen? What are the roots of the problem?

Many of the priests ordained in this country until the last few decades entered the seminary after the eighth grade in their local parish school. They were just barely entering puberty and adolescence when they were removed from their families and placed in a boarding school with other boys and taught by men. Their inter-gender experiences were pre-adolescent in many cases. Seminaries steered clear of any meaningful sex education as probable occasion of sin for the young men. The isolated environment was not conducive to developing healthy adult sexuality.

I recall many instances during my days in the seminary receiving less than subtle approaches by other men in the seminary. I quickly filed the information in my memory and was sure not to be alone with that person. My instincts were quite good, as many of these very men have been in trouble for homosexuality or pedophilia. (There is no convincing evidence that homosexuality and pedophilia are connected.) It was no big secret among the seminarians, or priests for that matter, that there was a problem with priests and sex. Years later men I had known in the seminary are now willing to talk about their suspicions and incidents that they had knowledge of at the time.

The percentage of homosexuals among the Catholic priests is considerably greater than in the general population. This is understandable since those with strong attraction to women are not as likely to survive to ordination. Yet the subject was never addressed directly in our training. I suspect there was a fear that knowledge of sexual things would be a source of temptation in an environment where even a fleeting sexual thought was considered a mortal sin. A number of men ordained in May were already in trouble before the summer was over. A classmate was ousted from his first assignment for making advances on altar boys within a month of his arrival at his first assignment. We never heard from him again. Interestingly enough is that, two years prior, another newly ordained was ousted from the same parish for the same reason.

It is interesting that during my first year at St. Francis Seminary, we were subjected to several days of psychological testing during Holy Week. It was an annual ritual for the first year philosophy students. We were never informed of the results of the testing and we had no idea of whether these were used in the screening process. If there were serious problems, they were either ignored or not revealed through the testing. At least there were not wholesale dismissals as a result of them. I often wondered why they waited until a man had completed most of the years of preparation before anyone questioned his psychological fitness. I am not aware that the data collected was used in any way to alter the curriculum to prepare the men for the ministry.

Combined with serious drinking problems that were also a priestly epidemic, the sexual aberrations of priests were a formula for disaster. Yet these were two problems that the Church of the 20th century found difficult to admit or to face. It is only when cases of pedophilia hit the front pages of the daily newspaper that the Church admits there is a problem, yet Rome has been loathe to admit the scope of the problem or to offer any remedy. Bishops would routinely reassign a priest when complaints arose, often several times, or he might be sent to a "retreat house" for rehabilitation either from a drinking problem or sexual violations. The laity were seldom if ever privy to the existence of these institutions. The manner in which each diocese responded to allegations of sexual abuse is nearly identical in every diocese where the matter has been examined. Apparently the paradigm for dealing with pedophilia was a secret directive from the Vatican, the secrecy, the pay-off to victims, reassignment of priests accused. It was all too similar to be accidental.

Hans Kung, one of the leading theologians of Vatican II raises the question of whether the decree of Vatican I back in 1870 that the pope is infallible makes it nearly impossible for the Church to modify its stance on anything. Papal infallibility has meant a Roman stubbornness in adhering to a position whether tenable or not. With worldwide shortage of priests an increasing number of Catholics are finding Sunday Mass and Eucharist unavailable in their parish communities. As the shortage grows, parishes will be consolidated or closed, and the faithful will be without regular services of the priest, or regular Eucharist. If the partial answer lies in married priests, is celibacy more important than sacrament? Is celibacy, which is not biblical, not theological in its foundation, not Apostolic in its roots nor universally applied even in the Church of Rome, more important than the central event of the church, namely Eucharist?

There are many upright men who would meet the qualifications of Paul's letter to Timothy who could be excellent, dedicated priests. When the pre-requisite is celibacy, the pool of candidates is greatly reduced. Are we compensating for this small pool of potential priests? Accepting some who would not have been approved in the past, some with serious psychological problems? Misfits? Are we attracting those who have problems dealing with their own sexuality and relationships to people of the opposite sex, men who have successfully repressed one of the most powerful human drives and emotions. Does priesthood provide a safe haven of respectability that would not be afforded in society otherwise?

Another factor is the issue of power from the Vatican down to the local bishop of the diocese, even to the pastor of the parish who has assistants under his authority. If one examines the Code of Canon Law promulgated in 1917 the model of the layered structure of authority was not democracy but rather the "benign monarchy" model espoused by medieval theologians based on their observations of the only government they knew at the time, the feudal system. It was far easier to maintain discipline and control over the lives of the priest if there was no spouse or family to be taken into the equation. For most of the twentieth century American Church this meant all the diocesan priests lived in parish supplied housing, under the control of the pastor, and often with only paltry income apart from housing and food.

Is there hope for a change? Of course we never abandon hope, but this is not one of the issues that one can expect will be resolved quickly.

Bishops the world over are hand-picked by Rome and certainly one of the factors is that the bishop hold views that are consistent with those of Rome and the majority of other bishops who represent positions far more conservative than the faithful in general.

The entire model is one of control, and seldom in history has a religious hierarchy been willing to relinquish whatever control they have over the believers. This remains true of the Catholic leaders from the local bishops all the way to the Vatican. Any change would mean a loss of power and control.

Is it all bad? Some think that in the past eras of priestly surplus the Church did not wisely use its manpower. Some served as little more than glorified parish secretaries, teachers, bus drivers and activity coordinators, handling tasks for which they were not always well suited or trained but were available simply because there were enough priests to fill whatever needs were perceived in the parishes. Many of the activities priests did in the past did not require the powers of ordination.

What are the trends? Certainly a greater participation of the laity in the operation of the parish as well as diocesan programs has been productive. Administrative functions, which few priests were prepared to perform well, are now handled by parish councils of laity. Many time-consuming activities such as the long hours in the confessional are for the most part a thing of the past. Gone too are the hours the priest spent saying his "breviary" – the prayers once chanted by monks in medieval abbeys and monasteries. Parts of these contained writings about the lives of the saint of the day that were more fiction than reality - pious garbage, but garbage nonetheless.

If there is hope it is that the role of the priest has changed. Still the vision of what the role of the priest should be is fuzzy indeed. Is it to be the " uniformed attendant at the spiritual filling station" that the local parish represents? Is it the "change agent" who works for social change, or change in the lives of his flock? Is it teacher? Is it administrator of programs? Is it one who presides at the rites of passage in life – baptism to celebrate life and acceptance into the family of believers, the sharing of life in Eucharist, celebration of love in marriage, or presiding over closure to life at funerals? Is it the role of priesthood to baptize, marry and bury? Is it putting on a good show on Sundays? Maybe part of the problem is that nobody seems to have a clear view of what exactly it is that a priest does, or should do, except to be celibate.

Despite the long years of schooling, the level of education of most priests left a lot to be desired. What did the young priest know upon ordination that would serve him well in his pastoral duties? Was it doctrine? For most the knowledge of the tenets of their faith was shallow and dogmatic. It followed a tradition of terse statements of doctrinal "correctness" that was the key to salvation, rather than living understanding and application of these beliefs to their daily lives. The "Catechism" that they learned in the parochial schools in its simple memorized statements constituted their working knowledge of their faith for the most part.

The training in moral matters was probably even more inadequate. A wag once said that Moses came down from the mountain with ten commandments, but that the Catholic Church recognized only two: the sixth and ninth. Seminary training decreed that even to think of anything sexual was sinful, such as thinking of the naked body of a woman other than your married spouse. All sexual transgressions were mortally sinful and would condemn one to hell. Teaching this in the parish schools and in confessional certainly led to a great deal of scrupulosity, particularly in those who were not quite playing with a full deck.

I always found it interesting that "de sexto" – the moral theology of sexuality, was reserved for the last year of our studies and taught by the Rector of the seminary himself. The textbook we used could only have been written by a celibate, who had no clue what he was talking about. We spent an entire class studying whether it was morally permissible for a couple to engage in penetration but with no pleasurable movement and withdrawing without ejaculation. The operative phrase was that there was no movement to give pleasure. Once you had experienced sexual pleasure, you had to complete the act and pregnancy must be a possible effect with no interference or it was mortally sinful. Even sexual foreplay required that intercourse be completed or it was mortally sinful. Unfortunately the entire course on sexuality dealt with finding sin in every aspect of human reproduction rather than on the most beautiful and wonderful of human experience, the love between man and woman. Sexuality and sin seemed to have been merged in the minds of Catholic moralists from top to bottom. Even today if a woman goes to the Vatican she would be turned back by the Swiss Guards if she is wearing shorts and would not be allowed in if she is wearing a sleeveless dress or without head covering. Does the Pope have a problem that he needs to be protected?

Apart from strident views on sexuality, few priests had any understanding of ethical issues in much of the rest of life. What was the morality of racism? In the 60's many respectable priests were certain that it was all right to keep "those people" in the inner city where they belonged. Business ethics were nearly unheard of, probably because the wealthy were generally benefactors of the parish and ought not be disturbed lest their contributions might be lessened. No one addressed the issues of greed at the expense of the exploited. What is more shocking is that no one was bothered by the narrow view of ethics either.

I remember preaching a sermon on hypocrisy and social conscience one Sunday, and I opened with the phrase

Mr. Business went to Church

He Never Missed a Sunday

But Mr. Business went to hell

For what he did on Monday."

Needless to say, it created quite a stir and was probably one of my most remembered homilies. I think I got the point across.

Counseling skills are valuable to the clergy but the priests were seldom if ever trained in these skills. There was a course on "Ascetics" – a hodgepodge of esoteric examination of mystics who lived long ago and far away. We were trained in Canon Law to know that there were certain sins that we could not forgive without special permission of the bishop, but we never received a single lecture on how to deal with the problems that their parishioners dealt with on a daily basis.

How does a celibate priest counsel a couple who have problems with sexual adjustment? What advice do you give to a woman whose children are being sexually abused by their father or mother's live in boyfriend? How do you console a family at the death of a child? or spouse? We were not prepared to do this. And tragically, prior to the 70's, Catholics were more likely to turn to their parish priests with their problems than go somewhere else. And the priests performed badly in most cases.

For example, if a teenager became pregnant she was usually shuffled off to a "home for unwed mothers." where she would be separated from the support of her family, have her baby and give the child up for adoption. The priests and Catholic Social Services would arrange for this, and in many cases paid for her care. But did anyone think about the young woman? Did anyone ask her if she would like to keep the child she carried for nine months, her own flesh and blood? Of course this would bring shame to the family and the priest would bring pressure to bear on the young woman to give the child up. We did no counseling of the young woman afterward and all too often she carried the trauma with her through life.

The alternative was the "hurry up marriage" in which one mistake was compounded by another, and given the Church's prohibition of divorce, many miserable lives that followed were little more than Church sanctioned shotgun marriages, done in the interest of the "respectability" of the family name.

With the heavy dose of religious exercises, daily Mass, rosary, meditation and devotions, there was a great emphasis on the spiritual formation of the priest to be. Yet in the inter-action with the members of the church and community, the pastoral skills required were not the same as those learned by attending Mass or fingering the beads of the rosary. Effective ministry required leadership skills, social skills, counseling ability, as well as effective communication and management skills.

In retrospect, the seminary trained us to go through the mechanics of the various rituals of the Church, from the Mass through the rest of the sacraments and blessings, without giving much thought to anything other than if the ritual was performed according to the script. We were schooled in being compliant and to mindlessly obey whatever authority was placed above us as if that authority was not only infallible but all-knowing and ever choosing the best course of action for us to follow.

Above all, we soon learned to go along and get along, not make any waves, and never rock the boat.

The role we were called upon to perform in the ministry was far different from that envisioned in the seminary curriculum we received. While the demands varied from parish to parish and even within the parish assignments, we were expected to do many things for which we had absolutely no preparation in our educational or experiential repertoire or had to deal with pastors who longed for the good old days of their youth when the priest ruled supreme in his parish and his authority was never called into question. Bungling and frustration were constant companions in the ministry. The romantic notions that attracted many to the seminary as teenagers faded into reality. It was difficult if not impossible to encourage a young man to begin the long journey to ordination for the priest who was himself unhappy with his lot.

Chapter Two

The Clerical State

In Biblical times there was a clergy class, the Pharisees and the priestly tribe of Levi. From a cursory reading of the gospels, they were not the favorites of Jesus. When he chose his apostles they were common folk, a couple of fishermen and a tax collector, to name a few. They were part timers, as evidenced by Peter going fishing even after the events of Calvary. Paul prided himself as a tent maker, a worker missionary we might call him today. In his letter to Timothy on the qualities of a bishop, he states that he have but one wife, not be a drunkard, be gentle and peaceful and not have a love of money.

Apparently the leaders or priests of the early Church were ordinary Christians who assumed positions of leadership. There is some evidence that not all these "presbyters" were male. While records of the early Church are sketchy, there seemed to have been an enhancement of the priestly caste in subsequent centuries but certainly there was nothing of the priestly caste of the modern Church.

Martyrdom was often a way of life for many early Christians. Persecution of one religious group by another has been more the rule than the exception in history. While all religions embrace tolerance in their tenets, that only applies if the other parties agree with its theological positions. Persecutions seemed to give vitality to the early Church. During this time and later there were men who fled the city to the countryside to reflect and pray. We refer to them as the "desert fathers"

– the early monks who saw their retreat as something of a replacement for martyrdom, which many Christians faced with persecutions in the cities. The idea of going off to the desert was not new. The Jewish Essenes, John the Baptist, and Jesus himself spent time in the desert. The desert fathers represented one thread in the fabric of the Church in their denial of the world around them. Certainly the monastic traditions have their roots firmly in the desert.

The monks took vows of poverty, chastity, obedience and stability. They were in reality the serfs of the abbey or the monastery. They owned nothing, and were tied to the land like serfs were to the nobles.

Monastic communities are ancient as well, with establishments at the foot of Mt. Sinai, Mt. Carmel, and European sites at Cluny and Monte Casino. Modern discoveries seem to indicate that the Essenes lived in a monastic community on the shores of the Dead Sea even centuries before the birth of Christ.

They were centers of prayer and contemplation and of study and learning Ancient libraries preserved there are some of the main links to the traditions of the past. There it was that a monk learned to read and write and perhaps copied manuscripts by hand. Writings and music composed by medieval monks became part of the worship tradition, hymns, musical compositions, poetry and the nocturnes of the Divine Office celebrated in the monastic communities. Of no small import was the onus of prayer for the benefactor and protector of the monastery the prince or king. Monks typically would rise before dawn to recite or chant the first "hours" of the divine office.

A development later in Europe was the expansion of church lands attached to the monasteries and later to the cathedrals. The monks raised their own crops and provided their own food. The owner of the land had serfs attached to the land serving the lord of the manor, or in the case of the church lands, the abbot of the monastery or bishop of the cathedral. One can see the inter-twining of cathedral and monastery: the shadow of many great cathedrals falls on the ruins of the abbey that often pre-existed the great churches. The Church was a powerful landowner, with slaves and serfs.

The noble families and the Church were intertwined in the Western Church. The oldest son inherited the title, while the second son was often chosen for an ecclesiastical career as bishop or abbot. The arrangement was one of control of wealth, influence and the lands of the Church within the noble families. Both the prince and the bishop were deemed to rule by "divine right." While celibacy was not the general rule for bishops and clergy, it was often imposed on the bishop or abbot lest control of church lands would fall outside the noble family. Marriages were generally arranged by the families, not rising out of the love of the parties involved, but to forge alliances to control their holdings and perhaps expand their influence.

A great surge forward in the influence of the monastery was the creation of the universities in the late Middle Ages in the 12th and 13th centuries. The revival of learning began with the Palatine school under Alcuin and Charlemagne. Another source of resurgence came from Spain where the writings of ancient Greeks preserved by Arabic and Jewish scholars, were translated into Latin and taught in the schools of Europe. This spurred the inquiring minds of Aquinas, Dominic, Scotus and others. They applied the principles of Aristotle and Plato to their Christian faith, compiling their efforts in "Summa's" or systematic compilations of Christian thought. The golden age of the Renaissance, the thirteenth century, was the high water mark of scholarship, art and spirituality in the medieval world. In Italy Marco Polo returned from the Orient with fantastic tales that stirred the imagination and trades of Europe, introducing exotic spices, fine silks and tales of a land far away where there were people who were unknown to Europeans.

The invention of the printing press in the 15th century brought dramatic change. Books could be reproduced more quickly and cheaply than ever before, and knowledge that had been confined to the monasteries on mountaintops became widely dispersed. The monopoly of the monks on learning gradually waned.

The explorations of Henry the Navigator and other Portuguese and Spanish sailors down the coast of Africa seemed to have changed little except that there was now a great land mass south of Europe and a sea route to the Orient. Considering the navigational tools available, some of these voyages are quite remarkable. The compass was still rudimentary, with most navigation done by the stars. However once you sailed into the southern half of the planet, the sky at night was as foreign as the lands beneath. There was no means to accurately measure longitude until the invention of the spring clock centuries later. While writers in ancient Egypt and Greece posed the theory that the earth was not flat as generally held, but was indeed round, ships and instruments needed for extend voyages simply did not exist and sailors were content to follow the shorelines of the continents.

The daring voyage of Columbus was a great leap forward for the expansion of European culture and influence and it ushered in changes in the role of the Church. Though Columbus went to his grave thinking he had discovered a new route to the East, the explorers who followed discovered a native population that was soon exploited. Along with the conquistadors were the missionaries, anxious to "save" the savages by introducing the Catholic faith throughout the lands and islands settled by the Spanish. These were the same clergy who were products of the Inquisition and not noted for their tolerance. They believed that Baptism, even if forced, was desirable since it saved the person from and eternity in hell. For most of the five hundred years of Christianity in the New World, a large portion of the priests and hierarchy were imported from elsewhere into Latin America, either from Europe of the United States.

When the scholarly Martin Luther posted his "theses" on the castle church door in Wittenberg, he was seeking debate of legitimate theological inquiry. Part of the debate centered on the practice of "indulgences" - prayers and good works to obtain remission of some of the retribution due to sins forgiven by a loving God who was still thought to extract some last measure of purification before the final reward in heaven. Among the good works were contributions to the building of St. Peter's in Rome: preachers scoured the German countryside soliciting funds and offering "indulgences" in return for donations.

The most notorious was a Dominican monk named Tetzel, whose preaching included a heavy dose of guilt and the promise of release from punishment in exchange for generous donations. In return for their donations, the faithful could free their departed relatives and friends from purgatory, that temporary place of suffering and purification between death and the time when a person was worthy of being admitted to the presence of God in heaven. Clearly Tetzel's mission was to raise money, and his most memorable line was "When the sound of gold in the kettle clinks, then the soul to heaven springs." It didn't sit well with many north of the Alps who saw it as another form of taxation by the Pope to build a magnificent monument in Rome, which was costing far more than the earliest estimates. While Luther had no intent to split with Rome and considered himself a Catholic until his last breath, the event touched off a rift that has been with us since. Like many religious splits in history, both sides went their separate ways, confident that theirs was the only correct one and that God was on their side.

Tetzel, to be sure, was not well liked, and Luther's challenge to debate took on added dimensions. First of all, it struck at the financial foundation of the Church of Rome. The Papal States at the time consisted of the middle section of the Italian peninsula, and the Pope had his armies, collected taxes, held serfs and peasants who tilled the land. Luther challenged the collection of funds under the guise of spiritual benefit as espoused by Rome and preached by Tetzel and others.

The entire matter might have been confined to a theological debate in the university except the German Princes saw an opportunity to wrest control of church lands from Rome and bring them more firmly under their own hand. There was more politics and economics involved than generally written about on both sides of the argument. When Henry VIII broke with Rome, one of his acts was to abolish the abbeys in England, thus wresting power from the Church and concentrating it in the crown.

What happened in the 16th century was a religious upheaval that would split the Church and have a ripple effect long into the future. The effect was theological and disciplinary. Other theologians in Europe, encouraged by the developments in Germany, challenged other areas of commonly accepted thinking by theologians loyal to Rome.

While the monks of the universities brought systematic order to theological thought, they also changed the concept of what it meant to be a Christian from the life-experience paradigm to one of dogmatic correctness. The heresy battles of the early Church defined the parameters of belief, but it was the medieval schools of theology that gave it a more intellectual framework. In each of the challenges, the Church reacted with Councils to clarify what the Christian community believed.

The revolt spread and challenged Rome in nearly every area north of the Alps. The reaction was not only a clarification but a firm resolve of the bishops who gathered in Council in the city of Trent in the 16th century to chart the course of the Church for the future. The main edicts of the Council, apart from the wholesale condemnation of those who did not agree were threefold.

First, the Mass was "frozen" in its current form in what became known as the "Tridentine Mass," after the Council of Trent. Latin was to be the language of the liturgy in contrast to Luther and the English scholars who translated the Bible into the vernacular and worshiped in their own tongue. From the Council of Trent to the second Vatican Council, there was no change. One could attend Mass in Mexico, Rome, or Chicago, and the only thing that changed was the accent of the priest celebrating it.

Medieval theologians taught that the essence of the Mass was the words of consecration said by the priest. Participation or even understanding by the faithful was unnecessary. The Mass was the "great mystery," a sacred rite. Conducting the Mass in Latin at a time when the language was no longer used by common people added a certain aura to that mystery. It was the ritual purity and correctness of doctrine that were important, not the participation or enrichment of the faithful.

The second accomplishment was the publication of a "Catechism" of the Council, which in terse statements defined the doctrine of the Church from beginning to end. This was to be the basis of all Catholic teaching from that time forward. If one compares the catechism of the Council to the one published by the American bishops who met in Baltimore in the latter half of the 19th century, they are nearly identical in content. A great premium was placed on doctrinal purity and correctness as the way to salvation. Anyone who questioned or disagreed was promptly censured. The watchdogs of Rome kept a vigilant eye on publications by religious scholars from that time forward.

Books on religious topics became subject to the bishop's "Imprimatur" - let it be printed after it had been scrutinized by a theologian in the diocese who gave his "nihil obstat" – there is nothing objectionable. The Vatican instituted an "Index of Forbidden Books," that were forbidden to Catholics under the pain of mortal sin. Included in these were theological books that did not conform to the conservative views of Rome and a number of works that were considered a bit too ribald for the faithful who might be led into sins of the flesh. Many political works found their way into the Index, including many of the works surrounding the French Revolution as well as the works by Machiavelli.

The stagnation of religious thought continued in the Church until well into the 20th century. Studies of archeology, comparative history and ancient documents were stifled because they led one to inquire into the authenticity of the Scriptures as the literal inspired word of God or challenged the teachings widely held by Catholic scholars of the past. From Galileo who was condemned for teaching that the earth actually circled the sun to the findings of Darwin that the creatures of the earth were not fashioned by the hand of God exactly as we find them today, scholarship was stifled and often condemned.

The third area of the Council's influence was disciplinary. Celibacy was reaffirmed and the training program established for priests was gradually formalized and brought under the direct control of Rome. Seminaries took the place of monasteries and universities as centers of formation for future priests. Their education was to be grounded in the philosophy and theology of the 13th century scholastics. Eventually seminary curriculum and environment were established throughout the world. Rome realized that to maintain its position of authority it needed to maintain disciplinary control over its priests and laity. The publication of the Code of Canon Law in 1917 was perhaps the apex of Vatican control.

The faith that was transported with the explorers and settlers to the new world after the Council reflected the vision of the Church and the feudal system of much of Europe at the time. The popular image of the missionary with the cross Christianizing savage tribes is probably a glamorized version of history not borne out by the facts. For example the missions of California were military outposts and work-stations in which the natives were held in servitude much like the peasants or serfs of Europe. There were some 300,000 natives in California when the first mission was established. A century later there were only about 30,000.

Slavery was not limited to African imports but had been prevalent with native populations before. Europe still had serfdom and peasants were still attached to the land until well into the 19th century in some countries. Entire native populations were wiped out by diseases, for which they had no immunity, while being "converted." There were missionaries with Pizarro and Cortez while they looted the native civilizations to enrich the nobles of Spain. In all this, the missionary spirit was born and would live for centuries, not only in Latin America, but also among the immigrants of North America, Africa, and the lands of the Pacific. The missionaries were more than innocent bystanders to the plunder and enslavement of the natives in the New World by the Spanish.

However the priests who served the immigrants of North America were somewhat different. The French brought their missionaries with ideals similar to the Spanish, to convert the heathen to the Christian faith. They met with limited success and a few met their deaths at the hands of natives in Canada and New York. Gradually the natives who remained were forced west and their place taken by immigrants from Europe.

Maryland was founded by English Catholics no longer welcome in England. Immigrants from other countries who sought religious freedom, Pilgrims, Quakers or whatever group was out of favor at the time came seeking a new life in a new world soon followed in other colonies. It is interesting that the colonists who came here to escape intolerance were hardly tolerant of one another's beliefs. When the Founding Fathers wrote the constitution they needed to insert an amendment that the government shall not establish a state religion.

Similar to the Spanish lands, the early American priests were Europeans from Germany, Italy and other lands whose Catholics settled in America. They brought with them the traditions of Europe. The clergy were given places of honor alongside the nobility. Some, like Marquette, were explorers as intent on exploration as on pastoral ministry. There were itinerant preachers who traveled from one group of Catholics to the next baptizing, hearing confessions, performing marriages and celebrating Mass at any place that was convenient and available. These priests generally followed the ethnic settlements of their own language.

The older parishes in many towns in Wisconsin have an ethnic origin as Polish, German, French, Italian or whatever. Often they were supported by benefactors from the old country, who in many cases paid for the construction of churches and convents and sent priests and nuns to serve their kinsmen who had emigrated to a new land.

Most immigrants were not well-educated people and their new homes in the wilderness afforded little opportunity for schooling beyond the basic necessities of reading, writing and simple arithmetic. The priests in these settlements were usually the most educated persons and were highly respected for their knowledge, leadership and position in the community. Many were talented men in fields other than theology. They were builders, designers, explorers, educators and arbitrators of disputes. The authority of the priest was nearly absolute in his own parish. There was a period of "lay trusteeism" in which conflicts arose between the bishops, the priests and the lay boards of the parishes who were the actual officers of the parish and could hire and fire the priests at will, held title to the property and control of the finances of the parish. This was changed so that the bishop, another diocesan official called the "vicar general," and the pastor were three of the five officers on the board of every parish, with two lay trustees holding the other votes. But conflicts arose nonetheless. While there may be some value to being beyond the reach of disputing factions in a parish, the structure put the pastor beyond accountability in all too many cases.

This was particularly true of the pastors who were "monsignors" – an honorary title bestowed by the Pope on the nomination by the bishop and usually given to a priest who had distinguished himself as leader of a large and successful parish, or who held an important office in the diocese. These priests were then deemed to be "members of the papal household," and could not be transferred or removed from a parish against their will without the permission of Rome. They were seldom moved, despite how they performed. It was a standing joke that one of these Monsignors told the bishop that he could not be removed from the parish against his consent because he was a Monsignor. The bishop is reputed to have replied: " I may not be able to remove you, but I could send you an assistant pastor who will break your heart."

One had to remember that the parish structure, as well as the hierarchy of the church was not designed on a model of participatory governance but rather on the model where position gave privilege by some divine right to serve for life, and that the peasants and serfs (people) served the needs of the lord and did not question the will of the master. Such was the case in many parishes. Certainly Canon Law, as promulgated in 1917 as the law of the Catholic Church, was structured on an authoritarian model with a vertical structure emanating down from the Vatican to the local pastors.

Quite a number of parishes had a history of being placed under "interdict" by the bishop over a dispute between the priest and the parish. Interdict was the most severe penalty imposed on a parish. It deprived them of the services of a priest and closed their parish church. This happened at St. Mary's in Fond du Lac during the 1800's when the Capuchin fathers from nearby Mt. Calvary got themselves appointed as pastors of the parish. A dispute rose over who would get the collections, the Capuchins or the parish. Police were stationed for a while during Mass on Sundays to keep the feuding factions apart. The bishop finally closed the parish and the dissidents formed a parish two blocks away, moving together two houses that served as a temporary Church. It operated for about a year before the bishop appointed a new pastor and reopened St. Mary's.

Conversations with older priests and laity, who lived through the "good old days," were filled with stories of the abuse of power by the priests in the parishes. While surely many of the immigrant priests were caring and saintly men, there were those who irritated members with their lack of tack and gruff manners and often sharp tongues. They became the role models for the authoritarian pastors who followed. It's fair to say that not every priest was up to the demands of the position. In addition to performing all the religious functions of the parish he was in charge of a school, cemetery, several parish organizations, the physical buildings, finances, often including a building program or onerous debts. It seemed that most Catholic parishes were strapped for cash throughout their existence. Catholics were not known for their generosity, partially because most of them were not people of means themselves and with big families did not have a great deal of income that was not already committed to the necessities of life.

The priestly influence extended into many areas of daily life. People came to the priest to have their religious articles such as a prayer book or rosary blessed. He was called upon to bless the homes of his people either when they were built or when they changed ownership. He had authority to grant dispensations from the Church rules that banned meat on Friday, work on Sundays and fasting during lent. Since all children were expected to attend Catholic Schools the permission of the priest was required to attend a public school, even college, and you could be sure that a stern lecture would be given before the dispensation.

The Church thrived on guilt that spewed out from the pulpit, in the parish school and in the confessional as a means of controlling the lives of the faithful. It was insidious and permeated the church from top to bottom. Priests made the congregation feel guilty and fearful of God's wrath and then offered to remove that guilt through confession, attendance at Sunday Mass and reciting certain prayers which had been approved by the Church as special "indulgences" to remove the retribution due to sin.

During the 60's the guilt machine began breaking down. One factor was the Vatican Council, which after centuries relaxed some of the rules that did not meet modern life. People could now eat meat on Fridays, relaxing a rule made in the 1500's and they no longer had to fast from midnight to receive Communion, the Lenten fast was trimmed down. Many of the faithful wondered what happened now to all those people who went to hell because they ate a hot dog on a Friday, or needed to take a glass of water in the morning before receiving Communion. Few if any realized that many of these practices rose out of necessity or custom some time in the distant past. For example, the Lenten fast had its roots in trying to conserve precious stores of food that were sure to run out before the new harvest, and meatless Fridays probably had its roots in the scarcity of meat in the diet of people in the past and was an effort to stretch supplies. During the 1960's, with changes coming out of the Vatican Council, people began to question the church's position on other matters as well.

Another factor in the breakdown of the guilt machine was that the faithful were better educated, read more and came in contact with more people of different religious persuasions who were good citizens, moral people but who had different views on certain questions of morality, particularly in the area of birth control, divorce and remarriage. They also began to see the inadequacy of the outdated morality of the Church in dealing with larger issues in society, such as discrimination, business fraud, environmental pollution, exploitation of workers and a wide range of medical ethical questions. They began to look for their moral beacons in places other than the local parish priests. They also noted that the Church was selective in the parts of Biblical morality they would adhere to and which to ignore. It really came down to what was acceptable at any particular time in the culture and mores of the people. Few religious leaders have had the courage to disturb the comfort of their parishioners when it will lessen the donations on the plate.

The growth of psychology and studies of sexual behavior shed an entirely new light on sexuality and morality. People began to wonder if it was really true that a fleeting sexual thought or look would condemn one to hell for all eternity or if every act that brought physical pleasure outside the marriage bed destroyed one's favor with an all loving God who created man and women with all their pleasurable parts. They began to question whether a celibate could really understand the complexities and needs of a healthy marital relationship. With spousal and child abuse finally being recognized, they questioned the Church's position on divorce and re-marriage. Was it right for a 25-year-old woman with children who left her husband because of beatings to have to spend her entire remaining life without the companionship and support of a loving spouse? Was this what God intended? Or was it based on the property rights of ancient peoples? Or was current practice rooted in cultural mores or survival necessities? It was not such a hardship when life expectancy was less than forty years, but when a 25 year old could expect to live another fifty years, was it the same thing? Yet Church law required that she get a special "dispensation" to even file for a separation or divorce and re-marriage was out of the question. However, re-marriage was allowed if a divorced person of another faith converted to the Church and married a Catholic.

One need only look at the parish church during the time when confessions are being heard today. Only a few bother to receive the sacrament, whereas in the early 60's the lines would be long, particularly around the holidays of Christmas and Easter. I'm not convinced that the Catholics of today are less moral than they were then. I suspect they carry less guilt around with them and their teenage boys and menopausal women are better able to cope with life without the burdens piled on them in confessional.

With the breakdown of the guilt machine, the power of the priestly caste waned. As young men no longer flocked to the seminaries, and the number of priests decreased, so did the power of the imperial priesthood. Parish Councils were now consulted on matters of parish ministry, expanding the role of the parish into areas of the lives of the parishioners in a role of service rather than mandates and controls. As priests aged they no longer had an ample supply of young assistants to do their bidding. The pastor often found himself alone with a large parish that once had three or four priests In smaller parishes he found himself charged with as many as three churches. He had to parcel his time and share many of the temporal duties of the parishes with the laity.

The struggle goes on. Some with a conservative point of view long for the good old days of the priestly caste and some bishops jealously guard their positions as one of divine right rather than a call to service of the people of the Church. But there is a crack in the monolith and one can only surmise what will happen in the next fifty years. There are times when the words of Marie Antoinette seem appropriate. When the starving poor in Paris cried out "Give us bread," she replied: "let them eat cake." When the people of the Church, facing a severe shortage of priests cry out "We want the Mass and Eucharist" what will be the response? Will it be consistent with the belief that Eucharist is central to the Catholic Community? Or will they continue to say: "let them have celibacy?"

While each of the men who began their journey towards ordination and beyond could tell a different story, there are some similarities among them. They are stories of family background, education in Catholic Schools and Seminaries, the power structure of the church, the impact of celibacy both in limiting the pool of potential candidates as well as affecting the quality. The story of each of us touches the jobs we were asked to do, often without the training needed, the conditions under which we were expected to live, the way the young priest was valued by the Church. There are many twists and turns in the road for everyone who has stumbled down this path, often with many painful steps along the way. Often the glance backward brings a certain sadness of what might have been. What might have been had the Church not lost a generation of its brightest and most capable priests, or its dedicated nuns who were the backbone of the parochial schools?

My personal saga begins with the small rural Catholic area in Wisconsin where the towns were named after the Catholic churches that were not only the biggest buildings in town, standing on the highest hill, but dominated the lives of the people as well. All of us to some extent are products of our environment. My home, my family, the rural community I lived in during my childhood certainly directly influenced my aspirations and ideals. I was born in what is called the "Holy Land."

Chapter Three

The Holy Land

Located among the hills east of Lake Winnebago in east central Wisconsin, the name is derived from the fact that all the towns are named after the Catholic Church that dominates the skyline — towns like St. Peter, Mt. Calvary, St. Cloud, Johnsburg (St. John's), Marytown, St. Joe, St. Anna, Charlesburg (St. Charles). The area was settled almost exclusively by German Catholic immigrants in the last half of the 19th century.

The first Europeans in the area were probably the French Canadians, who with Jean Nicolet established an outpost at Fort Howard, later named Green Bay. There is evidence that Marquette and Joliet skirted the area in their historic trip up the Fox and down the Wisconsin into the Mississippi. However, early settlements in the state centered on Fort Howard in the east and the lead mining areas of southwestern Wisconsin.

The lead mining area of the southwest part of the state was established early in the 19th century, particularly after the Blackhawk War. John Jacob Astor's company established a fur trading post in Prairie du Chien, the Villa Louis mansion in Cassville remains from its glory days. With the water routes of the Fox and Wisconsin, there was another important stopping point where the two rivers came within a mile of each other, a geographical fact that helped name the town: Portage. Wisconsin at one time built a barge canal between the two rivers, but by the time it was completed the railroad came through and the canal quickly fell into disrepair. Before the railroad, there was considerable canoe traffic on the rivers, and this included early exploration of Lake Winnebago and its shores.

The Italian Dominican priest, Samuel Mazzuchelli, who labored among the lead miners in the southwest, traveled through the area before heading to the lead miners. In his "Memoirs of a Missionary" he noted his visit to the Indians camped on Lake Winnebago to spear sturgeon. He wrote how they built their huts over a hole in the ice and dangled an ear of corn or a carved decoy in the clear water to lure the fish, spearing the ancient looking creature as it came to investigate, not much different from the tactics of the fishermen today.

The Native Americans lived in the lands along the East Shore of the lake. I remember Dad's farm had two steep gravel cones on the "back forty." We always referred to them as the "Indian Mounds" but they were actually glacial deposits of gravel and sand. Dad talked about finding arrowheads when he plowed the fields around them. In the 1950's when the hills were mined for gravel several skeletons were uncovered, and I am sure that some of them ended in the gravel crusher and are spread on a roadbed somewhere. It is a pity that the site was not explored as it was apparently a sacred place and had some archeological significance. When the Abler's, who farmed the land to the west, were digging foundations for a new shed, they also uncovered some remains.

A trading post was established at Fond du Lac in the 1820's and the first permanent home was built in 1836. Naturally the water route was over the lake and an overland route along the east shore, since there were no major streams or bodies of water to cross as there are west of the lake. The mid-point in the journey from Green Bay and Fond du Lac was an area that came to be known as Calumet. After the Indian lands east of the Fox River and Lake Winnebago, south to the mouth of the Milwaukee River were ceded to the government in the 1830's the government was selling land for a stated price of $1.25 per acre, and land speculators like Governor James Doty quickly laid claim to extensive tracts east of Lake Winnebago from Green Bay to Fond du Lac.

Early records mention Calumetville and Pipe, as well as an Indian settlements at Brothertown and Stockbridge as the halfway points from Green Bay to Fond du Lac on the overland route.

The first "Holylanders" were German farmers who came to the area in the early 1840's. They established a school and built a church dedicated to St. John the Baptist. The town became known as Johnsburg. The registry of the parish for baptisms, marriages and funerals recorded not only the names of the children and parents, but also their "kries" or district of origin in Germany. Most came from the area along the Mosel River in the area of Trier and Koblenz. No one knows why they came, but the period was one of political and religious turmoil in Europe.

We are able to trace most of the families of my ancestors on both sides, to a small area of Germany in the Saar area, in the area that abuts France, Luxemburg and Belgium. After the defeat of Napoleon, who had over-run the area in the early 19th century, the area was dominated by Lutheran Prussia. Perhaps the combination of political unrest, religious strife and hope of a better life brought them to a new land.

One of the first roads in the area was a military road from then Fort Howard (Green Bay), through the state to Prairie du Chien on the Mississippi. Streets in Fond du Lac and in Green Bay still bear the name Military Road. A railroad was built from Fond du Lac to Sheboygan in 1869 and linked several towns in the Holy Land. There were stops at Peebles, Silica, Malone, Calvary Station and St. Cloud. Passenger service was discontinued some time before World War II, but freight service continued until the early 1950's. The scars of the right of way are visible in a few places, particularly the cuts through hills just behind Dad's farm.

Two things were important to the settlers: their German heritage and their Catholic faith. We used to joke that "the fastest thing on two wheels was an Irish Protestant riding through the Holy Land on a bicycle." The people spoke German in their homes and learned their prayers and catechism in German. Sunday sermons were in German; in fact, German sermons were the norm in the parishes even after World War II. Any priest assigned to the area had better know how to hear confessions in German. Even into the 1960's, a great number of the people were bi-lingual.

My great grandparents were immigrants from Germany. My mother came from a farm family north of Johnsburg, a member of the Knaus family that settled in the middle of the 19th century. Great Grandpa Mathias Knaus was born in Germany, at a town called Frassdorf in 1819. Grandpa Peter Knaus born in 1853, was one of the original trustees of the parish in Johnsburg when they finally incorporated the parish after much squabbling over control of the Church. The family spoke German at home, and the parish school in Johnsburg taught the children in both German and English. Mother could write the old German cursive script.

Nicholas Schmitz was born in Drees, Germany. His oldest son, Johann, born in 1824 came to this country from the town of Ursfeld. His son Peter, born in 1858, was my grandfather, born in Johnsburg, but settled in St. Peter after the Civil War. The old farmhouse where dad was born and raised still stands, although the farm is no longer an active dairy farm. Like many other children, he walked the mile or so to the parish school in St. Peter each day.

I remember dad talking about building the parish school in St. Peter in the late 1920's and the arguments over whether the school would be a German or an English school. English won out, but not without a fight.

The parish churches were usually built on the highest point in the town, a visible symbol of the faith that dominated the people. They were the centers of much of the community life. Parishioners gathered regularly for Sunday Mass, often again for Vespers on Sunday evening, and then again for "Devotions" during the week.

Their brand of Catholicism was certainly tainted by late 19th century conservatism that seemed a blend of Victorianism and Calvinism, perhaps influenced by the 19th century theologian Jaansen who taught that man was inherently sinful and unworthy of God's favor and certainly was not worthy to receiver the Eucharist on a regular basis. While they attended Mass every Sunday, most of the people did not approach the Communion rail on a regular basis, and when they did, they were certain to have gone to confession the day or evening before. Usually they would take Communion on Christmas and Easter, so the lines at the confessional were sure to be long in the days before.

First Communion for children was generally delayed until the child was about fourteen. It was the rite of passage to adulthood, and a way of keeping the children in school until the eighth grade.

Parish organizations served an important social function. For the men there was the Holy Name society; for the women, the Christian Mothers. There was some sort of organization for the teenagers as well. The monthly meetings of each group were well attended and each organization had a monthly "Corporate Communion" at one of the Sunday Masses, sometimes followed by a breakfast and program in the church basement. One of the spiritual goals of these Corporate Communions was to encourage members to receive Communion on a regular basis. These organizations also formed the pool of workers for the parish picnics and other events that required large numbers of volunteers.

For Mass, the men sat on one side of the church and the women on the other, with the children in the front few pews, their behavior supervised by the nuns who taught in the parish school. Usually the older men would start filling the pews from the back and the pastors would jokingly refer to them as the "volunteer fire department." In those days women wore some form of head covering, particularly at Easter, when they would show off their spring finest. All sorts of headgear would appear from time to time, even young girls who devoutly pinned a handkerchief or a sheet of Kleenex to their hair with a bobby pin.

At one time there was a grocery store across the street from our parish church in St. Peter and some of the men of the parish would linger in the store until the priest finished his long-winded sermon. With the priest facing the back wall, away from the congregation, the men could sneak in unnoticed. However one priest apparently figured out what was happening. Each Sunday, before "High Mass," the priest came down the aisle and sprinkled the people with holy water as a reminder of their Baptism, a sprinkling known by its Latin name, "Asperges." One Sunday he marched down the aisle and out the front door of the church across the street and into the store, sprinkling the men who were congregated there instead of being at the start of Mass

In each parish, the social highlight of the year was the parish picnic, often held on the feast day of the Saint for whom the parish was named.

Parish members supplied most of the food for a chicken dinner; the women baked pies and prepared and served the food. The beer tent attracted the men, and if the sheriff wasn't looking, a gambling tent was erected, or at least a bingo tent. Often there was a polka band to supply music for dancing. There were simple games for the children operated by the teenagers of the parish. The annual picnic was a major fund-raiser.

Each town had at least one dance hall, and the wedding dances with "oompah" bands were traditionally open to the public. Posters announcing the wedding and the dance were distributed to the taverns in the area where they hung from a wire stretched along one of the walls. Young ladies would impose on a brother or parent to take them to the dance, hoping to get a ride home from one of the eligible young men in attendance.

Dad told of going to dances in horse and buggy days, when he would deliver the young lady to her home, and sit back in the buggy and go to sleep hoping the horse would remember the route home. He admitted that on more than one occasion he woke up the next morning in the yard of another farmer.

Since Catholics before Vatican II had to fast from midnight if they were to receive Communion, the Wedding Mass was held early in the day, usually nine o'clock, in the parish Church. Quite often weddings took place during the week. The majority of the people involved could be free as easily during the week as on the weekend. After the ceremony, the bridal party would drive to Fond du Lac for their formal wedding portraits in a studio. Old wedding photos show the same curved banister staircase as a prop. They must have used the same one for decades.

A lunch was then served for the bridal party and family, usually including uncles and aunts. The food was prepared by relatives or friends with the aid of the owner of the dance hall, with much of the food provided by the families. Usually it consisted of chicken, hot-dogs, potatoes and gravy and vegetables. Nothing fancy.

The afternoon was filled with the bride and groom maybe visiting a shut-in grandparent or relative and a bit of bar hopping at some of the area watering holes. Meanwhile back at the dance hall where the reception was being held, there was a small combo playing polkas and waltzes for the folks who were there for lunch and cared to stay through the afternoon. Mostly the men gathered around the bar for free beer and the latest news.

A larger crowd was invited to the dinner in the evening, often including first cousins and a wider circle of friends and neighbors, and in particular the families of people who had invited you to one of their family weddings in the past. The meal again was seldom fancy, and was generally prepared by women who were either relatives of friends coaxed into the kitchen for the day. It was not unusual to have several hundred people for the dinner and reception, often eating in shifts. I sometimes wondered if the bride and groom even got to see everyone. In retrospect, I have to wonder how the bride, who in some cases was a few months pregnant, survived the day-long ordeal.

Wedding dances drew crowds from the area. A deputy or two was engaged to keep the peace in many instances, and there was a charge for admission, which usually paid for the band. Posters in area taverns invited the public and since this was one of the few social opportunities in the Holy Land they were well attended.

With free flowing beer and plenty of testosterone one might expect that there would be some altercations in the parking lot and one would not be disappointed. Many a young man came home with a shiner or bloody knuckles and sometimes with a pretty good beating. Seldom if ever was any arrest made or charges filed.

There were a few other customs associated with weddings. One of them was a special ride after the ceremony. If an old horse and buggy could be found, the bridal party would get a ride around town for a few minutes. Sometimes, a decorated hay wagon would be substituted with a freshly washed John Deere pulling it.

When the couple returned from their honeymoon, friends and neighbors would greet them with a "shiveree" – making noise outside the house of the newlyweds until the groom would appear and there would be a party. You could get away with that in a rural community. Another custom was for someone to get into the house of the newlyweds, either on the wedding day or during the honeymoon, and decorate the place for them. Some of the decoration jobs got quite elaborate. Among them was filling the bathtub with Jello, putting saran wrap over the toilet bowl, unscrewing all the light bulbs and streamers of toilet paper sagging from wall to wall.

In one case where the newlyweds lived in an upstairs apartment, someone sneaked in and wired the doorbell switch to a pressure plate between the mattress and bedspring. Every time the couple would roll toward the middle the doorbell would ring. It took them a while to figure that one out.

Of particular interest in the marriages in the area is the fact that very few of them ended in divorce. Partly it was because of their religious belief that anyone who divorced was sure to be ostracized from the community, and condemned from the pulpit. Catholics had to get permission from the bishop to even seek a divorce. I'm not sure that this was a good thing in many cases where abusive relationships endured, often because there was no alternative with lives entangled with the economics of the farm and large families. On the other hand, most people were quite faithful to their spouses, if for no other reason than that if anybody did have an affair the whole world knew. The grapevine did not keep secrets.

If one analyzed the marriages in the Holy Land, a high percentage sprang from romances begun at church picnics or wedding dances. Young men found their brides among the women who lived within a few miles. For example the five brothers of the Schneider family in Silica married women who grew up within a mile of the Schneider home. Family trees didn't branch widely, and when a young couple met they were sure to look at their family trees before any serious dating. When a young man would talk to his parents about his new-found love, there were two questions they would ask: "Is she Catholic? and is she related to you?"

It was not uncommon for second cousins to marry. In fact there was concern raised in the 1960's about the "inbreeding" of close relatives over several generations and the effect on the health of the community. It seems there was a higher percentage of birth defects, particularly mental retardation, in the area than nearly anywhere else in the state. This was due in part to large families and births to older mothers, as well as only minimal pre-natal care and women giving birth when they were well in their forties. If one studied the genealogies of the families in the area, he'd find that the same families had been inter-marrying going back perhaps a couple hundred years, since most of the families came from the same small area in Germany before settling in the Holy Land. Family trees had not branched much in perhaps four hundred years.

Large families were the norm for Catholics in the area. It was not unusual for a couple to have more than a half-dozen children. In fact, it was the norm. Rare were the families with only two or three children. A dozen or more was not rare. Perhaps the aversion Catholics had toward birth control contributed to large families, certainly before the invention of the birth control pill in the 1960's, it was a major factor. Obviously the large families had many ramifications. Economically it kept many families in a lower financial status. It also had some effect on the education of the children who were sent off to work at an early age rather than continue their education beyond the parish school's eighth grade. Another aspect was that the men and women of the Holy Land had an ample supply of possible mates without going outside the Holy Land, adding another link that bound the families of the area together by family ties as well as their German heritage and Catholic faith.

Another bit of social glue that united the towns was the baseball teams fielded in each of the towns, with Sunday afternoon games filled with spirited rivalry. For many years teams simply passed the hat for donations to support their local teams, with the necessary stand for beer and soda. The tradition continues and though the teams attract some outside players from Fond du Lac, the players are mainly from their home towns.

The parish school was considered so important that it was often established prior to the building of the church. The custom was to offer grades one through eight. Resources were limited and even into the 1960's there were as many as three or four grades in the same room under the direction of one teacher. The parish paid for everything except "book rental" and personal supplies for the children. Holy Land

Catholics were not known for their generosity to the church, probably because few of them were affluent enough to be generous. Many of the farms were small and the families large. It was a struggle to support nine kids on an eighty-acre farm. I remember one bombastic pastor complaining about the meager Sunday collections. He complained: "If they ever devalue the quarter, our parish will go bankrupt."

There was no gym or science room, and the library consisted of a single shelf in the corner of the room. Many of the kids walked to school if they lived nearby, and a few of them walked several miles. They carried their lunches which would generally be a sandwich, maybe a piece of fruit and either a thermos or glass bottle of milk.

The desks were screwed to the wood floor in rows. The buildings were poorly lit and ventilated. Bathrooms were in the basement and the daily schedule included regular parades to the bathroom with one student appointed to be the "monitor" and report on kids who got out of line.

The school day began with Mass in the parish church with children escorted in lines to their assigned areas, the younger children in front, the older children generally in the choir loft. One of the nuns was trained to play the organ and direct the choir. Some of my classmates who had repeated a grade and were older than the rest of us and were going through their adolescent voice changes were excused from singing. They seemed to pass the time during Mass dropping spitballs or seeds on the people in the pews below, competing with one another over who could hit the bald head of one of the parishioners. I wonder about the educational benefit of the daily Mass or the religious significance of the experience.

Mass, at the time, was celebrated with the priest facing the far wall of the church, his back to the congregation with the sanctuary separated from the people by a "communion railing" where people would come to receive Communion. There was a linen cloth that the Mass servers would turn over to cover the narrow railing for Communion and the people would kneel in line along the rail as the priest carefully placed the Communion bread on the tongue of each of them.

Women were not allowed in the sanctuary during Mass with one exception: a bride on her wedding day. The entire ritual was conducted in Latin, a language none of the children understood. There were two types of Masses: the "Low Mass" which the priest recited in a low voice with altar boys responding in Latin at key points during the Mass, and the "High Mass" in which parts of the Mass were sung by the priest and the choir. Even with the "High Mass" most of the prayers said by the priest were "sotto voce"—in a soft voice, that no one beyond a few feet away could hear.

Popular theology taught that there was something mystic or magical about the Mass. The priest alone at the altar would say the words of consecration over the bread and wine, which would become the Body and Blood of Jesus. What the people in the pews did to occupy themselves while this was going on was not really related to the Mass. The children had little prayer books to read their prayers, while some of the older folks might have a "Missal" which had translations of the prayers the priest recited, or they would finger their rosary beads, repeating the "Hail Mary" and "Our Father." About the only participation required of those in attendance was to stand, sit or kneel at the proper times, sometimes signaled by the young boy "Mass Server" ringing a bell to alert (or wake up) the people in the pews that something important was happening. With the underlying theology of a transcendent and unapproachable God, as well as the unworthiness of our sinful human natures, there was no need or room for active participation. All that was required was that one be physically present while the sacred rites were being performed.

One quaint practice of the Catholic schools was the "spiritual bouquet" that children would dutifully give to their parents for Christmas, Mother's Day, Easter, etc. It consisted of a greeting card, and instead of a nice poem or a simple I love you, it included a list of things that the children promised to do for their parents such as attending Mass and receiving Communion a certain number of times, praying the rosary a certain number of times, and praying "ejaculations," short prayers to which an "indulgence" was attached. I often wondered about the adolescent boy who promised one hundred ejaculations to honor his dad on Father's Day. What are they teaching the kids now?

In spite of all of it, the quality of the education was not bad, due mainly to the solid teaching and discipline of the nuns who staffed the schools. But while many Catholics look back to these days with nostalgia, there were those whose school experience haunted them for life. Nearly every class had one or more children who repeated a grade, carrying with them the stigma of having "flunked" a grade. Years later these kids still carried the tag and their aspirations in life seemed to be limited by the lower expectations that marked them in the early grades in school. Living as adults in the same community also meant living with those who remembered the unpleasant things that happened to you in the parish school. With nearly forty students in one room in two or three grades, there was little help for the child who was struggling. The fact that many of them came from homes where German was the primary language compounded the problem. The handicapped were often not educated at all, but kept at home and merely fed and clothed, their parents convinced that their schooling would be a waste of time.

Nearly every child who came through the Catholic Schools has unpleasant memories of the nuns who taught there. Some nuns were authoritarian and did not hesitate to use the ruler on the hands or pull the short hairs at the back of the neck of a student to get attention. It seemed the boys always got the worst of it. The nuns, to be fair, worked under duress. They were not required to have the same educational qualifications as teachers today. Often they had two years of college and then attended summer school in an endless pursuit of a degree. Many were barely out of high school when they found themselves in a room filled with rambunctious children. Few had any training in theology. As a result, the weakest part of the curriculum was often religion. The study of religion became a blend of memorizing answers in the Baltimore Catechism and the pious stories of someone who lived far away and long ago. The parish priest would regularly visit the classrooms and quiz the children on their memorized answers to questions in their catechism. If the bishop happened by for confirmation, he too would quiz the children on their catechism lessons, as if having memorized the answers constituted the faith requirement needed for Confirmation.

The nuns lived in the convent next to the school or in part of the school building itself. They had little choice of what school or career they worked in or the people with whom they had to live. While most parishioners held nuns in awe, they were in fact quite isolated. Most of them came from small towns or farms or conservative working class families in the cities. They joined a religious order after eighth grade and spent the rest of their lives at the beck and call of their superiors, going wherever they were sent. Most of them taught in elementary schools, and I am sure that many envied those who were able to teach high school or college or enter some other profession that was more personally suitable and fulfilling than teaching three grades in one room in a rural farming community.

Many of them, seeing the lot of their mothers and older sisters, who had large families and worked on a farm with little chance for an education or respect saw the chance of an education and getting respect from the community attractive. They looked at the nuns who taught them in the schools and saw that they were better educated and respect-ed than other women in the community. Generally nuns lived in homes that were as nice or better than others in the area and most certainly were cleaner. Parishioners in the small towns were often generous to nuns who served the parishes. They would share their vegetables and on occasion some of the meat when they butchered a hog or cow. Yet in spite of it, the life of the nun in the parish was a rather Spartan one and quite isolated.

Apart from this, a steady dose of religion in the parochial schools convinced a large number of young girls that nuns were assured of a "higher place in heaven" because they dedicated their lives to the church. To be sure, it was a measure of pride for a nun to convince a young girl to enter the convent so there was some pressure. Parishes and families too, took special pride if there was a nun from their midst.

My family had a closer relationship with nuns than many. My older sisters, Alice and Loretta each spent some time in the convent. Alice was there only a short time and for the rest of her life never wanted anybody to know about it, even though a few pictures of her in her nun's habit kept showing up in photo albums from time to time. Loretta spent about two years in the same religious order, until the leaders of the order decided that her back problems were not conducive to the rigors of religious life and she was asked to leave. Apparently one needed to be in very good physical health to be a nun in those days. We also had two cousins from Johnsburg who spent their adult lives in the convent. When they returned home for a week or two during the summer to visit their parents, we were sure to be invited for a visit. Yet other than these social occasions, the nuns remained apart. They didn't entertain at their homes and were seldom if ever invited to the homes of parishioners. Few received assignments close to their families. Their lives were confined to the school, the parish church and the convents in which they lived.

My closest contact with young women in the years of their "formation" or training was at St. Mary's in Fond du Lac when I served as assistant pastor there. The Sisters of St. Agnes staffed the schools in town, and their convent or Motherhouse was next to the hospital. The "postulants" as women religious were called during their high school years, helped out with catechism classes on Saturdays at the parish. I could notice the change in the young women from year to year. At fourteen they were vivacious with a sparkle about life. But as their years of training progressed I saw the sparkle dim. They became less interested in their personal appearance and demeanor. It seemed to me that their personalities were gradually broken down to fit into the mould of a woman religious. Their clothing changed from what women of their day wore to the shapeless long religious habit that concealed their feminine anatomy. When they received their full habit their hair was shorn and their heads covered by a veil. They took a new name, symbolic of a new identity, often the name of some male saint. They all took the name "Mary" as their first name, so we had Sister Mary Oscar, Sister Mary Henry, Sister Mary Hubert, and the like. They did not use their family names, and each nun's name was different from the others in the Order. Some orders allowed the women to choose their own names, while others were given their names by their superiors. The young women would choose either their favorite Saint or come combination of their parent's first names which made for some interesting combinations.

What trauma accompanied the process of turning young girls into nuns? Maybe because the change was gradual, the women themselves did not detect it; but it was dramatic change. During their training, contact with their families was limited: a visitation day or two during the year and perhaps a short vacation in the summer. Even contacts with other

68

women in the same convent or religious order were tightly monitored. The young woman was not to socialize with those "outside her class" whether they be older or younger members of the order. Correspondence was limited and usually censored.

It was a process of strict control, preparing the woman for a lifetime of obedience without question to her superiors. Orders from a superior were to be carried out "immediately, cheerfully and without question." Looking back, one wonders that those who came through the process had any semblance of normalcy remaining.

I remember when I was child attending St. Peter's there were three teaching nuns and a "cook sister" who did the domestic chores for the group. The Mother House assigned them to their "mission" often without regard for their talents or wishes. One of them would be appointed the "superior" who made all decisions, often arbitrarily, about the school, the house, even down to the menu at dinner. Not having a car, the nuns were dependent on someone from the parish for transportation to shopping, doctor's appointments and the like. They wore the full religious habit, floor length, black, with a floor length "scapular" – a piece of cloth about as wide as the shoulders draped front and back. The collar was a stiff white affair that resembled a bib, fastening in back. The headgear was a combination of contraptions that concealed all but the front of the woman's face, covering the top and side of the head, as well as the neck. Atop all this was a black veil that reached down nearly to the waist in back. Around the waist was a wool rope fastened with a slip knot, and three knots in the piece that hung from the waist, for the three vows that she took upon entering the order: poverty, chastity and obedience. From this dangled a rosary with beads the size of small grapes. It jingled when she walked, which was nice for the kids in school—she couldn't sneak up behind them very easily. Generally she wore a crucifix around the neck, and on the ring finger of the left hand, a simple gold band, her "wedding ring" as a bride of Christ. On their feet they wore black "granny shoes" with shoe - laces and a heel of perhaps two inches. While it marked the woman as a nun wherever she went, it perhaps provided some modicum of safety, at least she felt some security in her religious habit.

Changes in religious garb began in the post-Vatican II era in the late 60's, much to the chagrin of Rome and many conservative Catholics who wanted to live in the past. Gradually habits were modified, and all but a few of the nuns discarded the old habits entirely. I am sure it was traumatic for some of them who for years had not worried about their figures or foundation garments nor worry about their hair or make-up. They perhaps felt somewhat naked without yards of cloth covering their arms and legs. Some, I am sure, clung to the romantic notions of nuns they had known in their childhood and had joined the convent to emulate. For some the old habit was a symbol to the world that automatically gave them identity and respect.

Among the more ludicrous garbs was the Daughters of Charity headgear, made famous in the TV show the Flying Nun, and earning the nickname "God's Geese." The outrageous headgear of white "wings" was actually adopted by the order's founder centuries ago because it resembled the sunbonnets worn by the French peasant women, with whom the order in their charitable works, wanted to identify.

Nuns in their habits were bound to be conspicuous wherever they went, being forced to listen to the endless babble of mindless faithful, particularly those who had had a few too many to drink, who assumed that if you wore a religious garb you would know every nun or priest in the world, or that you were interested in their stories of encounters with nuns or priests in their lives. There was no privacy, no place to get away. Their entire worldly possessions were to be stored away in a single trunk. In addition, the pastor of the parish often wielded a heavy hand as to what went on in school and if he did not like a particular nun he was sure to complain to the head of the order and have her replaced. If she didn't like her assignment, she would simply be told to "offer it up" for the poor souls in purgatory or some other platitude.

The nun's day began early, getting to school before the youngsters would arrive, then marching them all off to Mass, making sure their behavior was perfect and that no one talked or fidgeted during Mass and stayed in line and kept silence on the way to church and back. The nuns taught classes until noon and then rushed off for a quick lunch, eating in shifts so someone was always there to supervise the children. When class ended, there were papers to correct, lessons to plan, and generally two of the nuns would be assigned as sacristans for the parish church, laying out the vestments, decorating the altars, and making sure that all supplies were in order, taking care of the altar linens—a daily chore. For some reason their discipline did not allow one nun to be alone. If there were church services in the evening, they were expected to be in attendance.

In spite of it all, these women were the backbone of the parishes in which they served. They provided a solid education for the children. They provided a ray of hope for young women who aspired to be more than their mothers. They were women who were respected.

Until the 1950's, many Holy Land children stopped their education after eighth grade. They could read, do some simple arithmetic, write and knew their catechism lessons. So they were prepared for life. Few went to high school until the state began to mandate attendance. And it was rare for a child to go on to college. The prevailing attitude was that if the children became too well educated they would not want to work on the farms.

In 1970 I conducted the high school retreats for some of the Catholic sigh schools in Milwaukee and there were some follow-up gatherings with some of the kids. I remember meeting the father of one of the girls who was a university professor. He told me that he had worked on a study for the Catholic bishops in the 1950's on the religious orders of women. The part of the study that the bishops published was the one calling for what was termed "Sister Formation Program." This called for better educational preparation for the women who staffed our Catholic Schools, including solid grounding in theology, which they were sorely lacking.

The professor then went on to tell me the bishops suppressed the other half of the study which recommended that there be a moratorium on new convents for women religious and that no new facilities be planned that depended on women religious for staffing because the numbers were going to dramatically shrink in the future. He stated that the recommendations were based on the profile of the women entering convents and the decreasing percentage who actually completed their training. The actual membership in many religious communities began its decline already in the 1950's. He continued commenting on all the new convents and schools that required an increasing supply of nuns who were cheap labor in reality, most of them standing empty today or converted to other uses. Some of them were used for only a year or two as religious houses of study and formation.

With the large families, there was a surplus of helpers on the family farm and a shortage of resources to support them. Often young men were hired out to a local farmer after eighth grade, while many of the girls worked for families in the city, or with relatives as mother's helpers and baby sitters, and later house cleaners. I remember some of my older brothers working for area farmers that way, and some of my older sisters also worked for families in Fond du Lac.

The economics of the Holy Land was tied to the farms, and businesses that supported the farmers like feed mills, implement dealers, and the building trades. In the earlier days there was a blacksmith in each of the towns and, of course, the local grocery store and more than enough taverns to supply the refreshment needs. For some reason the area never did attract manufacturing jobs, though factories in the cities were happy to have the farm boys working for them. They were hard workers, honest, and didn't complain a lot.

When the state required children attend high school, young folks began to aspire for more than life on the farm, and as in many rural areas, kids from the Holy Land who went on to school seldom returned, finding their way into larger cities. At the same time, the quiet of the countryside enticed some to build new homes on the land they once plowed, and subdivisions sprang up, particularly around St. Peter where many of the hills offered a spectacular view of Lake Winnebago to the West.

Today, parishes are struggling. Many schools have closed or consolidated with other parishes as the supply of cheap labor in the person of nuns who staffed the schools declined; area social life no longer centers around parish churches or wedding dances.

There were some interesting characters in the lore of the Holy Land. Mother told of old Mrs. Theyerl from Johnsburg who reputedly practiced witchcraft around the turn of the 20th century. She was said to have a "buch" (book) with spells and incantations and potions and the lot. Whether there was any truth to mother's stories, we were never able to ascertain, but the fact is that she and many others who grew up in that area certainly believed there were witches among them.

Apparently there was some type of demonic possession in the old school building at St. Peters, with a young girl possessed by the devil. A special priest was brought in for the exorcism and then all was well. The woman later married and raised a large family, becoming one of the pillars of the parish.

The only doctor in the area was in Mt. Calvary, Dr. Baasen, who was married to mother's aunt Carrie. He was a gruff old man when I knew him, and tended the medical needs of most of the people in the Holy Land. His office was in the basement of their home. The walls in the waiting room were paneled with gray cement board, and there were two examining rooms. The place reeked of medicine and rubbing alcohol. He dispensed medicine and did some minor surgery in the office. In fact, he removed my tonsils in the office when I was about five or six. Other than for surgeries, he did not take appointments. People would merely show up at the office and wait their turn. This practice continued even when his successor, Joe Miller, built a new clinic on the edge of town. Baasen was the "old country doctor" who made house calls and delivered babies in the home. I was the only one of our family of eleven to be born in the hospital. Mother's Aunt Carrie served as his assistant and took care of the books. Mother maintained she did this because she wanted to know everybody's business.

Health care was rudimentary at best at the time. Childhood diseases were a part of growing up: measles, mumps, chicken pox, whopping cough – we nearly all got them before vaccines were invented. Nearly every summer there was an epidemic of polio, but that was more prevalent in the cities than on the farms, probably because of less contact with infected persons. Mental illness was neither recognized nor treated, other than acute cases being confined in mental hospitals. One of our neighbors suffered from post-partum depression after the birth of her second child and spent the rest of her life in a mental institution. Several families in the Holy Land had a member in the mental hospital. The state and each county maintained asylums for the mentally ill. Generally when a person was confined they were never heard from again. These were the days before the development of drug and other therapy. Many of the people so confined would today be in treatment and lead productive lives.

Growing up on a farm in a large family is often described in nostalgic terms, but the reality is that while there are memories to be treasured, there are also things we'd rather forget and things I never want to experience again.

Our family farm was something of a landmark on the east shore of Lake Winnebago. It had one of the longest barns in the area, and the land was a mixture of rather flat fields below the highway and sharp hills east of the road behind the buildings. Then there was the "back forty" which originally was a farm in itself.

The back forty was Dad & Mom's first farm and their first home. They took it over from Dad's sister, whose husband died of appendicitis a few months before mom and dad married. The Peter Schmitz clan settled on farms quite close to one another and close to the homestead. The little forty-acre farm was quite scenic, but too small to support a family by farming. In fact, Dad worked nights at the hospital in Fond du Lac tending the boilers for some of those early years. The farm was nestled between the hills with a creek running through the middle of it. The house was a Victorian style home, with a front porch, and a "summer kitchen" where meals could be prepared during the summer months on the wood stove without heating up the rest of the house. The building was never electrified, though I remember there was piping for gas lighting with gas supplied by a carbide generator of sorts in the basement. I don't remember it ever being used as such. Water was supplied from a shallow well dug next to the house with a hand pump on the kitchen sink. There was a small 30 X 40 foot barn set against the hillside with a cement silo which stood long after everything else was demolished, a chicken coop, the usual outhouse and something unique, a bee cellar dug into one of the hills behind the house. A gravel road wound its way into the valley and crossed the creek before it ended at the main highway. The only building I can remember was the house but there were foundations where other buildings once stood. I do remember that the house was rented out until the mid 1940's.

There were several apple trees near the house: the old varieties of apples such as "northern spies," "russets" and "banana apples" with a honey crab tree just behind the house, and a couple cherry and plum trees along the side. Most of the farms in the area had at least a few apple trees, but dad seemed to have more than most, though the old trees were not well cared for or pruned for years. Across the creek was another larger orchard with several different kinds of apples: wolf rivers, wealthy, greenings and snow apples. These were probably planted at a later date when that field was no longer tilled for crops. The fencerows held a couple wild plum species and the two valleys that coursed through the little farm had old hickory and butternut trees. We spent many hours as kids gathering the nuts and occasionally wandering onto the neighbor's land for butternuts as well.

In front of the old house was a yellow rose bush that flowered abundantly every summer. No one ever pruned it, watered it or fertilized it. Yet years after the house was torn down it still flowered, a defiant reminder that once a family lived here and cared about beauty. Only when the township bought the land for a dump and covered it with tons of landfill did the rosebush cease to brighten the landscape with brilliant yellow blooms. It would not surprise me if some day it pokes its persistent shoots though all the refuse and sprouts a triumphant bud to welcome the afternoon sun.

The creek was spring fed from an outcropping of limestone on the neighbor's land under the one of the bridges for the railroad that ran from Fond du Lac to Sheboygan. The water was generally clear, except when there was runoff from rain or spring thaw. Then it drained a watershed that stretched for over a mile to the east and drained perhaps a thousand acres of farmland. But we are certain it was polluted by cow pastures of three farms on its way to Lake Winnebago. There were a few small minnows and crayfish and an abundance of frogs. It was too small for any sizeable fish. As kids we used the creek for recreation and a source of fish bait with the crayfish and minnows. We spent many hours seining for minnows and crayfish or trying to catch frogs along the banks or just walking barefoot in the water. The hills were great for sledding during winter, scooting down snowdrifts. The slopes were quite steep and we could get a good fast ride for a short run.

Some time during the 1950's dad rented the back forty out to a gun club who used the area for rifle practice and on occasion there were some matches, so on weekends the hills would echo with the sharp report of heavy rifle fire. They seldom interfered with the cattle or any other activity on the land.

The old dirt road wound its way through the old farm, separating the house and barn, crossing the creek in the valley with a cement bridge with "tombstone" abutments, then turning west through the Abler woods, across another bridge, and ending on the highway. We maintained a right of way through the Abler land, so the road was kept open. We fenced the perimeter of the back forty, with a gate across the roadway. However this was one of the favorite party and "parking" lanes in the county, and we would often find the gate left open after some one had used the valley for a night time party. In fact, a Fond du Lac native, Maureen Daly in her novel Seventeenth Summer, describes the evening romancing in the lane that ended in an apple orchard with a creek nearby.

The hills were gravel and sand deposited by the last glaciers, and I remember gravel pits there, with a crusher operating in the mid 1940's as well as remnants of earlier excavations. During the 1950's other companies worked the pits and many of the roadbeds of area highways were graveled from our pits. While this was a boon to Dad financially, he never got paid for most of what was hauled out by the contractors during those years. In hindsight, it was a pity they hauled any of the hills away. The back forty, with its hills and gentle stream, broad valley and woods, was an idyllic place for a home, even a resort of some kind. Today that land would be worth perhaps a million as prime home sites, particularly the hilltops with a spectacular view of sunsets over Lake Winnebago.

About 1927 Dad bought the neighboring Briggs farm, with the huge barn, two large silos, a machine shed, chicken coop, a small house for the "hired man" and about 160 acres of land that joined the original forty acre farm. A few years later the township, with WPA funds, decided to straighten out the road that wound through the back forty, and made a cut through the hill, adding a cattle pass between the two parcels.

The hill east of the barn provided an unobstructed view of Lake Winnebago in its entirety. I remember working the land, watching the boats on the lake, and seeing the steam locomotives chugging from Oshkosh to Fond du Lac on a clear day. In the winter we could see the fishing shanties dot the lake. Quite often we would be able to see storms approach across the lake and head home before it began to rain. Today there's little there but a gaping hole where sand and gravel were hauled away.

Dad and mom talked about a German man named "Hans" who worked for them during the early thirties. In the aftermath of World War I they never really trusted him, and apparently Hans kept to himself. For some reason they suspected he was a German spy of some sort, but I often wondered what a spy would be doing working for a farm family in Wisconsin. Where he went when he left them remains a mystery.

The old "one room schoolhouse" stood along the highway in a grove of trees, probably built some time in the late 19th century. . My older brothers and sisters attended at least some grades in the old building, "Taycheedah Number 6." Each of the township schools had a number and was under the supervision of the County education office. In the early years the teacher often lived with Mom and Dad on the back forty, and dad served for many years on the school board as the clerk. It was a red brick building with one room, a wardrobe at the rear near the entrance, and a wood stove for heat. It was not electrified, and there was an old well on site that had been abandoned. A large outhouse with sides for boys and girls was at the corner of the property. I remember many of the School Board meetings were held in our kitchen during those years. When the school closed in the late 1940's, the building was sold and converted to a home. The buyer was a man who worked for the railroad in North Fond du Lac, and he rented it to his father, Mark Sherman. Mark was a character who deserves mention.

As Mark told the story, he got into a feud with his family and left the house as a teenager. When he returned five years later, his parents demanded to know where the hell he'd been and why hadn't he even contacted them. He left in a huff and didn't return for another five years. In the meantime, he rode the rails and lived in hobo jungles along the tracks. He would often demonstrate some of the tricks and skills he learned in his life on the road. During World War II he worked as a welder in the shipyards in Duluth, and seemed to have worked in the wheat fields of North Dakota during the threshing season in days when harvest was done with the old threshing machines and horses to pull the wagons across the fields.

When they were building an outdoor theater in Fond du Lac, Mark got a job as a laborer on the crew. The only problem was that he was working for two contractors at the same time, the general construction contractor and the electricians. All went well until he got laid off at the end of the job, or at the end of the construction season. When he went to file for unemployment compensation, he tried to collect from both contractors. The scam was up.

Our old farmhouse was built in the 19th century, with a single wing for a summer kitchen on the first floor and a walk-in attic on the second. If you wanted hot water there was a reservoir on the side of the wood stove and a copper wash boiler to heat it atop the stove. The first floor had a kitchen, dining room, living room, a formal parlor, and a single bedroom. The kitchen had a sink, with a single cold-water tap and a switch to turn on the pump if you wanted water from the well. There was a wood stove for cooking and for heat. A large icebox in the summer kitchen was used for food storage. I remember we had a hand-cranked cream separator that we used on occasion, particularly during World War II when butter was rationed. We'd separate the cream from the milk and churn our own butter.

The second floor had four bedrooms joined by a hallway with a cast iron space heater that provided the only heat for the upstairs. There was a bathroom, with a tub but no running water and no toilet. The basement contained the furnace and a woodpile, along with a pile of coal. This portion was cemented, and it was here that the old ringer type washing machine was located. The other portion of the basement was the fruit cellar with a dirt floor, plenty of shelves for preserves and canned fruits and vegetables, and a large cistern for rainwater used for laundry. There was a copper tank in the attic that I remember was used to store rainwater pumped from the cistern in the basement.

We usually had a large supply of vegetables and fruits canned and stored in the basement along with potatoes and carrots kept in the cooler parts and whatever apples we'd picked late in the season. We'd have carrots in a box covered with sand and bushels of apples that lasted until nearly spring. I remember mom and dad had apples pressed for cider and canned some of it. They usually stored cider in a wood stave barrel. Someone told them one year that if they stopped up the barrel tightly, the cider would stay sweet and not ferment. They decided to try it. One night we heard a low rumble and the house shook a bit. The barrel had exploded and we had the sweetest smelling basement around.

For some reason the basement section under the summer kitchen was not used, and at one time had been filled with stones picked off the fields. I suspect there may have been either water or foundation problems that they tried to correct by filling the space with stones.

The siding was gray cement stucco, until it was replaced with the asbestos siding about a year before it burned to the ground. There were two chimneys; one for the main furnace and the space heater on the second floor and a smaller one that vented the kitchen stove.

One memory I have of the house was the problem we had with rats. They were in the basement, with the dirt floor, and for some reason found their way between the walls to the walk-in attic upstairs. My bedroom was next to the attic and they had gnawed a corner out of the door and sometimes at night would run across my bed on their way to God knows where.

During the summer of 1947 a violent thunderstorm swept through in the middle of the night, spawning a tornado that dropped one of the large box elders over the north wing of the house with some slight damage, but causing quite a bit of damage to the barn and taking the machine shed, a three sided affair with a tin roof, and lifting it over a nearby tree like an umbrella. Lying atop one of the beams that formed the framework of the shed was a mower sickle, lying flat on the beam. We never did find that sickle after the storm.

With the shed in ruins, Dad decided to replace it and the attached chicken coop with a garage, pouring the foundation for it in November of that year and hoping to get construction completed. An early winter left the job with only the foundation poured before the snows came.

January 28, 1948 is a night all of us remember well. The temperature was about -20 degrees with a brisk west wind. I woke up in the middle of the night and smelled smoke. I turned on my light and saw the room was filled with smoke, and screamed "Fire" and everybody woke up and got out safely. Fire had started in the summer kitchen wing, probably from an electrical short in the ceiling and spread quickly. With the smoke in my room I left the house with only my pajamas and a coat that I grabbed on the way out. I remember Dad investigating the source of the fire – the "summer kitchen" in the north wing of the house. When he opened the door, the fire was falling from the ceiling, filling the room with flames quickly as he closed the door. We kids huddled in Bert's house trailer parked nearby until they pulled that away with a tractor because of the heat of the fire. We could see the fire progress through the building.

Before she left the building, Mom called the fire department which was a volunteer department in Mt. Calvary about 10 miles away. It took a half hour for them to arrive, and other than a small tank on the truck they had no water supply. Volunteers for the department loaded empty tanks on their pick-up trucks when the alarm went in, filled them with water, and headed to the fire. There was no available water supply near most fires. Despite their bravado and enthusiasm, the lack of water generally meant that they saved few buildings. By the time they arrived the house was engulfed, but with the asbestos siding, the flames were pretty well contained inside the building, but embers drifted skyward and landed on the barn roof. The firemen, knowing the house was gone, turned their hoses on the barn, coating the roof with ice and saving the structure from damage. Before the fire spread throughout the house my older brothers were able to rescue some of the furnishings in the main section. Two pieces are known to exist today: the dresser in my parent's bedroom and a rocker that was on the porch at the time.

When the sun rose, there were only smoldering ruins where once a home stood and the stub of the main chimney stood a few feet above the ground level, blackened amid the ashes. As they probed through the ashes they found a barrel filled with meat in salt brine in preparation for smoking in the old tin smoke house. The bacon and hams had been smoked all right and I remember eating some of it. Expensive smoking process though.

We kids spent the night at one of the homes along the beach and then lived with my sister Alice and her husband Ray in Peebles for a while. The neighbors all pitched in and we built a two-car garage over the foundation poured the fall before and we moved in. There were eight of us crowded together in this garage. We had a refrigerator, a stove and a space heater. A couple beds, mattresses and other furniture were given to us by neighbors. We were able to make do. This was home for the next six months, while the house was being rebuilt. I also remember wearing clothes we got from neighbors that didn't quite fit but kept me warm.

The whole family as well as neighbors pitched in to help rebuild the house. I remember pulling nails out of old boards salvaged from the house on the back forty that were used in the new house. Neighbors would stop during the day or sometimes at night to lend a hand with whatever needed to be done.

It was in the middle of the building project that our brother Francis was killed on his motor-cycle. He had spent Sunday afternoon at one of the taverns in St. Peter with a couple of his friends and for some reason they decided to take a drive to Mt. Calvary, about six miles away. There were three young men on his classic "Indian" motor-cycle when they hit a rough spot in the highway and missed a curve, landing in the ditch. Francis had a head injury and lay in a coma for a day. Surgery to relieve the pressure on his brain was not successful and he died the next night. The two passengers he had received only minor injuries. His death left deep wounds in the hearts of the family. He had been drafted in the army during World War II, joined Patton's Third Army shortly after the Battle of the Bulge, and though he probably never knew it, fought over some of the same ground that his ancestors came from along the Mosel River. He was wounded in action, receiving the Purple Heart and also was commended with the Silver Star for bravery for an incident in which he was on patrol to check out a farmhouse in the area. There were eighteen German officers inside, and he was able to take all of them prisoner. The general who presented the Silver Star was none other than George Patton, "Old Blood and Guts" as Fran referred to him.

I remember him telling of an incursion into Austria to save some horses before they fell into Russian hands. I never knew until many years later that the horses were the Lippizaner Stallions of the Spanish Riding School. Patton was a great horse lover and wanted to capture some of them.

A nostalgic memory is threshing time. We'd spend several days cutting the grain with a "binder" that cut the stalks and bundled them with twine. To properly dry them we'd have to go behind and stand the bundles in "shocks" to dry for threshing. If all went well, by the time we finished with the cutting the first fields would be dry enough for threshing. If it rained we'd have to go back into the fields and separate the shocks so the bundles would dry enough for threshing. One time I was spreading bundles from the shocks and stuck my pitchfork into one only to see a black and white ball of fur between the bundles. I think I set a record for short sprints with a pitchfork that day. Luckily the skunk was gone by the time we had to pitch the bundles in the wagon later in the day.

On threshing days we'd pitch the bundles into wagons, then unload them into the threshing machine that was parked just at the entrance of the granary so the grain could easily be put into the bins for storage, while the straw was blown into the barn or a stack nearby to be used for bedding. The threshing machines were noisy behemoths and the work was dusty and dirty. To do the work efficiently required several people. One person drove the tractor pulling the wagon for the bundles, (or in the olden days drove the team of horses,) others pitched the bundles on the wagon, another pitched the bundles into the machine, another watched the grain coming out the other end and tended the machine so nothing went wrong. If the grain was a bit wet it would clog the machine, or a belt would slip off a pulley, or the person feeding the machine would throw too much in at one time.

Before the advent of combines, threshing crews of several neighboring farmers would gather for the work, moving from farm to farm, and of course having a good noon meal wherever they went. The farmers would bring their own wagons and teams for the day. There generally was enough help so nobody had to work too hard. Actually, it was more of a social event, a sort of a communal celebration of the harvest that bred nostalgia. Dad was one of the first to realize that we'd probably get the work done quicker if we just had our own machine and did our own work. That was all right as long as there was enough help around to do it.

With most of the Schmitz clan living within a few miles of each other, they generally worked together when the need arose, whether gathering crops, butchering animals, or whatever. Uncle Joe lived on the next farm, Uncle Pete and Uncle Hugo lived less than two miles away, and Uncle Ben just over two miles away.

Not only did they work together, but they gathered for recreation as well. If one or the other came to visit there was sure to be a spirited game of sheepshead with a couple bottles of beer and a lunch at night. Uncle Joe had a boathouse at the lake which was a favorite spot for family picnics on Sunday afternoons in the summer. Lake Winnebago was warm and the water close to shore shallow so the kids could safely wade or swim. It seems that in the evening after the farm chores were done, the men would occasionally go in for a swim, taking with them a large drag net as the fish came in close to shore after the sun went down.. They'd make a loop with the net and then drag it into the boathouse. We always had enough fish to eat. With no cottages close by no one was the wiser.

They fished together on the lake in the summer and winter, both with hook and line and sturgeon spearing in the winter. Dad put out "set lines" for catfish consisting of a line stretched along the bottom of the lake and anchored on each end with a pole and flag at each end to identify it and locate it. He caught his share of catfish and late in the season bagged a few sturgeon as well. In fact, he caught more sturgeon illegally on the lines than he ever speared through the ice.

He loved to fish on nearby Lake Winnebago. I remember the old flat bottom boat he bought sometime in the 1940's. It was an old scow that always leaked, but it was good enough to row out a few hundred yards on a calm day. Later he bought a small outboard motor. Not owning any lake frontage, he was able to impose on the generosity of one of the neighbors to haul the boat ashore and store it there.

We had an old ice fishing shanty that we pulled out on the lake as soon as it was frozen solid enough to drive a car on the ice. Actually I can remember three such shanties that dad built. The first was covered with corrugated roofing tin and was recycled as a smokehouse until Dad's smoke fire got a bit too hot and burned much of the wood framing inside. The second one was all wood with a tar-paper roof. When the tornado destroyed the shed and the outhouse it contained, the fish-shanty was retired and served as the family privy. The third one lasted until Dad no longer did ice fishing.

Dad told the story of the old Model T Ford he and Uncle Ben Vogds were using to pull an ice shanty off the lake after the season. It was an old derelict of a car and they'd cut the body off, so there was just the frame, motor, wheels and a couple of seats. They were just a couple hundred feet off shore crossing a crack in the ice when the ice gave way, tossing them into the water. Dad panicked in the cold water, which came up to his chest, and Ben dragged him out of the water.

They figured the car wasn't worth much, so they simply unhitched the shanty and let the car sink below the ice. Many years later one of the cottage owners was wading off shore and stepped on something that seemed out of place. He dove under water and discovered the old Model T with a rusty chain attached to the rear bumper. It made the headlines of the paper, but no one seemed to know who left the thing there. We knew.

During hunting season the gang often spent Sunday afternoons hunting pheasants, rabbits, squirrels or whatever. They'd dress the game and usually gathered at one home or the other on Sunday night for a few hands of cards and a "feed" made from the game caught during the day. They enjoyed these Sunday gatherings immensely. In fact so much so that when the hunting season ended they wanted to continue the tradition. In the absence of game, someone would sneak into the farmyard of one of the families, filch a couple chickens, ducks, rabbits or whatever and then invite them over for a "feed."

Card playing was an important part of their social lives. A good old game of Sheepshead (Schaffskopf in German) was a part of every family gathering. The men would gather around the table, while the women folk prepared the food, did the dishes and watched after the children who often stood behind their parents watching the game. I often wonder if it was their love of the game or their lack of conversational skills that was at the root of the practice. It seemed a game of cards and a bottle of beer filled the time without the burden of trying to carry on a conversation, or at least the card game filled what might have been unpleasant gaps.

Neighboring farmers also worked together filling the silo with chopped corn stalks and they shared the labor when butchering hogs or cows. I remember the butchering days. It was a ritual ceremony of sorts, with the family gathering for the event. Looking back, I am amazed at the talent folks had for butchering and making sausages. Mom and dad would make several kinds of sausages, and I do not recall ever seeing a recipe for any of them.

Hogs were generally about two hundred pounds when they were ready to butcher. We'd get them in an enclosed pen and someone would take a rifle and shoot the hog in the head between the eyes. Naturally the hog would fall, though on more than one occasion the bullet missed the brain and the hog would squeal until another shot made its mark. Someone would run a sharp knife into the heart to drain out the blood. If they planned to make blood sausage, someone would catch the blood in a basin to be saved for later.

The hog was scalded in a barrel of water just the right temperature to loosen the hairs which would be scraped off with hog scrapers. (I still have a pair from the farm.) If the water was too hot, the hair would not come clean, and obviously, the same was true if the water wasn't hot enough. It generally took two men to dip the hog in the water, with a stout stick in the "gambol" of the hind legs for grip.

Once the hog was scalded and the hair scraped off, it would be hung up and gutted and the innards would be saved, the heart and liver put aside for sausage. The small intestines were cleaned and used as sausage casings and the stomach used for headcheese. If summer sausage was planned, the large intestines would be set aside as well. So only the lungs and pancreas were discarded.

Usually the women got the job of cleaning the intestines for sausage. They scraped them with a knife on a board to force the contents out of either end. Then washed the intestines in salt water and set them aside while the hogs hung outside to cool. (We always waited until colder weather to butcher.)

From the hogs they made bratwurst, liver sausage, summer sausage, and on occasion blood sausage and head -cheese. The hams, shoulders and bacon were put in a brine barrel and later smoked using either apple or hickory wood that dad set aside for the purpose. The rest of the hog was cut up. The head would be cut in half and there generally was a fight over who got to share the brains fried in butter. The rest of the head was cooked in a large copper boiler to be used in sausage. Even the ears were cleaned and ground up for liver sausage, as were the liver, heart and tongue. The fat was ground up and rendered for lard. Apart from a couple bones and some of the innards, there was little that went to waste. Dad used to say we used everything on the hog except the squeal.

Usually the beef we ate on the farm was not prime but rather one of the herd that was no longer productive and probably would not bring a good price on the market. This was generally the practice among the dairy farmers. The cows that were not good producers were either shipped off to the market or fattened and slaughtered for meat.

We raised sugar beets under contract with the sugar company which had a loading tipple in Fond du Lac near a railroad siding. The company hired migrant workers for the stoop work, hoeing and weeding the beets, though I remember years when the grown-ups would hoe the rows and we kids would come behind and thin the beets so there was only one per hill to give enough room for the plants to grow

By harvest time, in late fall the migrants had generally gone back to Texas or Mexico and the adults would dig the beets, lop off the tops and toss them on a wagon or truck to haul to the tipple. I recall the machinery we used: a special cultivator that tilled between the rows and a digger to break the soil and raise the mature beets in fall.

I remember a fencerow along the back lots of the lake cottages. The migrant workers would cut the weeds for us along the fence- row. Dad used to marvel at how well they kept that one fencerow cleaned for him. It was only years later that I realized the "weed" they were cutting was marijuana. No wonder they took such good care of it.

The routine with a dairy herd was much the same from the time the cows came into the barn in fall until they were turned out to pasture in spring. We got up early in the morning, milked the cows, then fed them silage made from chopped corn stalks and ground oats with perhaps some concentrated feed mixed in. In for breakfast, then return to give the cows hay, haul out the manure. At noon we'd give them more hay. Late afternoon we'd have to climb up the silo and fork down enough silage for the evening and next morning, and throw down enough hay for the next day, as well as straw for bedding. We'd feed the cows silage and ground oats again, eat supper, and return for milking. We'd put enough straw bedding under them for the night, and push hay before them and call it a night. In between we had to feed the calves, pigs and chickens and whatever other animals we were raising at the time.

Among the more exciting farm events was the birth of an animal. Little pigs were the cutest creatures and quite tame, but we had to look out for the sow who didn't always appreciate us picking up a piglet. If the piglet squealed, you'd better be outside the pen.

Usually a cow could give birth with no problems, but on occasion, particularly with a large calf and a small cow or heifer, the birth could be difficult. In these cases we would get a piece of rope, and reach in the cow's vagina until we could find the calf's feet, tie a slip knot around each one, and pull. Not pretty, but it got the job done.

The job of feeding the little calves generally went to the youngest of the family helping with the chores. For the first few days the calf would nurse with its mother. However the cow's milk was too valuable for calf feed, so we'd wean the calf to drink from a pail. Teaching a calf to drink from a pail was easy. We'd stand astride the calf and with a hand over its nose, allow it to suck on one finger and when it was sucking on the finger, push the nose into a pail of milk or calf feed mixture which was made from warm whey concentrate. Usually the calf would learn to drink from a pail easily.

In the early 1950's, when the Korean War broke out, brothers Les and Gene were drafted into service. That left Dottie, Lil and myself on the farm with Mom and Dad. I had just finished seventh grade, Dottie was sixteen, and Lil was only ten or eleven. We were really something of a family unto ourselves, having grown up when the rest of the family was gone. We were also the only kids our age for at lest a mile around. My closest classmate lived over two miles away. The only playmates we had growing up were our cousins who came to visit with their parents. People who knew our older siblings didn't always know that they were our brothers and sisters. It was a standing joke among the three of us that when anyone would ask about one of our older brothers or sisters, we would simply reply "They were from our Dad's first marriage." We never told that our dad was only married once, and no one asked.

We ended up doing a great deal of the farm work for the next few years. Our daily routine was getting up early, milking the cows, feeding them, and then hustle off to school. When we arrived home, it was the evening chores, feeding the animals, milking, and at least one night a week, rushing off to church for "devotions" or one kind or another, or praying the rosary kneeling in the kitchen. Gratefully I never had a lot of schoolwork to do, but often would stay up reading for hours after everybody else went to bed.

Memories of Christmas are generally happy ones, and our family was no exception. Dad would usually find a red cedar of suitable size and shape on the back forty and haul it home. I remember the tree base was an old cast iron flywheel from some machine or other, so the tree was never watered. Mom would put on lights and colored ornaments, and we'd get to put on tinsel. In the old house the tree was always in the formal parlor that was seldom used otherwise.

The evening was generally spent with the adults playing cards until it was time for Midnight Mass, which was a family tradition. A middle-of-the-night breakfast generally followed. In the morning we'd discover that Santa had brought us a few things that were under the tree.

The Christmas season was a time to visit aunts and uncles and see their Christmas trees, an afternoon visit, with a game of cards, a beer or two, while the kids played outside if the weather permitted, then a lunch and we'd finish in time to get back to the farm for the evening chores. It was these visits that cemented the bonds of extended families as well as celebrated the season.

If there was a Christmas crèche there was ritual that had to be observed. While the manger and Mary and Joseph could be put in place before Christmas, the shepherds and baby Jesus had to wait until Christmas Eve. The Magi, or "drei Koenig" as mother referred to them, were held back until January 6th, the celebration of Epiphany and the biblical arrival of the wise men from the East.

It was not unusual for families to keep their trees up until February 2nd, the feast of the purification of Mary, and officially the end of the Church's Christmas season. I wonder why, with the dry trees and lights, not more of them set afire during the season.

Of course, the Christmas tree itself had another use. February was the sturgeon spearing season on Lake Winnebago, and the trees were usually used to mark the roads over the ice, or to mark the holes cut in the ice to spear sturgeon when the shanty was moved so that nobody would drive into the open holes.

Digging through a box of old photos, their sepia edges often frayed or glossy prints with the serrated edges sometimes tucked in albums with the little corners glued in place to hold each photo. Some of people no one seems to recognize any more, some with names penciled on the back border, hoping that the name will mean something to future generations. Some look rather quaint like the formal wedding poses taken in a studio, other snapshots taken with cheap box cameras catching life on the run, but with the slow speed of film and camera the still pose was the norm. A few were carefully colored in the days before colored photography, giving a new vision of a black and white world. Periodically we sort through the accumulation of nearly a century of memories captured in inexpensive prints and stored away hoping to immortalize the memory of who we were.

Stored away in the file boxes of our human memories are pictures of our past, often subsequently colored by our love, our sense of duty toward those we love, and our penchant for wanting the lives we lived to be beautiful and happy, filled with the loving care of those who nurtured our lives. At best, we glance back over the path we've walked through eyes that have the "correction" of our lives, so that it might be easy to say "that's not exactly the way it was."

Looking back at Mom and Dad is difficult, since our most recent memories are bound to be the strongest. I'm sure that my memories will differ from those of my siblings. Coming from a large family, I hardly knew some of my older siblings. Veronica and Alice were married before I started school, and Bert and Francis were in the Army during World War II. So for most of my brothers and sisters, I really only knew them as adults.

Both Mom and Dad were born in the 19th century. Mom was forty when I was born, and dad was thirty-nine. My grandparents, except for Grandma Schmitz, I never knew, and have only vague memories of her living with us from time to time. It was the custom of elderly parents to move in with their children on a rotating basis when they could no longer live on their own.

In the old house on the farm, we had an old wood stove in the kitchen, and mom liked to bake. It was a necessity on the farm with a large family. We couldn't afford to buy everything in the store; it wasn't convenient, even if we could afford it. And certainly the quality wasn't the same. Her pies were superb, made from scratch. Her "kuchen" made with apples, or sometimes raspberries, were a favorite, and she'd make several pans.

She made her own donuts and often when she'd finished, she was lucky if there were any left as everyone had to have a sample, and with a large family and relatives who seemed to drop in from time to time, she was lucky to get a taste herself.

When Bert and Francis were drafted into the army during World War II, she worried about them, though she seldom showed it. There were occasions when she'd sneak off to her bedroom with her rosary, and if one of us would walk in on her, there were tears in her eyes.

She always managed the family finances, kept the books for the farm and wrote out checks for all the bills. There never seemed to be a lot of money around most of the time. Frankly Dad had too many cows for the feed he could raise on the acreage and by the time the grass was green in the spring, he no longer had feed for the cattle and turned them out to pasture with nothing more than the meager grass to eat, certainly not a high protein diet for a milking herd. Of course, milk production dropped dramatically during the summer until the cows calved in the fall and were again on a higher protein feed. It was a cycle repeated year after year.

I can hardly remember my mother being healthy. I remember her having trouble with her knees and going to the hospital for radiation treatments. I guess they used radiation for just about everything in those days, but the final diagnosis was that she had some cartilage damage that later required surgery.

She had surgery on her knee the same year that our house burned down, and in the same year was operated on for a large goiter. For some reason farmers didn't learn about iodine in the diet, though for years the children in school got their weekly iodine pill courtesy of the County Health department.

Just about the time she recovered from these surgeries, she was afflicted with arthritis and could hardly walk, much less work with her hands. For a woman who loved to crochet, this was devastating. Her activities were limited, and even her favorite hobby was taken from her.

In the fall of 1952, while I was away at the seminary, she had pneumonia, and finally was admitted to the hospital. After a series of tests, the diagnosis was leukemia. She was given a couple units of blood and massive doses of penicillin and sent home. Three weeks later she was back in the hospital for another series of transfusions, and over the next two years she would have forty-eight blood transfusions. One time, around Thanksgiving, she must have had a bad unit of blood, and she lost her sight. For about three weeks she was totally blind. When she returned to the hospital for another transfusion just before Christmas, her sight returned. No one ever explained what happened.

At least twice a week she would get a penicillin shot from the doctor in Mt. Calvary. This went on for years, and she knew everybody in the Holy Land who was sick and what was wrong with them; and she survived most of the people who met at the Doctor's office those years.

One thing I remember was that she had an insurance policy with the Catholic Knights. When they paid her first hospital bill, they also sent her notice that her insurance had been cancelled. We never totaled the entire cost of her illness, but it took most of the family income in those years.

She was one of the first patients to use cortisone, partly to relieve the inflammation from arthritis, and partly because I am sure the Doctor had no idea what to do next. For some reason her leukemia went into remission, and she would survive leukemia for fifteen years before it recurred. She died at home in 1967 at age sixty-nine. Her funeral packed the small church at St. Peter to capacity. Through her illness, our home was a gathering place not only of family, but friends and relatives who were always welcome to stop by.

Mom was a deeply religious person, with a simple faith that never questioned anything religious. It was probably easier then. The Church was pretty straight- forward. The Pope was infallible so whatever the priests said must be infallible too. The parish priest was the last word on everything from sin to marriage problems. He could forgive your sins and grant a dispensation from fasting during Lent or doing necessary farm work to bring in the crops on a Sunday. He ran the parish like his own little kingdom and nobody questioned him. It was a time of speculation about the message reportedly given to the children at Fatima in Portugal by the Blessed Virgin, which was embellished with cold war rhetoric about Russia being converted and there would be peace. Parish churches were certain to have an outdoor shrine to Mary beside the Church.

In addition to her simple religious beliefs, she also grew up with some curious superstitions and quite often the two were inter-twined. For example, she insisted that she eat herring on New Year's Eve for prosperity during the coming year. And if we had a foggy day, she marked it in her diary and would predict that it would return in exactly ninety days. We planted potatoes on Good Friday to insure a plentiful crop. She kept candles and holy water around the house that had been blessed by the priest, and during a violent thunderstorm she would be certain to light a blessed candle. Of course the candle had to be 100% beeswax and blessed by the priest on Candlemas Day.

If there was something going on at the church in St. Peter, we were in attendance. Sunday Mass and weekly confession, Tuesday Night "devotions" to Mary, the Mother of Perpetual Help and during Lent the Stations of the Cross on Wednesday Nights were as much a part of our life as eating and sleeping. In between we generally prayed the family rosary each night after supper. We fasted during Lent, having meat only at the main meal of the day.

The periodicals that came into the home were religious in nature: the Catholic Digest, the Catholic Herald Citizen, the Extension Magazine (dedicated to missionary work in this country) and one or the other magazine published by a religious order, generally sent along with an envelope for donations. I remember her reading only a few books. One of them was the life of Theresa Neumann, a German woman who reputedly had the stigmata (the wounds of Jesus) imprinted on her body, and was revered as a mystic. The other was about a Capuchin priest in Italy, Padre Pio, who had the same stigmata. The books went into great detail about the physical characteristics of the two. Mother was enthralled by their apparent sainthood.

During most years of her illness the parish priest would come once a week to bring her Communion and hear her confession. I doubt that she ever had anything wild to confess. She had a special admiration for any religious, whether nuns, priests or others who had dedicated their lives to their religious beliefs. When our cousins from Johnsburg would come home from the convent we were certain to pay them a visit. I am sure that it was with great pride that she followed my years through the seminary. Even though she was unable to visit for most of those years, I was certain to get a letter from her weekly letting me know what was happening back home on the farm.

Dad was a hard working man, muscular and stocky. I don't ever remember him running with much speed. Just a trot was about all he could manage, but he loved to take walks around his farm, usually on Sunday morning after Mass. He would check the progress of his crops, look at the fence lines, and check out the wildlife. Until the 1960's we rarely saw any deer in the area, but there were plenty of raccoons, squirrels, rabbits and pheasants. Come hunting season and Dad would spend his spare time hunting pheasant, rabbits and squirrels.

A memory that stays with us all is that when he would walk the fifty yards from the barn to the house after doing his morning milking, he would always be whistling on the way. Mom knew it was time to get breakfast on the table then. It was always the same melody too. I never learned the name of the tune; it was probably some song he learned in his youth.

For a farm that relied on keeping machinery in working order, Dad never seemed to have many tools beyond a couple old wrenches that probably came with some long gone machinery, a couple slot screw drivers, a crescent wrench and an assortment of ancient pliers. It always amazed me that he was able to keep his machinery in working order with so few tools.

He did work outside the farm on a couple occasions. Early in their marriage he worked at the hospital in Fond du Lac at night, tending the furnaces. During World War II he worked at the tannery in Fond du Lac. In the 1950's he drove a gravel truck for the people who operated the pits on the farm. He worked at this to qualify for his quarters of Social Security, since farmers were not included in Social Security until later. He worked long enough to get his forty calendar quarters of coverage.

A life-long Republican, he was much more conservative than his children. I remember the early 1950's during the McCarthy hearings and all the muck-raking going on in Washington. Each night dad would sit by our old radio (one that had survived the house fire) and listen to "Gabriel Heater and the News." The line was usually the same: the Communists had infiltrated the State Department and other government bodies and were influencing our government policies. Some of dad's anti-Communist bent came from his years working in the tannery, where he got the Union Newspaper and also a copy of the "Daily Worker" which was the publication of the Communist Party USA. Dad was convinced that the labor unions were working for the Communists. About the only thing he was ready to argue was the issue of labor unions.

Dad left school before he finished the eighth grade, apparently because the Schmitz family needed another hand on the farm. Like far too many of the "Holy Landers" the lack of education was a handicap he would live with the rest of his life. He was somewhat naïve and as a result was taken advantage of by many. For example, for years he sold tomatoes to the buyers from Chicago for fifty cents a bushel, and I am sure he could have gotten much more. When they were building roads around, the contractors were paying the men operating the pits fifteen to twenty-five cents per yard, while dad got only a dime a yard. I am certain that he never got paid more than a small fraction of what was hauled out. He seemed to be happy that he got paid anything for it. He now was getting more money than he earned farming the same hills.

In some things, both mom and dad had knowledge that we still recall with awe. For example, they would make several types of sausages without a recipe, and they were all very good. They butchered hogs and cows, and knew how to cut the animal into various cuts of meat. They remembered the proper temperature for scalding a hog to scrape off the hairs. They made their own soap from cooking grease and lye. Dad kept his apple trees in good health, with a series of sprays applied at different times, from early spring before the trees would bud (for fungus and scale) through the development of the fruit.

Like most of the people in the area, they had little concept of the value of antiques. Probably because these were the things that they used when they grew up, so they had no special significance. We threw things out in the dump that today would be worth a small fortune.

I remember after the house burned that they shopped for furniture at some of the auctions around Fond du Lac. They bought two gorgeous antique bedroom sets, with the high headboard and footboard. The first thing they did was to have them cut down so they looked a little more modern.

Like many people of their era and background, mom and dad were not demonstrative about their affections, either to each other or to their children after they reached a certain age. None of us remember Mom and Dad in an affectionate embrace or kissing one another. We kids certainly did not experience the warmth of a hug. Whether it was a holdover from the Victorian age they were born into or their stoic Germanic heritage, they simply were not openly affectionate. However, with eleven children, they certainly must have been close to each other on some occasions.

Often we hear stories of how wonderful it was to grow up on the farm. I don't know the origins of that romantic notion, but for us it was hardly based in the reality of hard work with little time to enjoy the things that most people think of as farm life.

Chapter Four

Seminary Days

They call it the "hill of happiness, " St. Lawrence Seminary, where nearly three hundred boys from high school freshmen to second year college students studied under the tutelage of the Capuchin priests, members of a religious order that at the time served two parishes in Milwaukee, one in Appleton, with monasteries in northern Wisconsin and Detroit, and missions in Nicaragua and South Dakota. The school is located atop the highest hill for miles around. To the south the wooded hillside slopes to a large swamp. Below the hill was a ball field and swimming pool fed by an artesian well. The pool had a sand or mud bottom so that when it was filled with swimmers, the water turned cloudy and murky. To the west and north was the village of Mt. Calvary, and to the east farmland that stretched to the horizon, much of it wooded swamp and reeds through which the Sheboygan River meandered its way to Lake Michigan.

The gothic steeple of the parish church dominated the landscape from the village side on the north, while from the south, the sun played on the cream colored brick of the seminary's four story main building, the "Laurentianum," built some time near the middle of the 19th century. The seminary dated back to 1860 and the main building was erected shortly after. A tower topped with an observatory and telescope defined the building on the east end and the aluminum painted dome caught the sun nearly a hundred feet above the ground. I remember a couple years in the 1950's when the tower was used by the Civil Defense as a lookout post for invading airplanes. There was someone on duty round the clock (most of them volunteers from the village) watching for incoming Russian bombers. They never came.

The gray stucco monastery to the north housed the priests and brothers. One side was the parish church and the monastery chapel, while the other three wings contained rooms for the brothers and priests who lived there. In the enclosed courtyard was a large fir tree that towered over the two-story structure.

The old gymnasium, St. Thomas Hall, was the only place on campus where there the entire student body, which numbered close to three hundred could gather. It was a multi-purpose building, used for basketball games, movies, general assemblies and plays. About two years before I arrived, the school averted a disaster in the building. During the showing of a Sunday night movie, the film caught in the projector and started on fire. The flames quickly spread along the walls, which were covered front to back with netting to protect the woodwork during basketball games. Luckily everyone got out in time and the fire department was able to extinguish the flames. I can still remember char marks on the basketball floor that they were not able to sand out after the flames. In the process of repairs, they built an addition with fireproof projection booths.

Like most of the young men beginning their long journey toward the priesthood, I was filled with a combination of ideals and bewilderment. This was my first time away from home, living with someone other than members of my own family. It was almost like landing in a foreign country, alone.

When I arrived as a student, I went to the main building to register, a formality consisting mainly of checking my name off a list and getting assigned to one of the dorms. My assigned dorm was St. Joseph's Hall, attached to the main building and built some time in the third quarter of the 19th century, shortly after the main building. It was vintage 19th century. There were some fifty beds lined up barracks style with less than two feet between them. Mine was next to the door leading to the rear entrance. We were each assigned a locker, the type found in schools, and all our possessions had to fit either in this twelve-inch wide locker or under our beds in a suitcase. There were no locks on the lockers. This was a seminary and students were expected to be paragons of virtue. Any theft was punished by expulsion. Frankly, I never had much that might have been worth stealing.

There was a washroom with about a dozen sinks on the first floor, which was meant to serve the fifty or so young men on the second floor as well as another thirty who slept on the third floor. There was a shower room on the first floor, but showers were allowed only on Wednesday and Saturday afternoons. Toilets for both floors were at one end of the dorm on the second floor, plus a couple of stalls and urinals on the first floor. Lord help the kid who had the flu and had to go.

To supervise the area, a priest had his small room just outside the dorm, and a "prefect" – an older student – also slept in the dorm and was assigned to keep order. Silence was to be observed after night prayers in the chapel and anyone caught talking or creating a commotion had to "kneel out" on the hard floors for as long as the prefect saw fit.

Each morning at 6:00 the priest in charge or the prefect would walk up and down the aisles ringing an old brass school bell to wake everybody. On return he checked that everybody was out of bed and getting dressed. We had twenty minutes to get dressed, wash up, brush our teeth, and if we were old enough to have whiskers, to shave, and be in the chapel for morning prayers. Quite a feat considering you spent at least half that time standing in line for a sink or urinal.

One abiding memory of the dorms was the pervasive body odor that settled during the night, as ventilation was not the best in these old buildings. With the boys sleeping with less than a yard between beds, the place reeked, especially on warm nights. Just imagine fifty bodies in the same room that only got an opportunity to shower on Wednesdays and Saturdays.

Morning prayers were in chapel, where each student had an assigned place, making it easy to check who was absent. It also meant that if the next person in the alphabet had a bad case of halitosis or body odor, you were stuck with it every day several times a day. If you came late you had to kneel out at the front of the chapel for the duration of whatever the spiritual exercise was.

There was a "meditation" read by the spiritual director from a microphone at the back of the chapel. These meditations were an assortment of pious sentimental garbage unfit for human consumption, and certainly with no grounding in spirituality or theology. After these "inspiring" tales, we were supposed to meditate for a few minutes, but most of us merely nodded off to sleep or daydreamed of something else. To be perfectly honest these little pious stories were insipid. Some of them were recurring themes, like the little verse.

"Mother Mary, dressed in blue,
Teach us how to pray
For God was just your little boy
And you know what to say."

There was the recurring theme of Mary as our Mother and Jesus was our brother. I often sat there in the pew early in the morning wondering if Jesus was my brother, then my brother was an only child. But then meditation was never meant to be logical, or perhaps even rational, just a way to commune with God. Frankly, I never did get the hang of it and I often wonder how many, if any, of my classmates did. My guess is most of them faked it or had some sort of self-delusions.

The meditation was followed by Mass, which would last about a half-hour or more. The Mass was in Latin with the altar facing the back wall. Usually it was a "low mass" in which the priest merely mumbled the prayers of the Mass in a low tone with no participation or music. Students were encouraged to follow along in their own prayer books or pray the rosary or any other pious devotion that seemed appropriate. There was little interaction between what was going on at the altar and what the people in the pews were doing. The priest was doing his little "magic act" and the only participation needed was when we filed to the communion railing and the priest placed the sacred wafer on our tongues. I remember being asked by someone at the time about at what point going to Mass every day became a meaningful and enjoyable experience. I never did answer the question. I am sure that most of the "good feeling" associated with the practice had little to do with anything other than this is "what you're supposed to do."

The priests rotated saying Mass in the mornings. The favorites of the students were the priests who were able to get through it relatively quickly. My least favorite, Fr. Alex, insisted on being as slow and deliberate as possible. His Mass always took at least fifteen minutes longer than everybody else. He explained that he wanted every Mass to be as careful and thoughtful as his First Mass had been and exacting details of every rubric had to be performed precisely. The word "scrupulous" comes to mind.

Following Mass there was a time of prayerful "thanksgiving" until the priest at the back of the chapel would rap on the pew as a signal for the students to file out, starting from the rear where the older students sat, and process in silence to the dining hall in the next building. Breakfast usually consisted of cold cereal and white bread. On occasion the choice would be warm cereal. All this was served in a stainless steel compartmentalized tray, the same kind used in prison dining rooms.

After breakfast no one was allowed in the buildings until the bell rang for classes, unless the weather was inclement. Many of us would take the opportunity to walk to the bottom of the hill while others would toss a football or baseball around or just stand around and talk with friends. In the winter we shivered in the cold winds that always whipped the top of the hill.

Our first class, held six days a week at 8:00 promptly, was usually Latin. We had Wednesday and Saturday afternoons free. There were no electives. Latin, German and Greek were the only languages taught. In science there was a year of physics, one of chemistry, and one of biology. Two years of math in high school and one in college, usually taught by a priest who often knew less than the students who read the next chapter. Being a private school, the instructors were not required to have a teaching degree or any expertise in the subject they taught and few of them did. One of them, Fr. Peter, seemed to have taught just about everything in the curriculum at one time or another. The Capuchin priests who staffed the school studied at Mt. Calvary and in the Capuchin seminary, and after ordination came back to teach, a kind of intellectual incest.

History and literature classes concentrated on Catholic history and Catholic authors usually to the neglect of the rest of the subject matter.

We studied the history of the Catholics in Maryland and the establishment of various dioceses around the country and traced the establishment of the missions in California, but little else of American history. In English we studied the Catholic writers and bemoaned the fact that there were no great Catholic writers in America. I remember Fr. Andrew who taught European History, and read barely a chapter ahead of the class in the text. He also taught a speech class, which half the time was a "dry run" for the sermon that he was planning to give on Sunday at some area parish. There was no phys-ed, but everyone had to play softball and basketball, regardless of their talents or wishes. This made for some interesting games, as some of the students had never played any of these sports.

I once read the school catalog and noted it bore little resemblance to what went on in the classrooms. In some classes we used out-of-print texts that were available only from those who had the course the year before. The catalog touted the large school library, which for the most part was contained in one small classroom and a pile of old books stashed away high in the tower leading to the observatory on one end of the main building.

Oddly, for a seminary, the weakest part of the curriculum was the study of religion itself. In high school, there was simply no religion class at all. In college we had one three-credit course on the life of Christ and another course on the history of the Mass. Both were decent, but there was nothing about Scripture or doctrine. Apparently the seminary thought that a heavy dose of religious exercises in chapel were sufficient and that knowledge was superfluous.

A few classes and professors come to mind when I think of the best and worst of the lot. I can't think of one in retrospect who might be considered excellent. Fr. Roman, who taught a civics class, had recently returned from the missions in Nicaragua and taught more about the snakes in the jungles of Latin America than he did on American Government. An interesting story teller, he certainly was not a teacher.

I remember getting a "B" in Physics, though I had the highest test scores in the class for the semester (a 98% average if I recall). I complained, but to no avail. The rest of the year my test scores were 100%, and I finally did get my "A" but probably only because I let it be known to the whole class that I got shafted. They all knew that I was always the one who knew the answers to the questions, and could figure out all the experiments better than Fr. Silas who bungled through the course work.

Fr. Ralph taught Latin and German. I remember a course on Cicero in which we covered only a single brief paragraph for a whole semester. We learned every exception to every rule and the root of every word in Greek, Sanskrit, Old Roman and its derivatives in French, Spanish, Old English and Anglo-Saxon, or whatever language Fr. Ralph saw in the dictionary that day. We never did study Cicero. He had to be the worst teacher I ever had, bar none, totally disorganized, without a curriculum guide, lesson plan, or any idea where he was going to be from day to day or at the end of the course.

He seemed to take pleasure in belittling and embarrassing the students. I remember one exam he gave to the class. There were fifty True and False questions, all of them true. I figured out after doing half of it that he was up to something, and was the only one in the class who got them all right. Not that I knew the material, but I knew Fr. Ralph. He was had a hard time covering his displeasure that I caught on to his perverse mind.

Fr. Louie was the professor of Greek, with white hair and a white beard, and a resonant, nasal, baritone voice. A native of Germany, he was popular among the parishes in the area for his German sermons. One summer he took a trip back to his native land. No one in his native Bavaria could understand a word he was saying.

We were in class all morning with a short break between classes, a fifteen minute break mid morning for bathroom runs, and class till noon. Half the student body would gather in chapel for rosary at noon, followed by lunch in the cafeteria. The other half of the student body would say their rosary at night, arriving in the cafeteria later to reduce the congestion in the dining room.

Afternoon classes resumed at 1:00 and ended at 3:00. If there was no scheduled class, we spent the time in study hall. We were free for an hour in the afternoon to play sports or whatever. At 4:30 we were called back to study hall by the ominous bell atop the main building.

A priest sat on a raised platform to supervise the study hall. In his absence one of the students would be appointed to keep order. Generally the priest in charge read a book or perhaps worked on his class notes for the following day. I remember Fr. Maurice who took advantage of the time for a short nap. One evening some of us got the idea to see if we could get everyone out of the study hall without him waking up. We slipped out in groups of three or four, and about a half hour later he woke up wondering what happened and where everybody went.

We had to obtain permission to go to the bathroom. Silence was to be observed at all times. If you talked or disturbed your neighbor and were caught, the priest ordered you to "kneel out" on the hard floor for as long as he thought necessary to mend your ways.

At 5:30 half the gang went to dinner while the other half went to chapel for rosary. We were free then until 7:00 when we returned to study hall for another hour and a half. At 8:30 we had night prayers in chapel followed by another pious "meditation" to give us holy thoughts during the night. We were expected to take a rosary to bed to occupy our hands and bring prayerful thoughts rather than those "impure" thoughts that young men were prone to.

The school had a system of speakers in each of the buildings and at various strategic locations outside. This was used to summon people to the main building. At times they would patch it in to the radio of phonograph and play music, or baseball games, or whatever the priests in charge wanted to do. For the last half hour of study hall in the evening they generally played music for us.

There were some lighter moments in my years on the hill. Bart, a kid from northern Wisconsin, was an astute woodsman and in the winter would trap rabbits which he would dress, freeze outside, wrap and ship home to his parents. During English class one day, Fr. Roland, who among the priests was probably the most cultured and urbane, noticed that Bart had his desk top up, with his head down in the storage space beneath. Fr. Roland, wondering what was going on with Bart in the back of the room, strolled back and forth in the aisle, talking all the time and when he was at the back of the room he saw what Bart was doing in his desk. He was dressing out a rabbit during English class!

Bart was expelled a couple of months later, but not for dressing rabbits. The school had a collection of civil war muskets and rifles stored behind the stage in the auditorium / gym. A couple of the muskets and an assortment of watches appeared in his trunk in the basement of a dorm and Bart was dismissed just days before the end of the school year. I lost track of Bart after that, but I did hear years later that he was doing time for some crime or other.

Frank was another interesting student. In our second year of college we had private rooms, and Frank always tried to be up and out of the building before everyone else. One night we changed all the clocks in the hallway, and someone slipped into his room when he went to the bathroom and reset his alarm clock. His alarm went off about 3:00 AM, but said 6:00, as did all the clocks in the hallway. So Frank washed up and headed across campus to the chapel. When he arrived, the place was dark. About an hour later he finally figured out what happened. Never did find out who did all the dirty work though.

The minor seminary (as opposed to the major seminary which taught philosophy and theology) was a six-year school, with high school freshmen to second year of college in the same school. In addition, there were "special" students, who had finished high school elsewhere but did not have Latin. They were, for the most part, older than the rest of us. They spent one year as "specials" concentrating on learning Latin. I remember one man from south Texas who had to be at least forty and had never seen snow. Poor guy nearly froze in winter. He even had battery heated socks in a vain effort to battle the elements. He lasted through the year but did not return the next. These "specials" apparently were a fertile ground for the good fathers to recruit candidates for their order.

We had a dress code of sorts. We had to wear shirts with collars and could not wear blue jeans. Shorts were only allowed for basketball games, and our shoes could not have cleats on the heels. Crew cuts were not allowed except with the permission of the rector, and no beards were allowed, which was comical since the Capuchins wore beards as part of their religious identity. (Incidentally the word "cappuccino" derives from the religious order.)

Since there were no laundry facilities on the hill, we either had to send our laundry home (which was easy for me with my family only ten miles away) or find some woman in the village who took in laundry for some of the students. A few students had theirs done in the village, while most sent theirs home by mail in "laundry boxes" designed for that purpose whether made of tempered cardboard or aluminum. The school had a truck going to and from the post office each day with a load of boxes. Regularly the box was returned by mail with some cookies or other treats from home.

On Sunday afternoons during the winter we had intra-mural basketball games in the gym, and visitors filled the seats to watch their sons on the court. I remember one Sunday when a classmate stood on the floor and removed his sweat pants. Unfortunately, he had forgotten to put on his trunks, and didn't realize it. I doubt if his mother came to another of his basketball games.

One of the priests, Fr. George, was quite the naturalist, and a noted ornithologist. He trapped birds and banded them for the Fish and Wildlife Service for years. We became friends early on and I learned a great deal about bird life from him.

It was common at the beginning of each school year to play some prank or other on the new freshmen. One year some of the older students took a group of naïve youngsters on a "snipe hunt" out in the swamp to capture the birds for Fr. George so he could band them. The new kids were placed in position with a burlap bag and flashlight to catch "snipe" as the other boys flushed them in their direction. When they came an hour late for the evening study hall, they explained that they were out catching "snipe" for Fr. George. Without hesitation, the priest in charge approached Fr. George and asked him why he was having students catch snipes for him in the dark instead of being in study hall. Fr. George had a good laugh at that one.

Another priest also served a little country parish in the town of St. Joe, a few miles away. One year he experimented with various leaves and wood -resins trying to create his own incense for use in the parish church. He tried many, and selected a number of leaves that burned with a pleasant aroma. He mixed them together and tried them out

Christmas Eve with the parish church filled to capacity. It wasn't long before the windows and doors were opened in the dead of winter. While the leaves and resins may have been all right alone, together they created quite a stench.

Tragedy struck twice during my years on the hill. The first occurred when a group of young men were trying their hand at shot-putt in preparation for the games at the annual "field day." A high school freshman either stepped in the path of the shot, or it was an errant toss, and it hit him in the head. He died a few hours later.

The other death happened when the school choir went on a picnic at a boy -scout camp along Lake Winnebago. Some of the lads took to the water in canoes, and when one capsized a young man drowned. They violated had the first scout rule of the water: always wear a life jacket.

Ever looking for a good line, the spiritual director, who read his sappy meditations to us morning and night, soon recalled inspirational stories of what the young men had told him about their great love for God and their exemplary virtue. I often didn't know whether to throw up or look for the miracles to begin happening so we could declare them saints. Of course, it was "God's will" to take these fine young men to heaven, rather than gross neglect on the part of the school to allow these activities to go unsupervised. No one thought to lay the blame on neglect on the part of the good "Fathers."

We seemed to have more than our share of troubled young men whose parents were only too happy to send them off to a boarding school where hopefully they would be out of trouble and maybe the priests could straighten them out. It seems that parents who had prob-lems with their children were certain that the discipline of the seminary and the priests who ran it would solve all their problems. I don't know if any of them were in trouble with the law or not, but some were strange to say the least. I remember a kid from Chicago who though being tall and well built, was about as effeminate a person as I had met up to that time in my life. Totally inept at anything physical, he tried to make his mark by being the "gung ho" religious person. There was a set of prayers often used by women religious at the time called the "Little

Office" which contained some psalms and prayers, sort of a watered down version of the "Divine Office" that priests were required to pray each day. The larger version began with the medieval monks chanting the psalms and reading Bible passages in the great cathedrals and abbeys of Europe. Jimmy religiously said his prayers each day, making sure that those around him noticed that he was praying, whether this was between class, or if he would make a trip to the chapel during recreation time. Mentally disturbed, I would say, trying to masquerade as a holy man. I often wonder if he ever made it to ordination, and it would be interesting to find out what kind of a misfit he was in the ministry if he did.

I must admit, for the most part we were rather disciplined and docile. If you were not, your stay could be cut short. There were many who were asked not to return at the end of summer or even during the vacations during the year. Seldom, if ever, did they reappear on the hill. There was never an explanation given to the students, and the usual guess was that the young man was "homesick."

Our mail was censored, both outgoing and incoming. So much for privacy! Letters were distributed in the evening study hall, and our-going mail was to be placed unsealed in a box, and we never quite knew if anyone read it. I am quite sure that if a letter smelled of perfume one of the priests would take a peek.

We were allowed to make phone calls only from the Rector's office, with permission, not exactly the setting for a romantic phone call to a girl-friend back home. And in-coming phone calls were rare, usually a message would be taken and the person called to the office to make a return collect call.

Whenever there was an emergency faculty meeting, we were certain someone would be gone the next day. Among the infractions, theft was the most common, and certainly not tolerated. However, just violating the strict rules by talking during times of silence, leaving the grounds without permission, or any number of infractions were grounds for expulsion. There was no appeal, and the expulsion could come without warning and at any time. After vacations we noticed kids who turned up missing. I am sure that many of them were asked not to return after the summer vacation.

Most of the expulsions were students in their first or second year of study. Often the student was called into the office of the Rector and given the news and told to pack his things quietly, given the opportunity to call his parents, and then escorted to a train or bus depot quietly. With many it was probably immaturity, while other troubled youth needed counseling and perhaps therapy. At the time there was no one on the staff trained to deal with behavior problems or even recognize them. It seemed the seminary bore no responsibility for any behavior that did not fit the mold. If one did not question, rebel, or challenge the status quo, it was considered virtuous. Obedience was championed as the highest virtue. Obviously they were trying to prepare us for a life of submission to authority in the Church where it was considered sinful to question or disobey anyone in authority. If you had a rebellious spirit or questioned the wisdom of the good fathers, you obviously did not have a "vocation." Voluntary or not, the attrition rate among seminarians was quite high, even in the 1950's.

The seminary was on the circuit for missionaries back in the country from their foreign assignments, either Capuchin fathers or from some other religious group. Usually there would be a 16mm film and the speaker would spin yarns about the glorious work his Order was doing in foreign lands, usually Africa, Latin America or the jungles of New Guinea.

I remember one religious order presented their show, and then talked about the stern discipline of the priests who, among other things, ate their meals standing rather than seated at a table. I wondered at the time if It made any difference to God how they ate. Each of the groups had their own distinctive religious garb or habit designed to set them aside from all others. While they all took a vow of poverty, I could never quite understand what that had to do with a custom made religious garb that certainly was not comfortable or practical and probably cost much more than conventional clothing.

One can appreciate the struggle to feed some three hundred hungry young men and another forty priests and brothers on a limited budget, and the dining room fare at St. Lawrence would not tempt an epicure. Fr. Gerald, the rector, was approached by a woman who wanted to start an order of women religious. He saw opportunity, and wrote the order's "rule" and helped them get established as a religious order and approved by the Church as such. There were about a dozen of them initially, and they found their work as cooks for the seminary and the priests, taking over the task that had once been done by the religious brothers of the order. From stories I heard from men who had been there years before, the nuns were an improvement but that isn't to say they were gourmet cooks.

I doubt if any of the women were well educated, and they were certainly not skilled in the culinary arts. Their favorite kitchen appliance was the steam kettle, with everything coming out tasteless and overdone. During the summer two of the priests went fishing and came back with a stringer of beautiful lake perch. Coming back late in the evening, they just put them in one of the coolers in the kitchen over night, planning to clean them the next morning and have them for dinner. Mid morning, they came to the kitchen and looked for their fish. They looked in the cooler and could not find their fish. Snooping around the kitchen, they found them swirling around in the steam kettle, head, scales, guts and all.

One staple was bread, bought from a bakery in Fond du Lac, which someone had to drive the fifteen miles each day to pick up. Between the bread, jelly and jam, we didn't starve. Though I remember the time when they apparently got a deal on some butter – it was rancid. That's a taste you never forget, even just a hint of it. Occasionally I was asked to make the trip to pick up the bread. Usually it was during foul winter weather because the priests knew that I was accustomed to driving in foul weather on country roads.

A local farmer supplied the milk, not pasteurized, of course. He would bring it each day in ten- gallon milk cans. He would also take away several cans of garbage for pig food. The amount of food he hauled away each day was a pretty good percentage of what had been served. Surprising, - that is unless you'd eaten some of the food. When health regulations forbid using garbage for hog food, they dug a hole in the swamp below the hill and dumped the garbage in it. Naturally a hole in the swamp filled with water, and the mixture ripened into a stench you could smell for a mile when the wind was right.

The other smell was the sewer system. Without municipal sewers at the time, everything drained into a large septic tank, which overflowed downhill through a narrow channel to a grove of willow trees at the bottom of the hill. When the weather turned warm, you didn't want to be close. The pool of untreated effluent covered a couple acres of willow trees and swamp, and had been there many years. Every now and then they would have to clean out the septic tank when it got filled, so they merely pumped out the contents into the channel, down to the bottom of the hill, where it all flowed untreated into the Sheboygan River.

To help support the seminary, the Capuchins were into mail solicitation fund raising. They mailed a couple of million pieces of mail each year, asking for donations for the "poor boys" seminary; most of the lads were from working class families. Much of the printing was done in a print shop maintained at the school. I helped out from time to time and learned the basics of printing. I also gained some inside knowledge on the "begging" industry and how they bought and sold lists or names, particularly of those who had been generous donors in the past. Some people wonder how they get on so many lists. The beggars all swap lists or buy them from one another. I learned that there was nearly as much money to be made selling donor lists as was provided by the donors themselves. I learned early that when you donated to one charity, you were likely to be on the list of several more.

Sundays were visiting days in the afternoons with the exception of the first Sunday of each month, when for some reason, there was no visiting, just boredom. We had two Masses on Sundays, with an hour study hall in the morning as well. Visiting hours usually ended before rosary and benediction in the afternoon, just before dinner, and there would be a Sunday movie in the gym at night.

For a couple of years I was one of the projectionists for the movies. We'd preview the films on Saturdays for the nuns and whatever priests wanted to catch the Saturday show if they were going to be out of town Sunday. The priest who oversaw the projection room kept a careful eye out for things that were not suitable for young impressionable boys. We would often cut part of a film (35 mm), show it to the students, and then splice it back in before we returned the film. There were times when the copies were quite butchered, and these were films that were rated PG and pre-selected for suitability for seminary students.

It was a big deal when the school bought a television set (black and white) and we were allowed to watch Bishop Sheen and on occasion Lawrence Welk. The set was locked away for the rest of the week.

As students we were supposed to have a "spiritual director;" but there was no clear idea of what this person should be doing. Obviously the priests were not trained counselors or therapists, so I wondered what they really did other than other than have friendly chats with the young men. As a new student I was given an appointment with the priest assigned as spiritual director. Frankly he gave me the creeps the moment I met him though I was at a loss to know why. When we met in his office, all he wanted to know about me was how frequently, when and where I masturbated. I never went back and through my seminary years never had an inclination to seek out spiritual direction again.

I did notice that the lads who had fair, boyish features and complexion seemed to be going in for spiritual direction more than the rest of the gang. Often it seemed these pious young men did not return after vacation at Christmas or Easter, or over the summer.

Years later, when a pedophilia scandal at the school hit the press, some of my doubts were confirmed. I talked to men I knew from my days there and asked if they had any suspicions when we were there. The same name came back in just about every case. I wasn't alone in my suspicions. Fortunately, I never had to endure the proof. I remember taking the physical exam as part of the entrance requirements. One of the items that raised an eyebrow on the doctor as well as myself was the requirement of a blood test for venereal disease. This was in the early 1950's and most of the lads entering the seminary were only fourteen years old. Did they have a problem then they were not willing to admit?

We were always warned about "particular friendships" so that if you were seen often enough with the same fellow student, one of the priests was bound to take you aside and warn you that this was not acceptable, and you should mingle with more of your classmates. Years later I finally figured out why.

Years later, when reading of the sexual problems of some priests, I wonder if the roots were in the system itself. For the most part these young men were from conservative homes, taught by nuns in Catholic schools. They had little social contact with women as adolescents. It would be safe to say they were at best sexually naïve perhaps a fertile ground for homosexuality and pedophilia. Certainly this was not the environment that would enlighten one about sexuality, with the movies censured, reading materials limited to selected books and carefully screened periodicals, sometimes with pictures of women cut out before they were allowed to be seen by the students. It is little wonder that many arrived at ordination emotionally immature and found it safer to develop relationships with young boys than with mature adults.

The model of saintliness at the time emanated from Pope Pius XII, who was always shown as an ascetic looking man in his full papal robes walking serenely, hands folded and never seeming to notice anyone around him. He seemed to be photographed in profile in an saintly pose, lost in thought, meditation, or whatever. It seemed he was always in a trance or in direct communication with God. I remember one of the priests at the seminary who was said to be a very holy man. My memories of him are that he was out of touch with the world he lived in and seemed to be walking around in a fog all the time, and spoke only in a soft voice, but when he was in chapel his hands were always perfectly folded with fingers pointed upward with the left thumb crossed over the right as was proper according to the rubrics on the matter. He seldom inter-acted with anyone that I can remember. I used to question myself about my own spirituality, thinking that I was too grounded in the real world to be spiritual. I wondered how someone could be said to be saintly who was simply living in a different world, sort of self-induced delusion or was there something that I just wasn't getting? Given the religious art of the 1950's that depicted male Saints and Jesus with soft, effeminate features, the role models taken from art certainly did not encourage manliness in those who aspired to be saintly. I didn't know anything about mental illness then and gays were still in the closet, but in retrospect I wonder how much of what passed as sanctity was in fact mental illness or non-heterosexual orientation.

Unfortunately many of these men went on to be ordained and served or rather abused parishioners, their assistants and the women who staffed their parish schools.

Report cards needed to be sent home, not only for a parent's signature but also the signature of the parish priest, apparently to keep communication open with the priest in the parish. Of course when the seminarian went home for vacations, he was always the center of attention in the parish and in the family, giving them bragging rights of sorts. He was also expected to be at Mass every day, and have the parish priest verify this at the end of the summer. Again the long arm of the seminary sought to control even when we were away on vacation.

Before each vacation, we were sure to get an extended lecture on the dangers of "losing one's vocation." Obviously the greatest danger was association with persons of the opposite gender, especially that horrible practice of dating. This did not pose much of a problem for some, whom I suspected had not yet come to grips with their own sexuality or were already swinging from the other side of the plate. Seminary life was a safe haven away from the fear of these inter-gender relationships. The basis of sexual problems of priests later in life surely had roots in these years. Some simply never reached emotional and sexual maturity, and later in life engaged in what might have been pre-puberty explorations with children in their charge. One wonders if the environment gave root to a higher incidence of homosexuality among priests later in life, or if young men with gay tendencies found it more attractive than life outside the walls.

The Capuchin priests were an interesting lot. By rule of the Order they usually were bearded, with some doing no trim at all, to a few who maintained a clean-shaven face. There was one, Fr. Crispin, who claimed to have never shaved in his life. A number of them maintained a small goatee. Few of them would have won any prizes for beard design or maintenance. None, to my memory, had handlebar moustaches. They prided themselves on being "poor monks" but I could not quite get the connection between the vow of poverty and being unkempt.

Their habit was an ankle length brown robe of coarse wool with a hood or "capuche" (thus the word Capuchin). At the waist it was bound by a cincture, a white woolen rope with a slip knot from which two ends dangled usually with a total of three knots, symbolic of their three vows of poverty, chastity and obedience to their superiors. Attached to the cincture they wore a large rosary with wooden beads that jingled as they walked. They generally had two "habits" – an everyday one and a dress one. They were not always the cleanest articles of clothing around, sometimes bearing remnants from three or four food groups down the front. In the winter most of them would wear trousers underneath, but for the rest of the year, they did not. On their feet they wore heavy leather sandals. Though in the winter some of them wore socks and even shoes, some of the hardy souls would brave the elements except in the coldest weather in sandals and bare feet. While they had the usual black suit and Roman collar, these were worn only on the occasions when they traveled. Around the school they always wore the garb of the order.

Health care was antiquated at best. There was an old German, Brother Goddard, who ran the infirmary, which consisted of six beds and one bathroom in one room in the old building. There was no medical equipment beyond a thermometer and a bottle of aspirin and certainly no medical training for brother Goddard who seemed to be more interested in his little raffles and sale of religious articles than in caring for the sick. Thank God I never got sick enough to be in bed during my years there. I was lucky: in all my years in the seminary I never missed a day of class because of illness.

There was a doctor's office in the village where Doctor Joe Miller practiced. He had been a student at the seminary until he fell in love with one of the young ladies from the village, married her and came back to the village to practice medicine and raise his family of a dozen. By today's standards, it was rudimentary medicine at best, but as far as I know, he treated the seminarians without charging a fee.

At the end of high school those who were entering the Capuchin Order departed for the novitiate, a year dedicated to studying the rule and discipline of the Order. After the novitiate, there were a series of "vows" of poverty, obedience to superiors and chastity. Their further studies were all done in the Order's own schools, taught by men whose training had been the same. The fathers were quite good at recruiting among the classes, particularly among those who seemed to need a lot of "spiritual direction."

The seminary is still there, one of two in the country that still accepts high school age students. In retrospect, I wonder that it has lasted, but it was the "feeder school" for the Capuchin order. The dropout rate was high in our day. Only a small percentage who entered as high school freshmen were ever ordained. Many left after high school. At each break or vacation there would be a number who didn't return, either by choice or otherwise. The good fathers were quite willing to expel anyone who didn't quite fit their idea of what a good seminarian should be. I used to wonder if they were asked to leave or could not face another day or year on the Hill of Happiness.

Class content reflected a "castle under siege" mentality that allowed for no temptations. I remember our biology professor teaching the section on human reproduction. He put his head down and mumbled for an hour, without once looking at the class, then told us to skip that chapter in the book because it would not be on the test. Of course, we then poured over that chapter in detail. We spent more time analyzing the earthworm than in learning about the bodies we inhabited.

Many of the men who spent time on the hill returned year after year for the alumni meetings and dripped with nostalgia about the best years of their lives spent with the good fathers. After ordination I visited the good fathers on the top of the hill, coming away with a strong feeling that I had made a good decision not to join that religious order. In fact, I felt downright uncomfortable with a group of them in their recreation room. Since then I have returned to see what has changed: a couple of new buildings, some of the old. The only fond memory I ever have any desire to relive is the spectacular view

Upon graduation from the "Hill of Happiness" students continued studies for the priesthood either with the Capuchin Order or in various "major" seminaries throughout the Midwest. Studying for the diocese of Milwaukee, I naturally enrolled in the diocesan seminary at St. Francis. Even though it was less than a hundred miles away, I knew very little about the school when I arrived other than the location, along the shores of Lake Michigan south of Milwaukee.

I remember receiving a detailed list of things to bring along, including having every item of clothing and linens marked with identifying tape for the laundry, Also we were required to have a "cassock" – a floor length garment with a "Roman collar," two "surplices" - a white wide-sleeved shirt that fit over the cassock for chapel services. Also required was a "biretta" – the funny looking black headpiece with three wings joined by a tassel in the middle. Each man had to purchase a "Zimmarra" – an ankle length woolen overcoat with a cape covering the shoulders. All were custom made by a tailor from Chicago, made in the manner of the overcoats worn by seminarians and priests in Rome.

The list also included a desk lamp, even specifying the wattage of the bulb allowed. Forbidden were record players, radios and television sets. We were to be educated in a vacuum isolated from the world in which we were to provide religious leadership. Individuality was considered a threat and conformity was raised to a level of virtue.

We were given room assignments upon arrival, and I proceeded to unpack and get my room in order. I was on the fourth floor of the north wing of a building that dated back to a time prior to the civil war. The seminary dated from 1856 and this was the original section of the building. The first order of business was "room inspection" by the Rector, Msgr. Frank, who made the rounds to all the rooms with the Dean of Students, Fr. Leroy in tow. If they noticed something more than the Spartan rooms, the student was told it was not allowed.

The rooms were "dorm size" with a basin and mirror, a bed, a desk with a bookshelf, a single chair and a steel locker for clothing. At 5:30 the bell summoned us to chapel for the recitation of the rosary. Dinner followed and we were assigned to tables with our classmates on a weekly rotation so that in the course of a few weeks we dined with every one of our classmates. The priests on the faculty rotated supervising the dining room for lunch and evening meals. They sat on a raised table near the middle of the hall. Their only apparent duty was to signal when the meal was finished. Of course each meal began and ended with prayers.

At the noon meal it was the custom to read the "Roman Martyrology" for the day, a recitation of the martyrs and saints of history and their deeds, real or fictional, mainly fictional and often mythical. We alternated between Latin and English. Other than learning the names of some ancient heroes, there was little point to the practice and certainly little historical evidence to support the text. Rome finally admitted such during the Vatican Council when they deleted a number of "saints" from the list because they probably existed only in pious myth. Among them were the beloved St. Christopher, St. Philomena and others. There was a bit of name changing on Catholic Churches for a while.

At 7:00 PM that first night we all gathered in the auditorium for the formal "reading of the rules" by the Dean of Students, Fr. Leroy. I remember it was sweltering hot as we gathered, decked out in our long black "cassocks" to listen to him drone on for two hours on all that was forbidden to us, nearly all peccadillos were grounds for dismissal. Included in the pages of mimeographed rules were maps of the campus indicating where it was permitted to walk, congregate or smoke a cigarette. Smoking was allowed in only one building, the basement of the gymnasium where there were card tables and chairs. We were required to wear our cassocks and Roman collars to chapel, meals, classes, and other times when we were out of our rooms, unless engaged in sports.

We were told in no uncertain terms that there was to be silence in the residence halls at all times, since these were houses of study. Visiting another student's room was not allowed. In fact if two students were caught in the same room it was grounds for dismissal. We were not to leave the grounds without permission, checking out and checking back in with the dean of students. The sole exception was that we could walk to the lake in the morning before class. Likewise it was forbidden to have visitors except when a visitation day was declared by the Rector, who did it once during my six years there and even then visitors were not allowed in the residence areas of the buildings, which actually comprised most of the buildings.

Each section of the residence halls was supervised by a "prefect," – one of the older students, whose job was to enforce the rules on the floor. For some reason, I was never chosen for that task. My guess is that I was not considered compliant enough to enforce the minutiae of the rules.

The faculty was staffed by priests from the Milwaukee diocese. Nearly all were educated at the Seminary with graduate work in Rome or at Catholic University in Washington. This did not encourage diversity of ideas; there was little encouragement to intellectual inquiry in the Church at the time. It was important to learn the "traditional and accepted" authors rather than investigate and question. In fact most of the philosophy and theology books used at the time were re-hashes of prior writings that had been used until they went out of print. It was the era when the American Church looked to Rome to educate its leaders and never questioned the wisdom or appropriateness of anything coming out of the Vatican. Most bishops in the country had at least some of their education in one of the schools in Rome, and a high percentage of the faculty of the seminaries studied there as well.

I remember the library had a copy of a monthly magazine titled "The Pope Speaks" which contained just about every word that Pius XII had said in the prior month. Another periodical was "Observatore Romano" the daily newspaper of the Vatican. Both were considered of such weight that they could never be called into question, probably on a par with the Bible. Both our philosophy and theology courses were based mainly on the thirteenth century writings of Thomas Aquinas, as if there had been no progress in thought for seven centuries, or that no one other than the Vatican had anything worth our while to study.

The American Church had established a theology school in Rome called the North American College and Rome encouraged each diocese to send students for their theology studies. Milwaukee generally sent one or two each year, and on occasion sent men to one or the other seminaries in Europe or to the Catholic University in Washington. These were the men who were more likely to be on the short list for diocesan offices in the chancery, teaching at the seminary, or might be on the short list of candidates for bishop. They were usually among the best students and ones who tended to be more conservative. Priests who were selected for diocesan offices or promotion to bishop were generally selected because they were considered "safe," and were not likely to rock the bark of Peter. A large percentage of the bishops in the country studied in Rome.

Our class schedule was brutal. I remember the first two years at St. Francis carrying twenty-five or twenty-six credit hours per semester, a number of them one or two credit courses. The bulk of the schedule consisted of philosophy courses in preparation for theology. We had two professors of philosophy: Fr. Jack, who played football at Marquette when they still had a team, and Fr. Victor, a short little man who spoke with a distinctive lisp. They were quite a pair.

Fr. Jack apparently liked to have a mid-morning nip and would sterilize the air in the first few rows of the room for late morning classes. He complained that on his seminary salary he could not afford to drink Scotch and lamented the fact that he was forced by poverty to drink brandy. Apparently he compensated in quantity what he lacked in quality. He had studied under the Dominicans who insisted there had been no evolution of thought since Thomas Aquinas, their bright star of the 13th century. While Fr. Jack would argue the point, his courses were none-the-less a rehash of Aquinas based on Latin textbooks written by a Dominican priest in Canada. He never mentioned any of the contemporary writers, since if they disagreed with Aquinas they were wrong to begin with.

Some years after my leaving St. Francis, Jack made headlines, but not for his scholarly pursuits. When the Pope (Paul VI) condemned all types of birth control as sinful, Jack made news when he publicly declared that he could not agree; he resigned his post and joined the Episcopal Church at their seminary in Nashotah. Apparently he was living at Nashotah House with no source of income, and was not welcomed with open arms by the Episcopalians at any rate. In fact, he must have been something of an embarrassment to the Episcopal diocese as well as the Catholic Bishop. He then made a public admission of the "error of his ways" and asked the bishop for forgiveness and readmission into the Catholic Diocese. He spent his remaining days as pastor of a small country parish.

Fr. Victor studied at the Catholic University in the early 1940's, under Bishop Fulton Sheen. His courses were almost entirely from his class notes from Sheen's courses. He spent weeks in one course trying to refute the theories of evolution and insisting that God created the world much the way we find it today. Evolution, he maintained, was simply an unproven theory without evidence to back it up.

He had a student as his teaching assistant each year. The student would run off the tests for him from the stack of mimeo masters he kept on file and would grade them. He never changed the mimeo masters from year to year, so after a few years everyone had copies of his tests. It didn't matter, since he didn't seem to count them toward the grade anyway. In the spring he regularly cancelled a late morning class passing on his excuse that he had an important meeting or funeral to attend. My window faced the parking lot where he parked his car and I remember him putting his golf clubs in the car. I can't remember any funerals on the golf course.

He assigned term papers for each course, but never looked at them. When we got the papers back, there was just a "V" in red on the cover. "V" apparently stood for "vidi" – I saw. Some of us got a paper from someone who took the course the year before, typed a new cover sheet, and handed it in. He never noticed. Some of the bolder ones would put a little spot of glue between each page and the papers came back with the little spots still intact. He never read them at all.

To fill in the course work, we had a course in Greek, one in the writings of the ancient Christian writers, one in archeology, English, history of education, speech, Gregorian chant, a basic course of sociology, German, a couple of courses in Latin literature, and biology.

We attended class from 8:00 till noon, and from 1:00 to 3:00. The theory was that since we never went anywhere or had any outside interests, we were expected to carry a large load. In practice, we were never able to do justice to the curriculum even if it had been any good, which in retrospect it wasn't.

We were free from 3:00 until 4:30, and during this recreation period we managed to squeeze in some sports: basketball, softball, football, bowling, handball or tennis depending on the season. There was a study period from 4:30 to 5:30, followed by evening rosary in chapel and dinner.

After my second year at St. Francis, the school sought accreditation by North Central to get recognition for academic credits. The only school in the country that would accept credits at the time was the Catholic University in Washington. North Central sent a team for their investigation and insisted on several changes. The academic load was far too heavy, so the number of classroom hours was cut down to no more than eighteen and everyone was given a bachelors degree upon the completion of their college. Prior to that, a bachelor's degree was voluntary and the student had to write an acceptable dissertation. I wrote mine for an English professor on H.L. Menken, writer and critic of the early 20th century.

On the other end of the spectrum, we had some students who had a failing grade in one course or the other and were required to go to summer school at Marquette University to make-up the credits if they wanted to continue their studies. At the time Marquette apparently had accommodating standards for seminarians in summer school. It was a standing joke that some of the men ordained had more academic credits from Marquette summer school than they did from the Seminary.

North Central accreditation perhaps lent some credibility to those who came after but did little for us. After we left St. Francis, the school offered a masters program for theology, but before it could have any real meaning the seminary enrollment was so small there were few to take advantage of it. The seminary welcomed the laity, not only in faculty roles, but as students as well and there were wholesale changes in curriculum

Each Friday we had a "holy hour" in the afternoon with prayers, hymns and a sermon by one of the faculty. Few of these sermons were memorable, with some exceptions. The first was by Fr. James who taught Latin and was the assistant dean of students. Everyone called him "Louie." His tests were as weird as he was and he was extremely self-conscious about them. He carefully counted each test paper he brought to the room and counted each one as it was returned to his desk after the student finished it. In the class behind us, someone took one of the papers and tossed it out the window. Louie went berserk when he couldn't find that last exam and kept the class in the room for a full hour after, hoping to pressure someone to admitting to having the test. No one budged, and he never did find out who had the test.

I never knew him to have a friend either on the faculty or among the student body. He was, in a word, strange. After he left the seminary faculty, he served in several parishes in the diocese. People I knew from the parishes had the same adjective: strange. He was one of the prime examples of a misfit who found refuge in the clergy.

The sermon of his that I remember was an extensive discourse on "pusillanimous timidity" as the barrier to spiritual growth. It was the topic of conversation for months. I don't know if anybody knew what he was talking about. Apparently he found the term some psychology magazine and thought it was the answer to student problems.

Fr.. Leroy entered the hall of fame which his comparison of the student for the priesthood to the rosebushes in front of the building. He described the bushes as long and spindly and producing no flowers. So the groundskeepers pruned them back to the stems, and nourished them with organic fertilizer from the nearby stockyards, and now look at the beautiful blossoms. Interpreted by the students: "First the seminary cuts you down, feeds you a lot of shit and expects you to come out smelling like a rose."

Fr. Leroy made the hall of fame with another talk. In the early 60's, the school had made arrangement with a science lab to collect urine from students for some scientific purpose. The lab placed large plastic bottles in each urinal in the residence halls with a funnel atop each. Fr. Leroy chose to make the announcement for the project in chapel. Apparently he thought in chapel the students were more likely to take it seriously.

In his usual stuttering speech, obviously uncomfortable, Fr. Leroy explained what the deal was about and how each of us "should be happy we can make a contribution to science. " The place went up for grabs. I never heard the purpose of the program nor any results. We could think of no scientific reason to collect the urine of a couple hundred men. It was before drug use came on the scene but I wondered if they were trying to discover if there was some contraband alcohol use or maybe to check the sperm count in the student population. Though some of my classmates were rather effeminate, I don't think any of them could have been pregnant. After a few weeks the plastic bottles were gone, but I was happy that I was able to make my contribution to science, especially at 5:30 in the morning.

We had some of the traditional Catholic religious exercises one might find in the parishes. It was part of the training that we experience all of the religious celebrations or rites of the Church so we would be able to implement them in our parish assignments. One I recall is the annual "All Soul's Day" on November 2nd. To pray for those poor souls in purgatory, we would parade to the cemetery on the grounds, through a winding path in the woods, all the time praying the rosary aloud. With nearly three hundred students lined up, it was impossible for those on either end of the line to hear what was being recited down the line, so it was mass confusion. Coming at the beginning of November, the weather was not always cooperative, and we'd often end up making the march in cold, often with a drizzle of rain, but marching to the cemetery we would recite he rosary aloud. No one really knew why. The men buried there had been there for generations. It was one of those religious traditions.

The other procession that we had every year was three days of special prayers called "Rogation Days." Traditionally, these were three days of special prayers for good crops before the planting season. Each day we would march off in a different direction, singing the "Litany of the Saints," invoking everyone listed there to pray for us. Again, spring weather can be unpredictable and we sometimes froze in the cold winds whipping off Lake Michigan. I remember one time there was a torrential downpour. Rather than staying in chapel and singing our litany there, the Rector directed the procession to wind through the corridors of the residence hall. We exited the chapel, went down the right wing of the building, down the stairwell to the basement to stairs at the end of the other wing, up those stairs, and back to the center and re-entered the chapel. At any rate we had our procession and were sure that God was pleased. I wasn't around to see if we had bountiful harvests in the hallways that year.

Probably the worst spiritual garbage was the Good Friday afternoon services. The Good Friday services some years earlier were the "tre horae" services, a series of devotions that consumed the hours from noon to three PM, the hours Jesus was said to have hung on the cross. The liturgy had been reformed to a shorter service held in the evening. However, the Seminary wondered what to do during those traditional hours, or probably more to the point, what to do to keep the students occupied through the day with no classes or religious services. Somewhere the Rector found a devotional service that we were obliged to attend. The devotion consisted of a series of insipid prayers to each of the five wounds of Jesus describing each wound in gory detail. I can still remember the recurring refrain several times with each of the five wounds of Jesus. The Rector would intone it, and the rest repeated it, an exchange that occurred several times in honor of each of the five wounds of Jesus.

"Have mercy on us, O Lord, Have mercy on us.
Have Mercy on the poor souls in Purgatory."

I do not recall a single seminarian who was inspired or did not have trouble suppressing the desire to throw up. The Rector had the only copy of the prayer book and never left it around the sacristy. I am sure if he had it would have disappeared. No one ever recalled seeing that particular religious exercise anywhere else in print.

We had weekly "spiritual conferences" given by Fr. Gabriel, the spiritual director of the place. He was a distinguished looking gentleman with a head of prematurely white hair, the son of a pioneering Irish family whose family "cottage" has been preserved at the outdoor historical museum at Old World Wisconsin. He wrote a column for the local Catholic newspaper in which he gave "moral" ratings to popular music. He never quite got a handle on anything more risqué than Pat Boone. He considered Rock and Roll to be decadent and appealing to the sensual appetites of the young. He once wrote to Readers Digest about their risqué humor and threatened to expose their immorality in the Catholic papers in Wisconsin if they didn't mend their ways.

As a spiritual director he obviously had no great qualifications and his "conferences" were monologs and made little sense. He would read them in a monotone, snorting occasionally, and not once looking at the audience. He had a wit at times, but I never remember him even cracking a smile when someone else told a joke.

Like most of the men assigned to the seminary, he was biding his time until he had enough seniority to become a pastor of a parish of his choosing. I often wondered if a couple of decades of isolation in the seminary was good preparation for the pastorate of a large parish. Those who left the seminary for parishes seldom distinguished themselves, and in most cases turned out to be disastrous. A few of them selected parishes in resort areas where they were able to be more relaxed, without the pressures of a large urban parish.

If there is a single word that describes life at St. Francis, it has to be "repressive." As students we lived in fear of the Rector, Msgr. Frank. So did the faculty. Msgr. Frank was in his mid fifties, quite over-weight with a puffy face. He walked with a definite limp. We never knew him to have a wide circle of friends, or even a friend among the faculty. When he walked from the refectory to his office or his apartment, he always seemed to walk alone, even though a half dozen other priests on the faculty lived in the same building. He made it clear that he was in command at the seminary. Even a minor infraction of the rules could bring expulsion and dash hopes of becoming a priest. Infractions included leaving the grounds without permission, having one's lights on after "lights out" at night, "particular friendships" and a host of other peccadillos. I remember one student, an ardent baseball fan, who secreted a portable radio in his room to listen to games at night. A secret room inspection by Fr. Leroy, while we were in chapel, uncovered the contraband radio, and the man was expelled. Apparently the notion of privacy was foreign to seminary discipline. When the Braves won the World Series in 1957 a trio of students slipped out at night to join the welcome party at the airport. They were terrified the next morning seeing their pictures on the front page of the morning paper standing next to the fence as the team alit from the plane. Apparently nobody noticed.

With no radio, newspapers or television, we were rather isolated from the world outside the seminary. Most of us wondered how this was a relevant preparation for the ministry. The reality was that the seminary, and the rector in particular, needed tight control if the men were to be molded into priests who would be submissive to anyone perceived to be in authority.

There was heavy emphasis placed on "obedience" which meant compliance with whatever rules the seminary wished to install at the moment. One of the favorite lines the Monsignor repeated over and over in his talks to the students was, "You're always right when you're obedient." It seemed to me that that same line was used as a defense at Nuremberg. In retrospect this obsession with control spewed down from the Vatican and permeated the Church at the time, based on the belief that your superiors always spoke for God. The Monsignor considered it a concession that we were allowed to talk at our meals. Many seminaries around the world had religious reading during meals.

A group of nuns from the convent next to the seminary did the cooking and laundry for students, cleaning for the priests on the faculty and provided the same services for the diocesan minor seminary nearby. As their numbers dwindled and the women aspired to more fulfilling careers, the order questioned their service to the seminary. They were curtly informed by the rector and the bishop's office that their order had been established (about a century before) to be of service to the seminary and the diocese expected that they would continue with that commitment. In reality, they were convenient and cheap labor.

Our Seminary choir was arguably among the best male choirs in the country and their rendition of Gregorian Chants was superb. However, no one ever heard it except for the seminarians and a handful of nuns who did our laundry and cooked our meals. It could have been a tremendous public relations and recruiting tool if it had only been used, but they sang only for the Lord and the edification of their fellow students.

Every other year the students put on one of Shakespeare's plays, and did a commendable job of it. There were only two performances; one for the student body and faculty, and another to which alumni priests were invited.

Each year we put on a Christmas program, including singing of Christmas carols by the choir and a one-act play written for the occasion. The ending of the play was the same every year, the reading of the Roman Martyrology for Christmas, under strict orders from the Rector. I remember writing the play one year with an "O'Henry" twist that was quite good. I had to change the ending to include the reading of the Martyrology, which really didn't fit at all, but he insisted that this be the ending of the play each year, so I had to re-write the last scene. The Martyrology is a stately piece but historically inaccurate in many details, yet every year this was the last section of the Christmas pageant.

Before ordination, we had retreats, a three or seven day spiritual exercise directed by some outside "retreat master;" three days for the entire student body, and seven days for those receiving "major orders" such as sub-deaconate, deaconate and priesthood. It was a time of intense prayer and meditation, with silence maintained throughout. There were no classes, but an overdose of preaching for the duration. One sermon before Mass, two more later in the morning, two in the afternoon and another in the evening. The retreat masters were adept at warning of the dangers of sin and describing the failings of priests in colorful detail. To compound the guilt if a priest sinned and continued to perform any of his sacerdotal duties, that too was a serious sin since a priest was to be free of mortal sin while performing any sacramental function including Mass, Confession or any other sacrament. I used to wonder, if you're going to hell anyway, would another sin make any difference? To be honest, I can hardly remember much of what they talked about, though a few talks still rattle around in my mind.

One preacher was describing the failings of a priest who had a drinking problem. He met with the man and offered to get him help but wondered what led him down the path of alcoholism. The alcoholic related a story of a woman of the parish who had tried to seduce him and stripped naked in the rectory in front of him. Upset over the incident the priest turned to drink. The retreat master assessed the situation. "Remember, if it's a choice between a woman and a bottle, you can always throw the bottle out in the morning."

After two years of philosophy, we entered a four-year course of theology. During the first year of theology, we were "tonsured" with a symbolic cutting of hair that enrolled us in the ranks of the clergy. It was a big deal, because at this time we had made a commitment to serve a particular diocese or religious order, usually the diocese that we were from. From that point on if one wanted to transfer to another diocese he needed the release of his own bishop. However there were a large number of students who opted to serve in another diocese, mainly because they could expect to have their own pastorate much sooner. In our day it was about five years in some dioceses while it was nearly a twenty-five year wait in Milwaukee. The process was simple: before tonsure, find a bishop or diocese that would accept you, and establish that diocese as your "domicile." Many men from large cities opted for the rural or semi-rural diocese where the wait for their own pastorate was far shorter than in the larger dioceses. We had many men from Chicago who "migrated" to the diocese of Madison or Green Bay.

During the summers, Milwaukee theology students attended a summer "Villa" or summer school. Other dioceses used their seminarians for teaching summer bible school, working at retreat houses and the like but Msgr. Schneider insisted on a "Villa." It was something of a rite of passage. The practice was Roman, where the Rector studied. Designed at one time to keep the students from temptation, they spent the summers at some "Villa" outside the city of Rome. Roman schools had abandoned the practice long before, but the monsignor insisted on continuing it here.

In our case the Villa was at a Cistercian retreat house on Lake Oconomowoc. The building was the mansion of an old sea captain, willed to the monks who built a monastery next door and a farm to raise their produce and animals. The farm was no longer operated by the monks, the land had been rented to a nearby farmer. They later sold the land and the handful of monks moved to the western part of the state. A developer bought the property and today it is an upscale subdivision.

We spent the entire month of July there. Of course, we had the same rules as at the seminary about leaving the grounds without permission, which we mainly ignored. Several of our number would sneak off to one of the bars in Okauchee for a drink or two, and sometimes put our voices together for a song fest which gathered not only applause but free beer from someone in the place. We would quietly sneak back into the place in the dark, and if you weren't up wind, no one was the wiser.

We had classes for an hour in the morning and were free for the rest of the day to enjoy the lake, swimming, playing ball, fishing, or whatever. The classes during my years there were given by Fr. Bob, who was a great story-teller, but his classes for the most part were a waste of time. I give him credit: he didn't take the Villa stuff seriously.

The Villa grounds were between Oconomowoc Lake and the main line railroad from Milwaukee to points west. At night, if the wind was in the right direction, it seemed much closer than it really was. One seminarian took his tape recorder out to the tracks one day, waited for the train and recorded it from the distant whistle to the bell on the crossing gate to the roar as the train thundered by. The dormitory on the third floor of the Villa was originally a ballroom for the manor and when the monks converted it to a retreat house they built rooms around the perimeter. The younger men slept in the ballroom while the older ones had semi-private rooms. In the middle of the night, someone put the speakers for the tape recorder outside his door, into the dormitory and turned the volume up full blast. Twenty or more men thought the train was coming right through the building, and the prankster took a midnight dip in the lake in his pajamas.

A classmate decided that the roof of the manor was a very private place for sun bathing, and he decided to get a "complete" tan. Unfortunately he was fair skinned, and got a good burn for his effort. For days he had difficulty sitting and smiling at the same time.

The diocese also owned a cottage next to the Cistercian's place, at one time a summer home for the bishop. The Rector always spent the month of July at the cottage; it was obvious he wanted to be in control at all times. When he left the seminary for a parish assignment, the Villa lasted a couple years more but the emphasis was on using the students to teach summer religion classes around the area. For many years, after his retirement, the retired archbishop lived in the cottage on the lake.

Theology courses were hardly an intellectually stimulating inquiry into the meaning of life, but rather a re-statement of the dogmas of the Church as defined by various Councils and Synods of the Church over the centuries. Each fragment of Catholic theology was given a rating as to its certainty. For example, if an article of faith was defined by a council of the Church, it was termed "Infallible" as defined by a particular Council, and maybe reaffirmed by later synods. The textbooks, written in Latin of course, footnoted every statement as to its verification in Church teaching. The emphasis was on doctrinal purity rather than relevance. It is a pity that the courses were not taught within the context of the development of Catholic theology. But that might have smacked of heresy to think that theology could in any way be a developing science or that what we came to believe in the Church actually developed out of real life situations. It was a time of great fear of censure from the Vatican, a fear that fostered paranoia among many teachers in Catholic institutions.

The pity of the training was that doctrinal correctness was paramount to the exclusion of all else, particularly to the importance or application of doctrine in the lives of the members of the Church. It mattered not that what was being defined had little relevance, as long as it was doctrinally correct. It seems that many religions sought the magical key to favor with their gods, whether this be the perfect ritual, the orthodox belief or the preferred words to use in prayers to earn God's favor. In the Catholic Church since the Council of Trent in the 16th century, the emphasis was on doctrinal purity and correctness.

130

Among some of the more interesting theological ratings was one called "theologically certain" which meant merely that most theologians agreed. Since most of them copied from one another or from the same sources, in reality it had little meaning except that this was the safe position to hold at the present time, whether or not it was actually true or even made sense. It was a position that had not been censured by the Vatican. Some of the dearest Catholic beliefs were considered "theologically certain." Purgatory is one that has never been defined by a Council of the Church but has merely been taught by theologians since the Middle Ages. Another interesting argument arose when there was no apparent scriptural basis for a belief; theologians would state that it was fitting —"decet" is the Latin word used. This was the argument presented that Mary was taken up to heaven body and soul after her death. Someone thought that it was fitting that Jesus would not let his own mother rot in a grave.

Lowest on the rating scale was "theological opinion," a rating given to things like "Limbo" because theologians couldn't explain what happened to the soul of the innocent child who died without being baptized, since they were "certain" that no un-baptized person could enter the sight of God in heaven.

One of our theology professors, Fr. John, was a brilliant theologian, but never wrote an article or book. In fact even his class notes were written in pencil so that if he were ever challenged he could easily change the notes on his index cards that he lectured from. It is interesting to note that he was the "censor librorum" (censor of books) for the diocese, and had to put his stamp of approval on books on religious topics before they could be published with the approval of the Church in Milwaukee.

Our church history professor, Msgr. Peter Leo, was a recognized scholar and authority on the Catholic Church in Wisconsin. A brilliant man who served as an army chaplain in France during World War I, he was the most scholarly of the faculty, and at the same time the one most interested in the lives and personalities of the students. However, in all due respect, he tended to be the champion of ramblers. Monday afternoons we often had outside speakers from 4:30 to 5:30. Peter Leo brought in the president of the Wisconsin Historical Society for the afternoon on the occasion of the publication of his latest book, the history of St. Francis Seminary, Halcyon Days. Of course, he personally introduced his friend, and rambled on at length about the wonderful traditions of the historical society and the impressive credentials of the president of that organization. By the time he finished his introduction, the entire hour was taken up and the speaker never got to say a word. For all his quirks, he was the man who gave me an appreciation for history, and was the only member of the faculty at the time who was respected outside the seminary for his scholarship.

After ordination, when I wrote the history of St. Mary's parish in Fond du Lac, I sent him a copy of my rough draft and asked for his comments. He sent it back with helpful notes and insights that I incorporated into the book. I gave him an autographed copy, which I believe is still in the library at the seminary.

Canon Law, taught by Fr. Al, was perhaps the least liked part of the curriculum. We pored through the Code of Canon law which was promulgated in 1917, mainly the work of Eugenio Pacelli, who later became Pope Pius XII. We spent three class hours per week for three years learning minutiae of Church law, most of which had little to do with the lives of the people in the Church and a lot to do with maintaining the control of priests by the hierarchy and the Vatican. The code itself was a volume of regulations, the violation of which had penalties ranging from suspension of priestly faculties to outright excommunication, and certainly including the element of mortal sin and hellfire for anyone who dared to challenge or disobey the authority of Holy Mother Church.

A great deal of the course had to do with the church law regarding marriage and the Church practice of granting annulments, a finding that there was not a valid contract of marriage in the first place. In actual practice at the time, very few annulments were granted by the diocesan "tribunal" which passed judgment on petitions. Milwaukee was known as one of the toughest tribunals in the country. One of the "judges" who sat on the tribunal of priests boasted that he had never voted for an annulment. If they were married before a priest and two witnesses, the marriage was valid in his eyes. Each case had to be approved by a review tribunal from another diocese, and if they disagreed the matter was submitted to Rome, and the total process could take many years, and though this was denied by church officials, could be costly. It is interesting that when the Church granted an annulment, declaring that there was no marriage, the children born of that union were nonetheless considered legitimate.

Much of the course dealt with "faculties" – the powers of the priest to perform certain functions like preaching, hearing confessions, performing other sacraments such as Marriage and Baptism, including a list of which sins could be forgiven by the local priest, and which required authorization from the bishop, the apostolic delegate in Washington or the Vatican itself. We spent weeks studying the "impediments" to ordination, one that was included was being an illegitimate child.

I wondered why a person would be considered a second-class Catholic simply because his mother was not married at the time of his birth. The strict legalism of the material was hardly an intellectual pursuit, and Fr. Al certainly made it unbearable. His tales of horror at the lives of priests who got in trouble because they violated Canon Law were sprinkled liberally throughout his lectures. His exams were impossible. He would deduct points for spelling, punctuation, even penmanship!

Obviously I didn't like him. Personally I found him more than a bit weird. His sermons were filled with flowery language and imagery that had little basis in theology and less relevance to the lives of the seminarians. On Sunday afternoons we would often see him driving through the grounds with his two brothers (neither of whom were married) and his mother who was in her seventies. This was his Sunday routine: dinner with mother, and a drive with mother and her two adult sons in Fr. Al's large luxury car. He would comment in class about the girls who walked through the grounds on their way to the Catholic girls high school on the lakefront, and that they were a source of temptation to the seminarians and that we should not look at them. (These were high school girls in school uniforms.) Another faculty member referred to them as "brazen hussies." I used to wonder what either of them would do if they were in the same room with a woman who was under sixty and not dressed in a nun's habit.

All the priests collected their mail in a common mailroom at the mid-morning break. Someone sent in a subscription to PLAYBOY magazine for Fr. Al. It came in a brown wrapper with PLAYBOY in big red letters on the outside. He tried to sneak it out, but a few of the others saw it and gave him a bit of ribbing. When the second month arrived, they were waiting for him. I guess he wrote in and cancelled it, or probably whoever ordered it told them to bill him later and he never paid the bill.

He left St. Francis and took a pastorate in Milwaukee and soon became known as the darling champion of the archconservatives of the Church. His name was associated with nearly every right wing group from the Veritas Forum, the Eagle Forum, and the John Birch Society. Rumor has it that at some point the bishop made him break with some of these organizations. However, his parish was the bastion of conservatism until the day of his death.

My final year at St. Francis coincided with the first session of the Vatican Council. Ironically few of our professors seemed to take any note of it or hold out great hope. Some of us who read the "experts" - theologians consulting with the bishops in Rome were expecting great things. The expectations of our own faculty were perhaps best summed up by one professor who stated "si aliquis aliquid dixerat, anathema sit" - If anybody said anything, they are condemned to hell.

Our hopes were dampened when Pope John XXIII, arguably the most progressive pope since the reformation, issued a reactionary encyclical requiring that all seminary courses be taught in Latin. Some of our faculty members tried to comply scrupulously, lecturing in Latin and doing it rather badly. Some said that this was the last gasp of the archconservatives in the Vatican to rein in the reforms of the Vatican Council. Apparently it was far more important to control course content, even the language in the seminaries than to have students actually master theology and Scripture. For most of us in the seminary at the time this was the first strong indication that Rome was out of touch with reality and cared more about control and uniformity than anything else.

I remember vividly the expectations of the first session with the brightest theologians of the world meeting to discuss the role of the Church in the modern world. One would expect that they would delve into the questions of relevance of the Church in modern life. Yet after months of debate and study, in a response to a world in which the majority of the population did not believe in God, the bishops of the world had one solitary accomplishment: they inserted the name of St. Joseph in the Canon of the Mass. It was a disappointment for those of us who expected them to address issues such as cooperation and unity among Christians and a positive approach to the Jews with whom Christians share important religious roots and beliefs. We anticipated there would be some collegiality emerging from the Council rather than the authoritarianism that had permeated the Church since the first Vatican Council in 1870, which declared that the Pope was infallible in matters of faith and morals. Many writers have stated this has made it difficult for the Vatican. Any change in doctrine or discipline must be shown that it does not contradict any prior position held by the Church. This was made even more difficult by the Code of Canon Law written mainly by Pius XII, which concentrated all authority in the offices of the Vatican.

It was a bittersweet time, with hopes of substantive change from the Council and the stark realization of the inability of the bishops to understand the problems and address the challenges of religion in the modern world. What optimism remained was due to the fact that the first session closed with another scheduled two years hence. Nearly a century of absolute rule by a Vatican that declared itself infallible would be hard to change.

The big day for seminarians was always the conferring of "Orders." There were a series of "minor orders:" porter, acolyte, lector and exorcist, conferred in the first two years of theology. The "biggie" was the sub-diaconate, the first of the "major orders" leading to the priesthood.

Before the "major" orders, each man was subjected to a "scrutinium," consisting mainly of an interview with the Rector in which he asked if we were entering into this freely and understood the obligations we were about to assume. While there was no one forcing us into ordination, there certainly was a great deal of pressure on the decision. We spent many years in preparation, in most cases up to eleven years in the seminary, with an education that had little value anywhere else. We had families who basked in the limelight of having a priest in the family soon, as if this was a reserved seat in the luxury boxes of heaven. It was not an exaggeration to say that as a young man lined up for ordination, the firm imprint of his mother's hand could be seen on his back.

The retreat before ordination to the "sub-diaconate" – the first of the major steps to the priesthood was an anxious time for most of us. This was the point of no return, when we fell under the Church rule of celibacy for life and assumed the obligation of reciting the "divine office" each day, a set or prayers and readings in Latin that were originally done by the monks in the medieval abbeys to mark the hours of the day. We spent one entire semester course just learning how to read the directions for the daily "breviary" using a printed "ordo" that specified which prayers and readings were required. The men from the Milwaukee diocese also were required to take a pledge to refrain from alcohol for the next five years with the exception of the sacramental wine during Mass. It was a pledge that few young priests kept.

Prayer and reflection did little to curb our anxieties. We had no clear idea of what assignments we might draw as newly ordained priests. In the final analysis most of us felt trapped. It was far easier to go through with ordination than to turn back at this point or one's own volition. We had spent many years in preparation for this day. There were the expectations of our families back home who would be disappointed if we chose to forego ordination. We tried to allay our feelings by telling ourselves that it was God's will and our decision was a "calling from God" and as long as we were permitted to go forward to ordination it must be God's will. Frankly, few of us knew what our lives would be like after ordination, serving in whatever niche the bishop needed to fill at that time. Some of us came from farms or small towns where the local parish had a single priest and we would be spending many years as assistant pastors in urban parishes where there were two or more priests, a ministry that was foreign to our experience.

The week of retreat and the ordination ceremony itself was for me a time of mixed emotions. There was the emotional high of the ceremony and its significance in my life, while at the same time a pervasive feeling that I had done something that in the eyes of the Church was irreversible, that I had committed myself to a life and to factors beyond my control that would affect that life, and I could not change any more.

My life ceased to be my own. Even years of indoctrination that we were chosen by God for this life and that our vocation was a gift did little to ease that anxiety.

There were cases of seminarians held back from "orders" for one reason or the other. Usually it was a matter of trying to curb the rebel spirit in the man. In one case a clandestine inspection of the man's room uncovered a few books that were a bit sexually explicit and he was forced to wait a few months before he could proceed to ordination. The books were not pornographic and by today's standards, hardly titillating at all.

In a few cases there were health problems. I remember one case of a man from the Green Bay diocese who found out the day before his ordination to the priesthood that the bishop would not ordain him. All the preparations for his "First Mass" celebration had been made, invitations to the celebrations sent out, and now after all the years of preparation he was denied ordination for some reason I was never able to learn.

Bishops and superiors could afford to be selective when there was an abundance of candidates for ordination. I remember one man who had impaired hearing in one ear. He had trouble finding a bishop who would accept him because it was felt he would have trouble hearing confessions (since most confessionals were two-sided and he would have to be able to hear out of both ears as he leaned from side to side.)

Ordinations, except for the final ordination to the priesthood, were all held in the seminary chapel. The bishop would arrive, the chapel prepared, the choir ready for the conferring of "orders." I always thought it was a pity that these ceremonies were not open to the public or done in the parishes of the young men being ordained. However to keep everything "neat and orderly" they were private. I think most of us would have been thrilled to have our parents and families celebrate the occasion, but it was entirely private, and the next day we returned to class at 8:00 AM.

The final year before ordination to the priesthood we concentrated on learning the "rubrics" of the various priestly functions. I remember

Fr. Gabriel teaching the proper way to conduct Mass. His directions were mainly on the proper position of the hands and the movement approved when giving a blessing or reciting prayers. It was important that it be done exactly as prescribed in the ritual books, particularly one written years before by a priest who taught the subject at the Catholic University in Washington, Fr. Wapplehorst. I often wondered why we had to be so precise, since the priest was facing the back wall for Mass anyway but it all had to conform to Wapplehorst. Wapplehorst's directions included advice for the master of ceremonies at a solemn high mass to carry a "cricket" clicker to give the signal for all the members of the ceremony to genuflect in exact synchronized movements which would edify the congregation, at least if they were not turned off by the noise of the clicker.

One of the highlights of the last year in the seminary was a course on Sacramental Theology taught by J.L. He had been on the faculty of the Catholic University in Washington DC and for some reason wore out his welcome there, and returned to Milwaukee. He was highly respected in theological circles as one of the most brilliant minds in the American Church, with a grasp not only of doctrine but also of the historical evolution of religious thought in the Church over the centuries.

The seminary Rector reluctantly agreed to let him teach a class to the "deacons" as we were called in the last year before ordination. It was without a doubt the finest course we had in the seminary, a stimulating intellectual inquiry, rather than re-hashing what someone had written decades or centuries before. It was the first course in six years at St. Francis that explored the thought of philosophers and theologians who lived after the 13th century as gaining some insight, rather than a condemnation hidden in a footnote and dismissed. Without exception the others followed the dictum that theological study ended with the death of Aquinas just as surely as revelation ended with the death of the last apostle. We were at last made aware that studies were being made on the historical context and reliability of the Bible and the development of religious thought in the Church through the centuries as well as contemporary religious thought outside the Catholic traditions.

One thing that he had that was sorely lacking in most of the faculty was a sense of humor. J. L. could be an iconoclast at times but seemed to be able to keep the tenets of the faith in perspective as something that developed over time rather than a body of religious truths that were given to the Apostles in their present form.

Near the end of the year someone got the idea that we would take over the class for a "roast" and mimic all his mannerisms and foibles. He enjoyed it thoroughly. Of course, I had a hand in writing most of the script which included the presentation of an apple with two bites taken out of it, appropriately dried out on my radiator for two weeks before. We presented this as archeological evidence that it was indeed an apple that Adam and Eve had eaten in the garden and that we were fortunate that this evidence had been preserved in the sterile and stagnant atmosphere of the seminary where nothing ever changed, even from the beginning of time.

We presented him with a certificate of appreciation from the St. Francis Seminary, which had over a hundred years of glorious tradition unencumbered by progress. Years later after he had left the active ministry, I met him at the home of some mutual friends, and he remembered every word of the parody we had done for his class.

My memories of St. Francis are memories of isolation, conformity and repression. By comparison with other seminaries around the country, St. Francis was considered one of the most repressive and isolated. Religious institutions at the time prided themselves in being "strict." It was a standing joke, that the only difference between the seminary and a prison was that in a prison you got to have visitors. I remember the occasion when our Rector visited St. John's Military Academy in one of the Milwaukee suburbs and reported his visit in one of his sermons with the highest praise for the military discipline that characterized the school, from the dress uniforms to the politeness of the students who addressed their superiors as "sir" and stood at attention in their presence.

We should have known that the atmosphere at the seminary was a prelude to how we were going to be treated in many of our assignments. The authoritarian model of the seminary carried over into the diocese in general and in most parishes in particular. The paradigm was formed in the seminary. If one of the despotic pastors had an assistant who did not conform, he was sure to complain that the seminary discipline was growing too lax. After all, the seminary was there to create subservient assistants to these pastors.

The education we received, to be honest, was mediocre at best. At the time the seminaries attracted some of the brightest and finest of young men. But the education we received did little to prepare us for the roles we would be called upon in our careers as priests. There were no electives, and most of the courses were the same as those taught a decade or more before, even using the same textbooks. While the isolation may have created conformity and reduced the dropout rate, it went completely counter to the interaction with people that the priest is called upon to do. We could probably argue with a fourth century heretic about whether Jesus was human or divine or both, but we were ill prepared to deal with the battered woman pregnant with her eighth child or the inherent racism of many of our parishioners. Such naiveté would cause great tension in some of our lives, while others would simply ignore it and become clerical functionaries, going through the motions of their ministry, oblivious to the world around them.

I was ordained May 25, 1963, at St. John's Cathedral. It was an impressive ceremony, with the seminary choir filling the vaults of the church with the Latin Hymn "Ecce Sacerdos Magnus" – Behold a great priest… as we marched down the aisle. It was the first ordination ceremony that my family was able to attend. The cavernous cathedral was filled with family members. The resonant voice of Archbishop Cousins intoned the ritual of ordination. "Tu est sacerdos in aeternum." - You are a priest forever. At long last, the journey was over. I was a priest.

Chapter Five

First Assignment

My First Mass in the parish church at St. Peter was a celebration for family, relatives and the parish community as well. I was the first man ordained from the parish in its ninety some years of existence, and with the exception of a distant relative, the only priest in the family. We invited all my aunts and uncles and first cousins and their spouses. Both Dad and Mother came from large families and their siblings had large families in turn, so there were over a hundred first cousins invited with their spouses.

The Solemn High Mass in the parish Church included many of the parish priests from the area as well as friends from the seminary. The Church never looked so grand, filled to capacity with standing room only, as the whole community was in a festive mood. We had lunch at a dance hall across the street and then returned and used the parish hall in the church basement for a reception in a less formal setting. My family was proud; the eyes of the community were filled with admiration.

The time between ordination and the arrival of the letter from the bishop giving the young priest his first assignment was an anxious one. The hype of the First Mass Celebration, and the adulation of relatives and parish members still had some glow, but the reality of that first parish assignment made us all nervous.

At the seminary, one topic of conversation was the "tough" assignments, and the problems always seemed centered not around the challenge of the work but rather around the pastor, housekeeper and living conditions in the parish rectory. Tales of horror drifted back from priests ordained in prior years and from classmates who belonged to these parishes. Some pastors were noted as rough assignments; they were convinced that their contribution to the Church was to "train" the new priests, and so they received a new assistant every year or two. The truth was that a year was all that any of the new priests could stand without a breakdown and there were more of them than anyone cared to admit. We knew where we did not want to be assigned but had no idea where we would actually end up, fearing the worst.

Assignments were made by someone in the Chancery office with no consultation with the priests involved in most cases. Pastors were often in the dark as to who would be assigned, and certainly the young priests were never consulted, or were bold enough to make a formal request, which certainly a newly ordained wound not dare to do. There seemed to be a rotation that an assistant pastor would be reassigned at least after seven years. These were times when authority seemed to be endowed with an aura of wisdom and divine right to make the appropriate decisions at all times, and if mistakes were made, it was "God's will." In fact, there seemed to be little difference in the mind of Church officials between God's will and their own autocratic and arbitrary management practice. I often wondered why God got blamed for all the foul-ups in the world.

We were poorly trained for the actual job of ministry, and the pastors, whose authority was near absolute, had no training in the functions of management in fiscal matters of the parish or pedagogy for the school and certainly not in the management of the parish staff. If things didn't work out the young priest was deemed to be at fault and was transferred. Problems were seldom addressed. The more senior assistant pastors learned the better assignments and after a few years learned to pull strings and get one that was amenable. The diocese also learned that assigning more experienced men to tough assignments would stir the waters, so the least desirable assignments fell to the newly ordained, often leaving emotional scars that would be with them their entire lives. There seemed to be an informal "fecal roster" on which priests would bounce from one undesirable assignment to the next, and if you complained about where you were, chances were that you might end up on that list. Any re-assignment off the regular rotation was suspect and the priest seldom received a desirable appointment.

The horror stories that filtered back to the seminary centered on life in the rectory, where all the priests, the pastor, and usually the pastor's "housekeeper" lived and worked. The standing joke was from the Psalms "ecce quam bonum, quamquam jucundum, habitare fratres in unum." Translated it means "behold how good and happy it is for brothers to live together." The joke was that it might be good (bonum) but we were damned if it was happy (jucundum). Later revelations about the sexual orientation and problems with priests put another twist to the phrase.

First of all, there was the pastor to contend with. Each pastor had his own philosophy about running the parish and how a young priest should deport himself. The system of appointing to pastorate was determined not by merit or track record but by seniority. There was no formal training for administering a parish as a pastor. One would think that newly ordained priests should be assigned to someone qualified to help the young priest launch his career in the ministry in as positive a manner as possible, but it rarely happened. In far too many cases, the pastor and his associates viewed themselves as adversaries and the young assistant pastors could not wait until the day when they would have something to say about their lives. Meanwhile their concept of pastorate was often warped by their experience and when they became pastors they often functioned exactly like the pastors they had detested when they served under them. These were the only role models they knew.

In the early 60's a young priest in an urban diocese could look forward to some twenty years or more in the service of an older pastor who had the position merely by seniority. This was the only qualification for the position of pastor. A pastor was seldom transferred to another assignment unless he requested it.

The system of seniority stifled career ambition on the one hand and on the other created a privileged caste system for the pastors and the under-privileged assistants. For example, the Milwaukee diocese had a rule that assistants were to be in the rectory no later than 11:00 p.m. When you considered that the priest had to be at least twenty-five years old at time of ordination, and the rule covered some who were nearly fifty, there certainly was no need. Yet there were pastors who dutifully locked the door at 11:00 with a double bolt so that the assistant who arrived late had to wait outside or wake the pastor and apologize for being tardy. Under the best of conditions if one arrived after the "witching hour" it was sure to be noted. It is interesting that in the same era, the diocese published "Guidelines for Teens" which recommended a 12:00 curfew for teens on weekends. I guess they felt that out high school students were more mature than the assistant pastors of their parishes. Being treated as adolescents by their bosses was a fertile ground not only for criticism and discontent, but often gave rise to juvenile behavior on the part of the assistants as well.

The pastor made all work assignments. He would seldom take the early Mass unless he wanted to get out of town for some reason. The young priest drew the assignments for Sunday afternoon Baptisms (though the pastor dutifully collected the money or stipends given, since these by diocesan law belonged to the pastor alone.) Because it was assumed that the young priest would be "better with kids" he would be put in charge of activities for teenagers and young adults, Mass servers and scouts, regardless of his aptitude or desire. Most of us were ill prepared for youth work from seminary training. We entered the seminary after eighth grade and the isolation of the seminary prevented interaction with our peers during their adolescence and early adulthood. We had limited experience in dealing with teenagers. Many of the moral problems of priests had their roots in this lack of preparation and use of prudent safeguards.

The age difference between pastors and assistants often created problems. With no retirement plans, the older priests hung on as long as they were able, often being more than a half-century older than their charges. It was not unusual for a young priest on assignment needing to care for a sickly pastor in addition to the parish duties. The Church had no paradigm for priests retiring and only meager financial support for those who could no longer function in their priestly roles. Very few actually retired.

Because the newly ordained never quite knew when the assignment would arrive, he would generally stay close to home during the interim between ordination and assignment letter. I remember when my letter arrived. I was assigned to St. Mary's in Fond du Lac. This was good news and bad news. I was the first priest from the area to be assigned this close to home. This was fine to some extent but many of my relatives and friends were members of the parish and there was little doubt that I would live in a fishbowl. People from the Holy Land often moved to the city for their jobs, or many sold their farms and retired in town. There were a lot of relatives and parents of kids I went to school with who were members of the parish. Whatever I said or did would be sure to flow from parish to family and vice versa. If I wanted to go to a movie or have a drink or two in a bar, word was certain to filter back to my family or to the rectory.

My first visit to the parish rectory was memorable. Hank, the pastor, in his mid 60's, was congenial, and his sister Susie, who was somewhere in her high seventies or eighties, was the rectory housekeeper and cook. She had been with Hank since his first pastorate nearly forty years before. The other priest, Roger, had been there about six years.

Ed, whom I was replacing, was immensely popular, a great preacher, and very active in the community. He had been there seven years, the usual limit on tenure for an assistant. He was taking a position at the seminary and the religious education department of the diocese. He left behind a foundation I was able to build on during my tenure. I remember my conversation with him. He said, "Don't try to be me, just be yourself. And when people talk about me, be kind." It served me well.

I was to spend the next five years at the parish. Initially my quarters consisted of a tiny bedroom with a small adjoining office/sitting room. Roger and I shared a bath across the hall. Roger's quarters were much larger, with a larger bedroom and sitting room. Roger took it on himself to "show me the ropes" which included introduction to key people in the parish and some of the "inside dope" on how things got done, including hearing confessions. He explained in graphic detail the various expressions used for forbidden sexual acts. He didn't have a clue!

I still remember his explanation of "necking" and "petting" – necking being anything above the waist and petting anything below the waist. His explanation of a "blow job" was that "this is when one male inserts his penis in the anus of another, and at the moment of peak excitement the man on the receiving end blows a fart, giving incredible pleasure to the other person."

Roger was a likeable but big fellow, more than a bit naïve, who could put on weight just thinking about food. Usually after the holidays he'd go to one of the doctors in the parish and get a prescription for "thyroid pills" so he could lose the weight he had gained over the holidays. I noticed that he became nervous and agitated while on the pills, and hardly slept at all. Years later I realized that the "thyroid pills" he was taking were probably amphetamines.

Each summer he took his mom and dad on a trip for his vacation and was sure to have 8mm movies of the entire trip when he returned. His idea of a vacation was to show mom and dad the scenery in another part of the country.

He generally spent his days off visiting his parents but on occasion he would come back from a visit with some of his classmates whom he admired since they had more prestigious positions in the diocese, such as head of a small program, faculty of a Catholic high school or whatever. For the next day or two we would hear that the diocese had great things in store for him according to his classmates. I wonder if his classmates found that as amusing as I did. Roger and I spent two years together at St. Mary's, and I think I have seen him only once or twice since.

While I was there, Hank decided that he needed a larger rectory. The reason was that as he was getting older, he needed another priest for the parish. So the parish spent some $300,000 to build an addition to the rectory. The addition included three apartments for the assistants on the second floor, and a larger living room for Hank, along with a sitting room and bedroom for him, and a single office to replace one that became a passageway from the old building to the new. Today there's one priest to serve the parish, with a lot of empty rooms. At the time of construction, the parish could have bought several houses on the block for about $15,000. In fact, they owned one, which was occupied by the head janitor. There was a joke among the clergy: "The Protestants have their better halves, but the priests have their better quarters." More expensive, but not always better.

In many ways St. Mary's during my tenure was one of the more successful parishes in the area. Our parish school was quite good, due mainly to a staff of dedicated teachers. St. Mary's parish school had sixteen classrooms and in my first year there had some 960 kids in school, grades 1-8. Actually there was a double shift that year for first graders. The Sisters of St. Agnes staffed the school as they did all of the parishes in the city where their Mother House was located as well. There were a couple of female lay teachers and a male band instructor who split his time between the grade school and St. Mary's Springs High School. There was also a school nurse who worked part time. For the most part the school had a good reputation, though by today's standards it was lacking in several areas. It had two sections per grade, and at its peak enrollment there were sixty children per classroom! With little resources except their textbooks and iron discipline, the nuns and lay teachers did their best to provide a good education.

The school itself is a study in history. The parish opened its first school in the 1860's in a wooden structure that pre-dated the old wooden church. In the 1880's they built a brick school that also had an auditorium on the second floor, which was quite common with parish schools built before thought was given to fire codes. The red brick school became known as the "Old Dutch College." A stone convent across the street housed the nuns who staffed the school. When the parish built a new residence for the nuns in the 1950's they were chagrined to learn that the nuns actually had title to the building that had housed them in the past.

In the 1920's, a young priest by the name of Phil Rose began efforts to raise money to build a new school. The crash of 1929 and the depression that followed delayed the project and there were rumors that the pastor, Fr. Gershbach and his brother Frank, who helped with the parish administration, had lost the money in the stock market. It caused quite a stir in the 1930's and created some rift in the parish. In the late 30's the project was delayed because of the high cost of construction. World War II put the project back another few years and finally, in 1948, they laid the cornerstone for the new school, a showplace for its time.

In my second year at St. Mary's we got a new principal, Sister Rogeria, a nun who had spent twenty years or so working for the diocesan education office, which wasn't known for its progressive educational ideas. Sister Rogeria was a local woman whose family came from St. Peter and we had some common relatives so I was an immediate hit with her. She was a fine reading teacher but was naïve about administration and other parts of the principal's job. For some crazy reason I thought I could pull a little practical joke on her, and we could have a good laugh.

I had copied a record of the "Gukenheimer Sauerkraut Band" which did some clever spoofs of popular and classical musical themes ala Spike Jones. I thought it hilarious and brought the tape to her office one of the first days of school and told her I had recorded the school band last spring and would she like to hear it. She beamed with excitement and I knew I was in trouble. I played their rendition of one of Liszt's Hungarian Rhapsodies, and she sat there with a big smile on her face.

"Isn't it wonderful how our children play so well." She looked so proud I didn't have the heart to tell her she'd been had. My gut cramping from holding back laughter I promised to let her hear the rest of the tape another day. I didn't heave the heart to admit the truth.

On the way out of her office, I met some of the 8th grade girls who heard the music.

"What in the world was that?" one of them asked.

"It's a joke," I whispered. "She thinks it's our school band. Don't spoil it." Thank God the kids didn't tell. I never did find out her thoughts once she realized she'd been had.

Sometimes the volunteers around a parish can be more trouble than they are worth, and at other times downright dangerous. When I was put in charge of the kids athletic programs at St. Mary's I inherited the volunteers, and a couple people who apparently were paid a minimal amount for various jobs. We had a youth hockey team, both a grade school and high school boys basketball, and a grade school football team. Getting volunteers to staff them didn't seem to be much of a problem.

I did have some reservations about the equipment manager who took care of the locker rooms for the boy's basketball teams. He had keys to the building and made sure that the kids behaved in the locker and shower rooms. However, he was there when I came to the parish, and nobody seemed to have the same doubts that I did. The guy was not athletic, he was single, about forty years old and lived with mom and dad. The kids used to talk about him quite a bit, as kids often do, and in this case the rumors were pretty specific and widespread among the kids. There had to be something to them. I don't remember what he did for a living, but he gave me the creeps from the moment I met him.

One night while the kids were practicing, there was some problem with a car in the parking lot and the police came to investigate. While I was talking to the officer at the entrance to the gym, he noticed the equipment manager and asked me what he was doing there. When I explained, the officer grabbed me by the arm and said, "Let's go out to the squad so we can talk privately." I thought I was under arrest or something, but he was a big burly guy so I went along.

In the car he began to explain to me that the city police had been collecting evidence on the man for years for molesting boys, but they were never able to get enough to make an arrest. He had a reputation all over town. That was all I needed, and our equipment manager was gone as soon as I could arrange it. I simply eliminated the position. The coaches were in charge of the locker rooms, and our school janitors would clean the place as they did anyway.

I often wondered why my predecessors hadn't questioned the wisdom of having this guy around. I know they had to have known because they heard confessions of the kids as well as I did. Maybe they were hiding behind that seal of confession a bit too scrupulously. It was interesting how the rumors died down after he was no longer the equipment manager. Did he move on?

An organization of married couples, the Christian Family Movement helped members deal with problems of family living in a changing church and changing community. It became a training ground for the leaders of the parish, attracting young and active couples. Not only were the couples able to meet with other young Catholic couples and share their insights into parenting, but they also took an active role in the parish and social problems in the community. I was the regional coordinator for the diocese, working to coordinate planning and activities. We were invited to establish the movement in the Episcopal diocese of Fond du Lac. This was not only unique in the movement but proved to be a successful ecumenical sharing and a great benefit for both the Catholics and Episcopalians. When the Episcopal diocese began to revise and update their liturgy the bishop of the diocese asked me to be a consultant to their clergy on bringing about the changes.

What was interesting working with the Episcopal church was the discovery that the differences among Episcopalians was sometimes greater than the difference between them and the Catholics, and perhaps the same could be said for the wide divergence of opinions and practice among the Catholics of that time.

The parish also hosted a group of lay missionary "Papal Volunteers" in training for service to the Church in Latin America. They were housed in a large house down the block from the parish and were studying languages and other topics that hopefully would help them in the missionary field. We also had a group of young singles, the Young Catholic Workers, who explored social issues and sought to bring their faith into the workplace.

A movement that began with the Hispanics called the "Cursillo" movement was active in the parish, seeking to help men and women live their religious beliefs in their families and the community. It was quite a change from the norm at the time when Catholics were expected to "pray, pay and obey." The movement attracted people with leadership potential from around the diocese. We were developing a group of men and women who wanted to take an active part in their parishes and who wanted to put the principles of their faith into practices in their daily lives and in their communities. Among their activities were regular visits to the prisons nearby working with the chaplain, and in some cases providing needed support services to the families of the incarcerated men and women. I was quite active with the group as a guest speaker in their regular retreats for men and women. This took me all over the diocese as the retreats were held throughout the area, including a number of programs put on in state prisons in the area. At the close of each "Cursillo" on Sunday night, all those who had gone through the Cursillo in the past were invited to the closing. It was a moving religious experience as the new "cursillistas" were welcomed into the group. It was almost a church within a church, and had quite a interesting resemblance to some of the Pentecostal movement: emotionally charged, personal relationship with Jesus, and rather basic beliefs that were never questioned.

It seems the movement drifted to the more liberal side as men and women tried to find relevance of their faith in their daily lives. They began to realize how inadequate the conservative institutional church had become in addressing the issues of their lives. Obviously, few of the older priests in the diocese were involved, and thus few pastors.

The retreats or "cusillos" (Short course) ran from Thursday night through Sunday. They were intense, starting early in the morning and going late into the night, with prayers, singing, and plenty of well presented sermons given by laymen and a few by priests. The group would be confined, sleeping, eating, worshipping and praying together with little or no time alone. The result was a predictable emotional high, resulting from the group dynamic more than from their religious faith. But everyone felt good going away with a new enthusiasm for the Church. These groups were at the cutting edge of what was happening in society at the time, prodding their conservative, white suburban Church into the reality of the modern world and its problems.

Among the social projects the "cursillistas" were involved in were missionary projects to some of the parishes in the mountains of Appalachia and the South. One of our parish families took a week or two traveling to a town in Tennessee, helping with repair of the parish buildings and teaching religion classes to the children and adults.

They met a single mother with about a half-dozen children, and thought they could make a better life for the family. When they returned to Fond du Lac they bought a large home on the south end of town that had once been a funeral home. They bought the house and made needed repairs and decided to open it as a home for single older men. Who would run the place? They turned to their friend in Tennessee and brought her to Fond du Lac. She proceeded to do the cooking, laundry etc. for the men at the rooming house and all was apparently well. That is until word got around that she was servicing the men personally for a fee as well as cooking their meals. A girl has to make a living!

The Church at the time was quite racist. I remember the racism in the seminary. In class after class people other than white Caucasians were considered "missionary projects" and something less than the white middle class that populated our parishes. When the Christian Family Movement's guides for the year spent a few meetings on racism there was a lot of resistance. I remember Fr. Roger being totally disgusted that they would choose such a topic for a good part of the year. After all, we didn't have any blacks in Fond du Lac. I asked him if there was perhaps a reason why there were none. He didn't know. I knew that like most of the cities in the area, Fond du Lac had an ordinance that no Negro could be in town over-night. There were no blacks because we didn't want any.

Fr. Groppi, a personal friend, was leading the open housing marches in Milwaukee and was considered a pariah by the institutional church. He was undoubtedly the most hated priest in the country. Yet personally he was a gentle, loving man who spent his summers while in the seminary working as a volunteer at a camp for children from the inner city. It seemed nearly everywhere in the country I went, even years later, his name was certain to evoke some of the most un-Christian feelings, even among the most deeply religious Catholics. In practice there was little doubt that the Church was inherently racist.

Our traditional parish groups included Boy Scouts and Girl Scouts. I was a card carrying Girl Scout for a number of years having, served on the Council Board as their clergy advisor. When we married, Jo Ann told me that my girl scouting days were over.

Our religious education program for the children attending public schools was second to none. In fact I was part of a team who taught religious educators from other parishes in courses at Marian College. We had religious education programs for High School students on Monday nights, for Junior High on Tuesdays, and Saturdays for kids in the elementary grades. It made for a pretty busy schedule since we had nearly two thousand kids in the programs. We did it all with volunteer teachers and no paid professionals. Yet we ran one of the finest programs in the diocese.

We did some things that were far ahead of their time, like providing special education for children with handicaps. Our program to teach religion to the mentally handicapped was unique in the 1960's. When word got out that we were doing something for them, they came from the entire area. We were able to recruit tutors for each of the children from among our high school students. A side benefit of this, in addition to keeping the kids involved with the Church, was that a good percentage of these tutors went on to college and became teachers.

Our Saturday morning classes filled the school building to overflowing. We used just about every space available. The kids would be in class for an hour and a half. Many of the parents brought their kids from outlying areas, since the parish did reach out into the countryside. What did the parents do while the kids were in class?

We came up with the idea to have programs for parents while the children were in class. I started it during my first year running the program, and we sent out invitations to the parents to join us for an overview of the program for the year and offered them something to do while the kids were in class. While attendance varied from week to week, we had about a hundred parents each week come to learn more about their religion while the kids were learning about theirs.

A couple of things we did were rather effective. If the kids did some project or artwork, we were sure to have it displayed for the parents to see. I would take my camera to classes and come back the next week with slides to show the parents what was going on. One of the benefits of the program was that the parents who attended often volunteered as teachers the next year. With over a hundred teachers involved in the program, I never had a problem finding good teachers.

Another program I was in charge of was the school lunch program. There were only two paid people in a program that fed about 600 kids each day: the head cook and the bookkeeper. The rest were volunteers, mainly the elderly widows who lived in the neighborhood. They were more than willing to come for a couple hours a few days a week to help with the cooking and serving of the meals. Most of them were excellent cooks. It gave them something to do and a social outlet with their friends. They also got a free meal, which they probably would not have cooked if they stayed at home.

In appreciation each year we had a dinner for them at the end of the year. We had little gifts and prizes for everyone, played bingo, and the like. The first year I ran the program we decided to spike the punch a bit. The ladies had the time of their lives. In fact a couple of them were a bit tipsy, but every one of them was sure to say it was the best party they ever had. Only the head cook and I knew that the punch was spiked. And we never told.

One of my tasks was the monthly "sick calls" to bring communion to the shut-ins of the parish. It seems that the area around St. Mary's had a lot of informal nursing homes at the time where a woman would take in three or more boarders who were not able to live on their own. For the most part they were well cared for, though there were conditions in some that would not pass any health inspections. There were times when I would rather have mailed the Communion wafer, but I "did my job." And did it quickly I am sure. I often wished I could have spent more time visiting the shut-ins or done more to improve their situations

This task generally fell to the assistants who did this early in the morning after the first Mass, arriving at people's homes somewhere shortly after 7:00 AM. (People still had to fast from midnight before receiving Communion.) The routine was the same: hear the person's confession. (What trouble could an eighty -year old woman who couldn't go anywhere get into?) We'd distribute a communion wafer and be on our way. At least it maintained some connection for the shut in with the church and brought some solace to them. I look back and realize I might have accomplished far more good by a friendly visit that lasted more than the few minutes it took me to hear a confession and distribute communion. I never realized the loneliness that must have been as devastating as the effects of the aging process for these people.

A few cases stand out in my memory even years later. One woman lived in a little shack with her brother on the northwest side of town. The little house was always a mess. The St. Vincent de Paul Society and nearly every other help group knew the woman and her brother as always being in dire need.

I was called by the undertaker, when she was found her dead one morning. She had purses hanging from hooks all around the little shack. Each purse was stuffed with cash. Apparently she hoarded all the money she and her brother received from whatever source. There was something over $200,000 when it was all counted. Most of it I am sure went to the welfare agencies that gave her some support over the years. I doubt if any of the charities that supported them ever got a dime. I wonder if family members ended up with it?

We had several nursing homes in the parish and I got the job of bringing communion to the people in them, and once a month I would have Mass in their chapel. Knowing the impaired state of the people who required nursing care, I wondered why we ever bothered to hear their confessions.

In retrospect, this was part of the culture of the Church at the time. There was something "spiritual" or magic about going through the motions of the ritual exactly as written out by someone in Rome in the past, with little thought to whether or not these actions or prayers had any benefit or known effect in the lives of the people involved. It probably was based on the assumption that if the Church told God to forgive, He would, and if the Church told God to favor someone with a greater reward in heaven He would certainly do so. I guess we had a lot of pull with the Almighty or at least we acted like we did.

One of the "priestly duties" of the youngest priest on the staff was to rinse the small linens used during Mass to wipe the chalice and the like. There was a phobia that some particle of consecrated bread floating around somewhere where might be touched by unconsecrated hands or worse and the linens had to be properly rinsed. In the anteroom of the sanctuary, a room called the sacristy, there was a small sink that drained directly into the ground. It was only into this little sink that one could pour the water used to wash the priest's fingers during Mass, and this was the final repository of the water used to wash the altar linens. If one of the Communion wafers fell to the floor during distribution of communion, it was placed in an "ablution cup" filled with water, which was ultimately disposed of in this sink. All the cloth used either on the altar, for wiping the vessels, or even covering the communion rail was of pure linen. I'm not quite sure why, but this was what the rubrics prescribed and no one questioned it.

The veneration of the communion particles was quite deep in the lore of the Church well into the 1960's. The inside of the vessels that touched the Communion bread and the wine had to be inlaid with gold, and the chalices were specially anointed by the bishop before use. Lay people were not allowed to touch the Communion bread. Only those whose fingers were anointed with the oils of ordination were allowed to do so. The priest would distribute communion by placing each wafer on the tongue of the communicant. It's a wonder that more disease wasn't spread, or maybe nobody noticed for the centuries the practice continued.

Each church had a communion railing that separated the sanctuary from the rest of the church. In the old Orthodox churches this was an actual door or "rood" screen that was closed during part of the Mass signifying that what was going on at the altar was too sacred for the laity to observe, somewhat reminiscent of the high priest of the Jewish temple entering into the Holy of Holies alone.

During Mass, the young lads who were mass servers would cover the rail with a linen cloth that was attached on one side so it could easily turn over the railing. People would then come at the proper time, kneel at the rail in a line and wait as the priest went back and forth on the line placing a wafer on the tongue of each person there to receive it. The Mass server would walk next to the priest and hold a "paten," which was a saucer with a handle, under the chin of the person in case some fragment or a "host" should fall. The priest would then brush these into the chalice before he rinsed it with wine and water. One wonders about the theology of these practices, but that's the way it was.

The Church thrived on certain mythologies. One of the myths perpetuated for years among priests and reinforced in their Catholic schools was the importance of a priest being at the deathbed to hear the last confession, and if the person were still able to swallow, to give them Communion for the last time, (called Viaticum – for the journey) The priest was also to anoint the person with oils blessed by the bishop on Holy Thursday and kept in each parish. The anointing was called "Extreme Unction" – an attempt to Anglicize a Latin term. It was believed if these things were done, the person was assured of going to heaven straight way and not having to linger in "purgatory."

In parishes close to hospitals without resident chaplains, the parish priest could be called whenever a person was admitted to the emergency ward or appeared near death. Some zealous priests used to carry the little vials of oils in their cars just in case they came upon an accident and arrived before the lawyers. I'm not aware that any of them were ever able to get through the police barricades to administer the last rites while the person was bleeding to death on the pavement.

At St. Mary's, Monsignor Hank was scrupulous about having someone in the house at all times to answer the phone or doorbell just in case a "sick call" came in. In five years there, I remember being called out once, on a Saturday morning. When I arrived at the house the police and undertaker and coroner were gathered. The man, who lived alone had committed suicide a day or two before. I took a deep breath and threw up. I often wondered if Hank's insistence that one of his associates be available at all times was his fear that he might be the one to respond to such a call. A few years before, one of his assistants was called out to a home where a mother had hanged her child and herself in the basement of their home. The woman had been seeing one of the parish priests about her marital problems, and he apparently followed closely the Church's view that "until death do us part" regardless of what it did to the people involved.

No doubt the practice of the "last rights" at the last moments of life was not only bad theology but also a terrible waste of personnel. Most parishes did not have a secretary to do clerical work or serve as receptionist. This was the job of the young priests. If someone wanted a record of a Baptism to file for Social Security (because it cost a couple of bucks to get a birth certificate from the register of deeds) or to schedule a Mass in memory of a loved one, a priest had to be there. We didn't have regular office hours, so they might arrive at any time convenient to them. Some came at inconvenient times, especially Sunday afternoons during football season. You could almost count on a vagrant showing up asking for a handout with a hard luck story I heard many times. While at first I was sympathetic to them, I soon realized that I was giving away a sizeable percentage of my meager monthly income and I noticed that Hank never opened the door, so he never had to give anything to the panhandlers. Apparently word got around with the regulars that there was a new priest at St. Mary's, and they came out of the woodwork, or should I say the bars on Main Street, where they could buy a bottle cheap wine if they were lucky enough to get a little handout.

You never knew who was going to show up at the parish rectory. We had the usual assortment of beggars, mostly local winos, and during the summer months a few migrants making their way through town. You could always tell when there was a big storm and the migrants who worked in the fields and canneries around the area would come into town. Our doorbell was sure to ring. On occasion we'd get someone who would ask for lodging for the night and we'd give him or her a slip to the Calumet Hotel, a seedy place down by the railroad tracks. I learned later that they'd trade this for another hit of wine or something and the hotel really didn't want them either. This was before drugs were common. Of course, Hank never answered the door and anything that we gave to the beggars came out of our own pockets. After months or years of this, I began to recognize the same people coming by at different times of the year. They made their circuit. There was a wooded area along the river and the railroad tracks where a few shacks were home to some of the locals and migrants as they came through town. It seems they all knew where to go for a handout. These were probably the local homeless.

In the mid 60's a national magazine featured an article about a family that traveled the entire country for a number of years, begging food and money from the local Catholic priests in every town they went. They prided themselves on living high and taking advantage of the easy mark that we were.

On other occasions there were slick sounding scams, fast-talking hustlers who had a hard luck story that never held up with a few simple questions and they went their merry way quickly. And there were the town wackos who needed to talk to a priest and who made the rounds of every parish in town. One day a man showed up and wanted to know if Father Kircher was available. When I told him that Fr. Kircher had died about fifteen years ago, he lowered his head and said he was sad to hear that. "He was my regular confessor," he said quietly. I wanted to ask when it was that he was to confession last, but I didn't.

I soon had a reputation for a sympathetic ear and willingness to help people get the professional care they needed, so I became the first stop for marital and personality problems and a few closet alcoholics who didn't want to admit their problem. Sometimes helping one with a problem opened the door to a whole lot of others, like the occasion when a young lesbian woman stopped in and talked about her problems dealing with guilt. I listened and apparently didn't yell at her or try to heap more guilt on her but tried to help her understand that there probably wasn't anything perverse about who she was and she should just get on with life as best she could and that who she went to bed with probably wasn't anybody else's business. Apparently she was not alone, because over the next few months, there was a definite increase in women with similar problems who came to confession to me on Saturdays.

No doubt the most interesting one came one rainy Friday night. There had been a terrific thunderstorm and heavy downpour late in the afternoon that knocked out power in a good portion of the city. Just after supper a couple came to the door and wanted to talk to the pastor. They looked like someone in the family had died or something, crying and distraught. I was only too glad to hand them off to Hank. He talked with them a few minutes and called me in. I wanted to say, "Thanks a lot." I didn't know what was going on.

Well, the story began to unwind as they opened up with me. Apparently there were some funny goings on in their home on 6th street. It was a two-story house with a walk-in attic in a wing of the house off the main section. At night there were rapping noises coming from this attic that sometimes went on for hours on end and the poor people were terrified. At times, when the man searched the attic he found nothing, and on some occasions the light in the attic would not work, but the next day everything would be OK. The two girls in the family got the notion to ask this "spook" questions and whatever it was rapped out answers. This really freaked everybody out.

Sunday morning the father laid out his suit on the bed to get dressed for church. When he turned around to get something out of the closet his suit was gone. They later found it in the walk-in attic. It seemed at night things would fly off the knick-knack shelves in the living room for no good reason. What brought the issue to a head that particular day was this: the father dug some potatoes in the garden and was going to take them to his parents who lived out in the country a couple of miles. He carried the basket from the basement to the landing at the back door, and noticing that it looked like rain, he went up to a closet to get his jacket. When he came down, the potatoes were back down in the basement.

Not knowing what else to do, I agreed to come to their house and bless the place. So I put on my cassock and a surplice, gathered a priestly stole, a holy water bottle and ritual book, and followed them to their home. By now it was getting dark, and the power was still out. I was walking through their house by candlelight and with a holy water sprinkler blessing the house. I even went into the dark attic and sprinkled it liberally with holy water. After I completed the blessing tour, I sat and talked with the family about the situation. The happenings seemed to occur only when the two daughters were at home. I suspected they had something to do with the strange happenings. So I went into lengthy discussions about poltergeists and the powers of the human mind to effect paranormal events, such as rapping and the like, and that whatever it was it certainly seemed harmless, so there was nothing to fear. I didn't think it was a matter of demonic possession.

I left and drove back to St. Mary's. On the way all I could think of was that if there had been a clap of thunder while I was going through that house, I would have probably filled my pants. Years later I met the people again and asked them if there was any further problem with the poltergeists. They assured me that there was no problem whatsoever after that night. I just chalked that one up to "Met ghost, conquered same." All in a Friday night's work!

The parish staff tried to connect our parishioners to the Church when the opportunity presented itself. One of those opportunities was when the parents brought their newborn in for Baptism. Often we'd never see them again until the child was ready for school or First Communion, if ever. So we instituted a program where a group of women would visit the mothers of these children and bring them a packet of information and services available if the need should arise. Just a low-key, friendly visit. Most of the new mothers loved it. Often a friendship developed between an experienced mother and a new mom that was greatly appreciated. There were not a lot of resources available to new mothers on parenting in the 1960's except advice from mom.

A facet of the program was parent education. We put on a series of programs for parents of young children, covering a variety of subjects. One year the women printed up a program listing all the sessions and the presenters. There was a pediatrician, a dentist, a public health nurse, a psychologist, and myself. They wanted a program on teaching children about sexuality from a Christian point of view. The title of my presentation was "A Christian Viewpoint on Sex" Each of the presenters had a little bio in the brochure, and there was a line in bold print "All our speakers are experts in their fields and come with extensive experience."

One night my presentation on the need for sex education went quite well but then it came time for questions. A hand went up.

"Father, it says in this brochure that all the speakers come with extensive experience. Can you tell us, where did you get all that experience?" We had a good laugh and I never did answer that question.

One of the interesting characters in the parish owned a large construction firm. George Hutter was an amazing man in many ways. He could recall on any of his far- flung projects, which men worked on what building down to the carpenter who hung the doors in a hospital in Nebraska.

He was a generous supporter of several worthwhile projects in town and the parish, including the scouting programs. My memory of him is receiving phone calls at the rectory. His secretary would place his calls, and announce very loudly "One moment for George Hutter Senior." When George would come on the phone I could lay the receiver on the desk and walk ten feet away and hear every word he said.

George was a great storyteller, and one of his favorites involved the building of the new Marian College in Fond du Lac. He was giving a tour of the construction site to the Mother Superior one day as he did frequently. As they were surveying the new buildings under construction she turned to him and said:

"Mr. Hutter, some of our young nuns are offended by the coarse language that some of your men use. Could you talk to them about that?"

Hutter replied, "Sister, you have to understand these are construction workers, and they're going to call a spade a spade."

"Mr. Hutter" the nun replied, "I just heard the guy over there call it a F_ _ _ing shovel."

For the most part, life in the rectory was quite boring. The young priests always had the early Masses, which was either at 6:00 or 6:15 each morning. The only people who showed up were a couple of old people who lived in the neighborhood and who couldn't sleep, and one or the other devout soul who came before going off to work. In a church designed to hold about a thousand, we often had as few as a dozen for the early Mass. Because the "stipend" for a High Mass which was partially sung by the priest and choir was $5.00 rather than $1.00 for the Low Mass which was recited by the priest, most parish Masses were High Masses. In most cases the organist was paid as much as the priest's stipend by the parish. It was often ridiculous with the priest at one end of a cavernous church and the only other person in church was the organist in the choir loft at the other end, with perhaps a sprinkling of elderly persons scattered around in the pews. I often wondered if this was what Christ meant when he told his apostles "Do this in memory of me."

Mass was followed with breakfast and then off to teach a religion class or two in the school before lunch. One of us would stay in the rectory to answer the phone and doorbell, and since Hank reserved a lot of things to himself, about half the time it was either to greet the people and call him, or tell them he was out, when in fact he was either taking his afternoon nap, which he did religiously from about 1:00 to 3:00 each day, or he was off to the race track, which he did for a couple of days each month when the ponies were running.

Afternoons were a drag, a good time to nap, to read, or as Roger used to do, build model boats complete with the intricate riggings. It was during these boring afternoons that I wrote the history of St.

Mary's for the centennial celebrations. Late afternoons, there were often "devotions" of one kind or another, particularly during October, Lent and the month of May.

The "devotions" consisted of a set of sentimental prayers rattled off in mindless fashion such as the rosary, or during Lent a set of prayers at each of the fourteen "Stations of the Cross" that hung along the side walls of every Catholic Church recalling the events of the last hours of the life of Jesus beginning with his agonizing in the garden and ending with his body taken down from the cross. It probably was intended to instill guilt in the faithful. The prayers overflowed with morbid emotion and were bound to inspire guilt in the faithful, a handful scattered throughout the cavernous church.

Dinner followed and if we had a meeting or appointment, that took care of the evening. In between we had to recite the prayers of the "breviary" which was a remnant of the Middle Ages when the monks in the abbey would chant their prayers at the hours of the day. Priests were expected to recite these prayers daily (under pain of sin, no doubt) and in Latin. I often wondered why it was that every violation of a Church law was considered a mortal sin. I could never figure that out. After the Vatican Council it was the progressive thing to write the bishop and receive permission to recite it in English. I was even more progressive. I just went ahead and did it. I figured if the bishop could give permission to some why not give it to all as was done in every other diocese around the state and save the paperwork. I guess it was a matter of authority and control.

The translations were pretty bad; trying to put flowery Medieval Latin poetry into modern English just didn't work. Perhaps the poetry didn't make a lot of sense in Latin either, but few priests had that facility with the language to know the difference between bad and good Latin poetry. It may have sounded nice when sung or chanted but made little sense when translated and read, much like the lyrics of many songs hardly make sense when recited without the music.

The parish of the 60's did not make good use of its priests. No one seemed to have a good idea of what exactly a priest was supposed to be doing. Staffing needs were often based on the number of Sunday

Masses needed to accommodate the parish or the lines at the confessional on Saturdays or the number of people on the parish roster. We had this structure or system that evolved in the American Church in the 20th century and we were at a loss to evaluate it or make any changes. We were trained to be attendants at the "spiritual filling station" and glorified parish secretaries. At least we had something to occupy our time.

During my tenure, the parish celebrated its centennial, and in preparation for it, I took on myself to write the history of the parish. I spent countless hours in the public library scanning through microfilm of newspaper articles, going to the seminary library to sift through materials on the diocese, as well as hours with parish records dating back to the 1860's, along with interviews with long time members who had pictures and other memorabilia that shed some light on the history. When it was finally published it was a serious book that stands with the best of local history on the Catholic Church in the area. I have noticed that whenever a subsequent history of the area is written, I am quoted.

As a priest, I considered myself a good preacher. Each priest in the diocese would receive his annual "Sermon Outlines" for each Sunday of the year to cover sections of Catholic doctrine. There was a cycle of a few years with one year covering the Commandments, the next the Sacraments and another on the Virtues etc. Usually they were written by one of the priests at the seminary, or rather copied from an earlier version by merely changing the dates of the particular Sundays. For the most part they were uninspiring, yet most priests followed them slavishly. Perhaps one of the secrets to whatever success I had was that I preached what I believed in and found it impossible to mouth something that I did not agree with. I found that one key to good delivery lay in speaking directly to particular individuals I had picked out in the audience, including some as far back in the audience as I could safely identify. This helped immensely with eye contact and kept these people awake usually.

Yet there was only one time that I felt I really got through to the entire audience. I had the last Mass on a summer Sunday when the temperature was well into the nineties, with high humidity. By the last Mass, which was packed to the doors, the building was a sauna. I looked out and saw everybody fanning themselves with parish bulletins or whatever else they could find. I was wringing wet in the heavy vestments. I paused and looked over the crowd when it came time for the sermon. I started my sermon:

"It's hot today. You're thinking it's too hot to listen to a sermon. I've got on all these vestments and I'm thinking it's too hot to preach one. If there wasn't one place hotter, neither you nor I would be here. Just remember that. God Bless you." I still think that was my best effort.

After the Vatican Council there was enthusiasm for inter-faith collaboration, and I was a board member of the Fond du Lac Area Clergy association, which included most of the Protestant clergy, a few of the Catholic clergy (mainly the younger ones) and the local Jewish Rabbi. If the truth were known, I was on better terms with the rabbi and ministers than with most of the Catholic priests in the area.

Sometimes my ecumenical spirit and common sense got me in trouble. I remember attending a funeral in a Lutheran church for the mother of a parishioner who was active in the parish. The entire family, including grandma, were good friends. The only two Lutherans in the church were the minister and the woman in the coffin. The pastor asked me if I would do one of the readings and say a few words of consolation for the family. I saw no objections and did it. Word got back to Hank that I had been there, and he wanted to know if I had received permission from the chancery office to attend the funeral. Actually priests in other dioceses and even in our own diocese had been doing this for years, and we were behind the times, adhering to the long-term suspicion and aversion to our fellow Christians.

Even in the late 60's it was considered sinful for a Catholic to attend any service other than in a Catholic Church, even for a funeral or wedding. I found such bigotry appalling, especially when the Church was trying to mend the fences of division. I wondered if the Christian Church could be believable if it was not one.

On the diocesan level I was a member of the first ecumenical committee to increase understanding and cooperation among various religious groups. Unfortunately, the powers of the diocese were mired deeply in the monolithic posture of the church and much of our work came to naught. I was on the committee that sought to improve relations with other faiths. I headed the sub-committee which dealt with the

Catholic cemeteries and the existing rule that Catholics and only Catholics could be buried there and that a priest was not to go to a non-sectarian cemetery to bless the grave and conduct graveside ceremonies.

I was of the opinion that it really didn't matter where the body would be laid to decay and there was nothing wrong the priest offering a blessing for the site and saying a few prayers for the deceased. The benefits to the grieving family were well worth making the change in the diocesan regulation. Certainly the separation of family graves by religion didn't make a lot of sense. So we proposed changes that would allow the priest to conduct graveside ceremonies wherever the family chose to bring the remains for final rest. We submitted our recommendations to the Chancery office, which at that time was the final word on everything. Collegiality hadn't yet even begun to sprout, much less flourish. At our next meeting a few weeks later we had our reply.

The matter was taken under consideration and the proposed change could not be made "because the diocese owned several large cemeteries, in addition to those owned by parishes throughout the area. If we allowed people to be buried anywhere they choose, it could result in a loss of business for the diocesan cemeteries." So much for Ecumenism!

There's an old Portuguese proverb that "God writes straight with crooked lines." Sometimes the lines were very crooked. This should have been the theme for the fund raising effort to build a new Catholic High School in Fond du Lac. Somewhere in the mid-60's, a fund raiser from Milwaukee got the idea that a new Catholic high school in town would be a great project and contacted Hank and his friend Fr. Ray from Sacred Heart Parish to obtain their support.

About five years before, nearby St. Joseph Parish, which at that time had a ninth grade in the parish school, conducted a survey about interest in building a boys' high school in town to go along with St. Mary's Springs which was run by the nuns. While there appeared to be some support, the survey of interest was limited to the parish and certainly not a scientific sampling. At any rate, this survey was resurrected as a basis for public interest in building a new St. Mary's Springs High school.

The phone calls kept coming to the rectory and there were private meetings with Hank and his friend Ray and the fund-raiser. I had strong suspicions that the fund-raiser paid for a winter vacation for Ray and Hank in Mexico that year, and suddenly their support was firmly behind going ahead with a fund raising drive. With the interest of the only two pastors in town who had any influence, the project seemed to have some spark of life, though there were serious critics.

One of the questions raised was the ability of the Sisters of St. Agnes, whose numbers were dropping off dramatically, to staff such a school. If they built it, could they afford to staff it with lay teachers? The answer poured out as if rehearsed: they would get the Capuchin Brothers from Mt. Calvary to teach the boys. Sounded good but was it? First of all, no one ever bothered to ask the Capuchins if they were interested in staffing a school with their brothers. The only high school the Capuchins ever staffed was their own seminary, and for a short time, a small high school at St. Benedict's in Milwaukee, and these schools were staffed by priests. The other problem was that the Capuchin Brothers were few, and most did menial tasks around the monasteries. The brothers were men who aspired to religious life, but in general did not have the mental capacity to pursue studies for the priesthood and certainly were not trained as high school teachers.

I was kept pretty well out of the loop as a young assistant, and perhaps because I asked a few pertinent questions, I was soon branded as an opponent of the project, which certainly was not true, though I had my doubts.

A big dinner was held at the hotel for the "outstanding Catholics" of the area. For some reason I didn't get an invite. About the only people invited were those with deep pockets. They heard some hired gun of a Monsignor from Nebraska talk about the need for a Catholic high school in Fond du Lac. The fact that the invitees were the financial elite left a bad taste in the community. Questions about who was paying for all this surely were pertinent.

At any rate, the month of the big pledge drive came and teams of parishioners swarmed through the city and countryside in search of pledges and checks. The project failed miserably. They did not raise 10% of what they would need. It was dead on arrival. The cash collected went to pay for the fund-raisers.

Next the pastors in town met and agreed that the parishes would underwrite the cost of building an addition to the High School. There was never a vote by the people in the parishes, but they were all saddled with the debt for the school that few of the families could afford for their children. Somewhere in the back of my mind the thought occurred that the Sisters of St. Agnes had somehow blackmailed the pastors in the matter. After all, they staffed every parochial school in town and the Catholic high school was an important source link between the parish schools and Marian College, which they also ran, as well as providing an important source for new recruits to their order.

I wondered years later how Ray and Hank were able to pull this one off. But then I looked around at who the priests in town were at the time. At St. Joe's, the monsignor was just hanging on. He prided himself as an educator and five years earlier had tried to build a Boy's high school for his parish. This was vindication.

St. Patrick's pastor was a sickly old man, and assigned to the parish were Father Don, who had more enthusiasm than common sense, and Father Paul, who for some reason reminded me of a beached elephant seal, though not as mobile and Paul didn't have the social graces of his animal counterpart. Neither Don nor Paul were known for their scholarly pursuits. The other parish, St. Louis, was staffed by priests from a French-Canadian order who seemed to live in their own little world.

So there really was no one who questioned the wisdom of the project or the idea of saddling ordinary parishioners with a debt for a school their families could never afford to attend. The project went forward, and the addition was built. And yes, the Capuchin Brothers have not staffed the classes for boys.

Standing in front of a church full of people can be interesting at times. I remember two weddings in particular. Back when people had to fast from midnight and could not even have a drink of water before Communion, it was a struggle for the late morning weddings. (Before the Council, there were no evening weddings or Masses.) One Saturday I had the last Wedding, which was at 12:00 noon. It was a warm June day, and apparently the bridal party had celebrated a bit the night before and I suspected the bride was a couple months pregnant. During the

Mass, the groom turned ashen colored and fainted. The bride seeing this, toppled on top of him; the best man bent over to see what was going on and fell on top of the two of them. So I had three people passed out on the floor of the sanctuary. We waited a few minutes, and they recovered a bit, but I had them sit down for the rest of the ceremony, which I think I did in record time.

The other one I remember was one of my CCD teachers, a good friend and I knew the entire family, as well as most of the relatives and friends. It was a big wedding and the church was quite full. When it came to the vows, I couldn't for the life of me remember her first name. I paused a bit, and leaned over to the groom and asked "what's her name?" He got a big grin on his face and told me quietly, "Pat." Saved the day. This was the last time that I neglected to write out the names of the bride and groom in my book before the ceremony.

When the altar faced the back wall there were few distractions, but when we turned around to face the people in the late 60's, it was a challenge to filter out distractions from what was going on in the pews ahead of me and remember where I was at any given time. In the back of my mind there was always a fear that I was going to miss something because I was watching the people instead of what I was doing. It was a challenge to drink cheap warm wine on an empty stomach and not wretch at the early Mass, especially if you had a sensitive stomach to begin with.

Another challenge was to keep a straight face when I could see what was going on in the pews ahead of me, in particular the antics of small children who had to be bored out of their minds. I remember one instance where a little girl apparently wet her panties and took them off and handed them to her mother. I think I pulled a muscle in my abdomen that morning.

Other embarrassing moments would come when the choir was singing the "Gloria" or "Creed" during which we would sit with the Mass Servers to the side of the sanctuary. On more than one occasion I nodded off, but when I trained the servers I always told them to be alert to that situation and to give me a nudge. I knew other priests who were so sound asleep that it took a while to get them to wake up.

When wireless microphones became a church fixture, there were a number of priests who forgot to turn them off when they left the altar, and the whole church could hear what they were saying in the sacristy. Occasionally the parish got an earful, like the priest who was talking to another priest in the sacristy and asked, "Did you get a load of that sexy babe in the front on the right? Wow did she have a pair of boobs." Luckily most of the people had left the church by then.

During my last year at St. Mary's, Fr. Dick was assigned to the parish, replacing Fr. Jim, who asked for a transfer after one year with Hank. Dick was newly ordained and came from the seminary with lots of new ideas, a world of enthusiasm and a spirit of change that was sweeping the Church and the seminary in the late 60's.

Being a Sheboygan native, as were Hank and Susie, dinner conversations invariably drifted to the Sheboygan that Hank and Susie remembered, not that things had changed much there in the last fifty years.

Dick was a fun guy, very personable, and got along well with people, but sometimes his friendships got him in trouble. He loved to party, though it became evident that his tolerance for alcohol wasn't great. The local FM station DJ's would take requests on their evening shows and Dick worked out a code with a couple of parishioners so that if there was a party going on, they could invite him without making a phone call to the rectory. For example, someone would call with a request from Ed and Carol to the gang on Marquette Street, and the song would be "Cabaret." This meant there was a party going on and we were invited. Years later I met one of the DJ's and told him about the scheme. He didn't have a clue, but I am sure the word got around to a number of other people.

One night Dick and I were at a party, which I left early, while Dick stayed on. I was sound asleep when I felt a hand on my shoulder. It was Dick.

"John" he said, "I need your help."
"What's up?" I asked, "Are you sick or something?"

"No" he replied, "I wrecked my car."

"Where is it?"

"In the garage" he whispered. He didn't want anyone in the house to know about it. Fr. Jerry was sleeping in the next suite and Hank was downstairs.

"Where did it happen? Are you hurt?"

"I hit the side of the garage, and I'm OK."

The garage was attached to the side of the school gym, and we all had automatic door openers, and apparently Dick opened the door, but didn't make it in. I got up and looked out the window. The door was closed, and there didn't seem to be any damage to the building. Dick was nervous.

"I don't want Hank to find out about this." He was sure his image would be smirched if that happened. I didn't want to wake the house by making an inspection in the middle of the night, and I knew his insurance agent. So I told Dick not to worry, I would talk to Ed early in the morning and we'd get it taken care off.

I had the early Mass and knew that Ed was always up before 7:00, so I called him at 6:45 and explained the situation to him and asked him if he could get a tow truck over to the garage shortly after 8:00, when Hank and Susie would be in church for the 8:00 Mass. Ed said he could take care of it. 8:05 a tow truck pulled onto the playground and I went out and opened the door for them. He took the car to Gibson's garage down the street a couple of blocks. Nobody ever knew a thing about it except Dick, Ed and the guys at Gibson's in the body shop.

When I looked at the car I wondered how he got it into the garage. There were solid tempered brick pillars about two feet wide between the garage doors and Dick hit one right between the headlights. He never touched the door and the only visible signs of impact were a bit of body trim that the janitor picked up next to the garage. From the damage on the car it was fortunate he didn't make it through the door because with the impact and speed he might have ended up going through the block wall right onto the gym floor. Now that would have been difficult to cover up.

I had a number of friends in the Jaycees, considered becoming their chaplain and knew they were holding a demolition derby at the fairgrounds on Memorial Day, just two weeks ahead. It was a great event and a wonderful fundraiser for their charities. I got an entry blank and filled in Dick's name with Gibson garage as the sponsor, and mailed it to him. I watched when it came in and promptly ended in the wastebasket. Damn, it didn't work.

I talked to a friend and told him what I'd done and asked him if he could rattle the cage a bit. He called Dick and posed as Gene from Gibson's garage, asking what size crash helmet he wore and told him to be out at the fairgrounds at 10:00 so he could get familiar with the car and get the rules down before the start of the race. Dick did a double take and tried to say he wasn't entered and all that. Finally in desperation he said, "This is Father Richard Kirsch from St. Mary's"

"I know" came the reply "and we're fixing your car and we've paid $250 entry fee for you to drive so you'd better be there."

Dick hung up the phone and dug through his waste basked to find the entry blank. Sure enough, it looked authentic, and the next thing I knew he was on the phone calling everybody who might know someone in the Jaycees. Nobody knew what he was talking about but told him that the committee was handling all that stuff. Nobody could help him out, of course.

Memorial Day came and Dick asked me if he could switch and take the early Mass. It had to be the shortest one on record, and before any of the people were out of church, Dick was on his way out of the city. He didn't come back until very late at night.

A week or two later his car was finally done, and when he went to pick it up there was a trophy on the front seat, about two feet high, inscribed "1968 Jaycees Demolition Derby. Father Richard Kirsch, Participant."

About five years later we were both married, and happened to meet at Ed Riegert's for a party. I said to Ed "You know, it's been about five years, do you think it's about time we tell Dick who signed him up for that demolition derby." Dick turned white and then red and broke down laughing. He had no idea we were behind the whole thing and were the only ones who knew about it. By the way, Hank never learned about the crash either.

After I left Fond du Lac, Dick had some hard times. The new pastor asked for St. Mary's because he had a cottage on Lake Winnebago and loved to spend his summers fishing. He was one of those priests whose world passed by with the Vatican Council, and some say with the 20th century. Without me to provide the leadership or back up, Dick was lost and clashed bitterly with his new boss. In his frustration, Dick turned to partying more than was healthy. In fact, on one trip back home he ran off the road and ended up in the hospital. While his wounds were not life threatening, his recovery was slow because he couldn't face going back to the rectory.

When he asked for reassignment, he got another lulu. The pastor at his new parish left town quietly in a plea bargain against charges of pedophilia. "Leave town and we'll sweep it under the rug" was the thinking of the law enforcement at that time. It wasn't long before Dick took a leave of absence and went back to school working on his masters degree, another fine young priest sacrificed.

For whatever reason, even some thirty years after I left the parish, people still have kind things to say about my five years there. Personally I have always felt that my transfer was done in spite and interrupted a ministry that was just beginning to blossom. Our parish was vibrant and alive. My influence in the community was beginning to reach out beyond the confines of the parish rectory. Programs that I arranged for the Knights of Columbus drew hundreds from the community. Our marriage enrichment program for young married couples was years ahead of its time. Our religious education program for children attending public schools was outstanding including programs for the parents at the same time. I was respected, loved by the people, and effective in my ministry. I have always suspected that Hank was intensely jealous of my popularity. I had to be popular. A good number of the parish members were relatives. Nevertheless Hank wanted me out of the parish, and I had no say in the matter. Like many young priests, I was expendable, not even worthy of the courtesy of consultation.

People in the parish years later still remember the days of my tenure with kindness. Many of the things that we accomplished fell by the wayside in the next generation of priests who served at the parish. I felt that I left my mark at least in this: I know that whenever the people of the community delve into the history of their parish, my work on the parish history will be the source book they will use.

Chapter Six

Hank and Susie

Most of the pastors in the 1960's had a "housekeeper" who did the cooking, cleaning and laundry for the priests in the rectory. Quite often she was a relative, perhaps a sister, or it might be a single woman or widow who had been serving the pastor for many years. Generally these women were protective of their boss and possessive of the parish house. At St. Mary's, Hank had his sister Susie as his housekeeper, a position she evidently wanted from the day he entered the seminary. She had joined him at his first pastorate many years before.

Eating two meals a day with the pair, who seldom left the house, the table conversations were bound to deteriorate into breaking small talk down into fragments, particularly when there was little common ground for discussion.

Hank was interesting in many ways, but he never quite got around to laughing at himself, which is a pity because there was so much about him that was hilarious. For example, at lunch one day I mentioned that I had gotten a new watch that used batteries rather than a stem-winder. Hank went into a long discussion of his watch, one of those "self winding" watches in which the mainspring was wound by wrist movement. He complained that as long as he had this watch, he always had to wind it. He got a little unnerved when I couldn't stop laughing. He never moved enough to wind his own watch.

His daily schedule was a rigid routine. He would rise at about 7:30 and have the 8:00 AM Mass, which during the school year was attended by the 800 or so children in the 16 classroom school. After Mass he would have breakfast and spend a little time reading the morning paper or saying his prayers from his "Breviary."

The mail would arrive about 10:00 and he would sort through the mail and open what pertained to him. This would take until nearly lunch time as he would read all the junk mail as well. If he received an invitation to some event he did not want to attend, he would try to get the stamp off the return envelope rather than reply.

He might find a few minutes to walk over to the school though he never taught religion classes. He told me once he wouldn't know what to say to children any more. I believed him.

After lunch he would spend a little more time with the paper, surely checking out the results at the racetracks, and it was time for his nap, which he took from 1:00 to 3:00, never to be disturbed. After his nap it was time for a couple more prayers and perhaps an appointment or two and it was time for supper.

One function he reserved to himself was to give "marriage instructions" to each couple on the day before their wedding, which was generally on a Saturday. He met with the couples at 4:00 PM in his office, and he would talk to them for about an hour. I often wanted to secrete a microphone in his office to hear what he actually said to them. I am sure that it contained a good deal about birth control and making certain that their children were raised as good Catholics. Personally, I thought that on the eve of their wedding, couples were hardly receptive to long sermonizing, and had their minds on something else. If he was intending to give them instructions on sexuality, they certainly had more experience than Hank did.

In the evening he might have a meeting with the Trustees, the Christian Mothers, Holy Name or Ushers societies, at which he would spend some time socializing and then return to the rectory, read the rest of the paper, watch a little television and retire about midnight. He was usually up to see that the last of the assistants were in before he retired. (We were required to be in by 11:00 PM by diocesan rule.)

In reality, Hank had little interest outside the parish and what he perceived as his priestly duties. He had a few friends in the parish, mainly the affluent, and the only laity who ever came to visit was the occasional visit from his brother from Sheboygan. He seldom left the parish confines. He had one friend among the priests in the area, Fr. Ray, with whom he made his monthly trips to Chicago race-tracks and took his winter vacations in warmer climes. I didn't recognize it at the time but he must have been very lonely with few outside interests, something that was very common among the celibate clergy of the Church.

I remember the day when Hank got the letter from the bishop telling him that he was to receive the honorary title of "Monsignor." Hank was a bit embarrassed and probably rightfully wondered why he had been signaled out for the honor. After all, about all he had accomplished was to remain in the fold for nearly fifty years. Other than the accidental pastorate of a large parish, he certainly did little, at least in recent years, to distinguish himself among his peers, but then neither had some of the others who were awarded the title.

Actually there was little consequence to the honor. One of them was that the bishop could not remove him from his pastorate without either his consent or approval from Rome. There were a couple around who put the bishop to that test, but in general the man who received the title either headed up a diocesan program of some prestige or was near retirement and not likely to be moved anyway. It was at the time an honorary title not tied to any particular achievement or office in many cases.

It took a few days for Hank to get into the act, order his ceremonial robes with the purple cape and a cassock with purple buttons and the like. These, of course, had to be special ordered and cost him a pretty bundle. A discreet call from someone at the Chancery office hinted that a substantial financial offering was expected by the Holy Father in gratitude for the honor. There was a gala celebration for the official conferral of the honor with cards of congratulations and gifts from dutiful parishioners that probably covered most of the expenses.

Within a few weeks he was insisting that we call him Monsignor when addressing him and he got more comfortable wearing his red and purple trimmed garb. For a while at least, he felt he had made an important contribution to the Church, though I am sure he was quite at a loss to figure out exactly what it was, other than going through the motions of daily Mass and saying his prayers.

Hank and I did not agree on more than a few issues. For example when he insisted on building a huge addition to the rectory, but then would not approve a few dollars to furnish it. I had a new apartment complete with bath, bedroom and sitting room but no furniture. I ended up buying a small desk for my room and a couple of chairs to sit on. The parish never paid for them.

I was in charge of printing the weekly bulletin on an old mimeo machine. The machine broke down and was beyond repair. We had a hand-crank machine in the school, which was on its last legs too, but Hank wasn't about to have the parish supply another one. We could make do with the old machine or the hand-cranked model.

When the repairman for the mimeo came to check the machine he told me he had just received an offset press in trade, which was in excellent condition, and he offered it to me for a good price. I bought it and began doing the bulletin from that machine, which was a great improvement over what we had prior. I had learned printing in the seminary years before and knew how to operate an offset. Hank wasn't about to pay for it. The matter came to a head when one of the trustees got a bill for offset press ink and supplies. He asked Hank about it and he told them it was a machine I had bought for the bulletin. Over his objections they paid me for the machine.

A more serious issue we clashed over was the way we treated young women who found themselves pregnant before marriage. Hank was of the school where you pressure them into getting married and if that isn't possible, send the girl away to have the child and give the child up for adoption. No support, no counseling, no sympathy. It was this sex thing. If you did it, you take the consequences. Gratefully, I didn't get involved in many of these cases, but one I did handle got me branded as a radical.

The case involved the daughter of a prominent businessman and good friend of Hank. The parents came to Hank with their story, dragging the poor girl with them. His reaction was true to form, but nothing was resolved, and a date was set for the wedding. Two days later she showed up at the rectory, wanting to talk to me. No, she didn't want to get married, and no, she didn't want to give her baby for adoption. It was her child and she wanted to raise that child herself, knowing that it would not be easy. This was nearly a decade before Roe vs. Wade.

Rebel that I was, I told her that only she could make that decision. Certainly if there was undue pressure on her to marry, that was immoral, and the marriage would probably not be valid if that was the case. I also told her that only she could give her child to someone else. It was hers to give birth to, to love, and provide with a home. She asked me if I would support her in that decision. Of course I would. Would I talk with her parents? I was trapped. We made an appointment, and I laid the cards on the table. They soon saw that it was her decision and not theirs. While there might be some discomfort on the part of the family, the pain of giving one's child away was certainly greater, and forcing an unwise marriage would be cruel at best. They finally agreed.

When Hank found out he blew his stack. What right did I have to interfere in a case that he had already taken care of? He had given her the alternatives that her parents wanted, either marry the guy or give the kid up for adoption. I was so astounded at his total lack of sensitivity that I found it hard to respond. I did notice that the family's relationship with Hank cooled considerably. At least the parents had some sense. The woman had her child and raised it with help from her family.

Hank's sister Susie was the rectory cook and housekeeper. In her mid-70's when I arrived, she had been with Hank since his first pastorate some forty years before. She was a spinster, and had to be the world's worst cook. I remember how she would broil pork chops until they were dry, then put them in the grease of the drip pan and let them soak while she went off to church to say her prayers, came back and served them dripping with grease.

On occasion she would serve small steaks, broiled well enough, but the problem was that as soon as she took the broiler pan out of the oven she doused it with ammonia to clean it, and the fumes nearly drove everyone out of the house. She couldn't smell. She had had a sinus infection years before and under went surgery, which left her without much sense of smell. It showed.

I remember a parishioner who owned a bakery and delivered her bakery orders to the rectory. Good bakery, but I learned years later that Susie never paid for any of it, and poor Louie, who was a friend of Hank's, was too embarrassed to complain. In fact, I wonder how much of what she served in the rectory was actually paid for. I know that much of the food was taken from the school lunch program. Meat, potatoes, butter, flour, and whatever was available from the government surplus, the school lunch program supplied what was needed for the parish priests.

Susie was in her early eighties and still queen of the hive when she fell and broke a hip. I thought she'd never come home from the hospital, but with a plate in her hip, she was back home in less than two weeks. Meanwhile the parish hired Peggy, a little Lebanese lady who lived across the street to do the housekeeping chores. Her parents were among the first and most respected of the small Lebanese community in the city.

One thing improved immediately, the quality of the cooking. Peggy didn't get to pocket what she didn't spend like Susie did, and she also paid for all the food. Even with that the meals were much better.

For some reason, Peggy worshiped the ground I walked on, and we got on well. One thing we shared was our dislike for the domineering Susie, who in spite of her infirmity, tried to maintain a firm hold on the rectory. We had a lot of fun over that. Peggy would refer to her under her breath as "the bitch" which was probably kinder than she deserved.

One day when she was making her grocery list while I was having breakfast I added ALPO to her list. She shopped at a store run by another Lebanese family, and they would look at the list and help her get the things from the shelves if they had time. She came home with a can of ALPO. It was a standing joke from then on, with that can of ALPO showing up in the most mysterious places.

Occasionally, when Peggy finished her work in the kitchen, we'd invite her to have a drink upstairs with the assistants. One night she had a couple of Southern Comfort Manhattans and had trouble trying to walk. I agreed to walk her home and make sure she got there. The last thing I needed was a drunken woman on the sidewalk outside the rectory or even worse in the rectory the next morning. We made it across the street. I opened the door and made sure she got in and headed her to her bedroom. She asked me later if I knew how she got out of her clothes that night. She was fully dressed when I left her, but I let her wonder about that one.

! remember one day she asked me if she could talk to me privately about something. I wondered what happened. She pulled out a letter from the Social Security Administration telling her to come down to register for widow's benefits, which she was entitled to since she was age sixty. I didn't see a problem but then she told me the truth: she had lied about her age when she got married. The records of the Lebanese parish were lost in the fire and the only record of her age was on their marriage certificate. I asked her how bad it was. She told me she was only fifteen when she got married, but she told the people at the courthouse that she was twenty-one and that all records were lost in the church fire. So there she was, fifty-four and entitled to Social Security benefits. What if they found out the truth?

Once I knew that there were no records anywhere that could prove otherwise, I told her that she'd made one big lie, and if she tried to change that, they were sure to catch up with her and maybe find out that her marriage wasn't legal either. The only thing she could do was to apply for the benefit and keep her mouth shut. Well, that's what she did, and accepted the fact that she became old before her time.

Toward the end of their tenure at St. Mary's life was pretty rough on Hank and Susie. She was definitely deteriorating mentally and Hank was slipping, probably worrying about her. But at the core of it there seemed to be a jealousy he found hard to handle. He was beginning to find that people would seek me out with their problems rather than go to him, and after all he was the pastor and a Monsignor to boot. Other than minimal administrative duties and the few functions that he reserved to himself, such as setting dates for marriages and enrolling new members to the parish, he had little to do and did little. My lines at the confessional were long while his were almost non-existent. I was active in the Ecumenical Clergy Council in town, a friend of the Rabbi and Episcopal bishop as well as a large number of Protestant clergy. I put on a series of programs for the Knights of Columbus that were immensely popular, wrote articles for the newspaper, and was popular with the people. I really didn't have any competition. Besides Hank we had two other priests on staff. Dick was new and didn't have the contacts or relationships that had taken me a few years to build, and Jerry, who was to be charitable, a mess. Jerry came to St. Mary's after suffering a breakdown at another assignment. He spent nearly a year "on the shelf" after his breakdown before the bishop gave him another assignment. He had a habit of latching on to a family and spending most of his free time at their home. About the only thing he did other than the ministerial things around the parish was teach a few classes at St. Mary's Springs High School.

For whatever reason, Hank wanted me out of St. Mary's and went to the bishop with that request. He was informed that as far as they knew I was doing a very good job and they had heard nothing to the contrary. Hank thought he would push the subject and said with a bit of anger in his voice, "Either he goes or I resign." The bishop looked at him and said, I'll accept your resignation and assign you as chaplain of the Catholic Home (a small retirement home in the city for Catholics). Hank got his retirement, which was more for Susie than for Hank and they both moved to the Catholic Home and I got a transfer to Kenosha.

Generally when a priest leaves a parish they have a farewell party for him at the parish. When my letter came, Hank would hear nothing of a farewell. But friends in the Knights of Columbus decided that I should have one and invited anyone who wanted to come with an announcement in the newspaper and K of C bulletin. We had a few kegs of beer and snacks and the place was filled all night long. Half the Protestant clergy in town came to pay their respects, and a large number of people from the parish. It was quite impressive. Notably absent: Hank.

Chapter Seven

Confessions

One thing the seminary did not prepare us for was that when a newly ordained priest came to town his first few sessions in the confessional were bound to be quite interesting, even bizarre. People racked by guilt and who were afraid to go to one of the more experienced priests would try out the new guy in hopes he'd have a bit more understanding approach, or should I say, naïve. If they could get absolution from the new priest they could go on with their lives. We memorized the "words of absolution" in Latin, but received very little training beyond that.

I clearly remember the first couple of weeks. Farmers confessing to having sex with animals, marital infidelity, victims of pedophilia filled with guilt and fear, a pregnant woman who was having an affair with a priest who was the father of her unborn child, a parade of women practicing birth control, which in 1963 was considered the big sin of the day. Large Catholic families were the norm. At the time we had an "Auxiliary bishop" who derisively referred to small homes as "B.C. Houses" because the couples who lived there obviously had to practice birth control since there was not enough room for large families. Of course his parish was in one of the most affluent areas of town with large homes where few people had to worry about supporting their children in style regardless of the size of the family. In spite of his title and position, he was the arch-typical insensitive bishop who disdained his people unless they were white, affluent and obedient

It was ironic that a celibate clergy were laying down the rules for what was licit or not in the sexual relations of their people. Years later, an outspoken secretary of agriculture got in trouble for his comments about the Church and its teachings on sexuality when he said about the Pope "You donna playa da game you donna maka da rules." This and a couple of his racist comments got him fired by the president. Yet secretly most of the Catholics agreed with him. Celibate priests often had no clue about human sexuality and the physical intimacy between man and woman.

Gradually after the first few weeks the routine settled down to a litany of "pecadillos" and non-sins such as forgetting to say prayers in the morning or losing one's temper. Most people confessed having "impure thoughts," which was considered mortally sinful. The "biggies" would return at Christmas and Easter. We referred to them as the flowers of the church: the poinsettia and Easter lily. Generally these were marginal Catholics who came to Church or at least participated in the Sacraments only at Christmas and Easter. Church law dictated that a Catholic confess his sins at least once a year and receive Communion during the Easter Season.

Every Saturday afternoon from 3:00 to 5:30 and from 7:00 to 9:00, as well as each morning after the early Mass for a half hour or so, we'd sit in the little box, which did have a vent fan. People would kneel on one side, separated from the priest by a screen with a cloth over it to conceal identity of the penitents. Of course, there was a little "peep hole" in the door so I could see who was next or who had just left. After a while I could recognize voices and vices. The worst was the parade of odors. Farmers with manure smell, elderly ladies doused with cheap perfumes that clashed the next one who came, onions, garlic, and someone who had stopped at the bar for some bottled fortitude...all these scents wafted through the box on the way to the vent. Of course, people shopped around for a priest who for some reason was a better match for what they wanted. Naturally, this didn't include harsh words or long "penance" which consisted mainly of a few prayers or for a big sinner it was to say the entire rosary. If a priest scolded a sinner, he was almost certain that person would go to another priest the next time. Confession, in practice, had little to do with effecting any change in their lives and probably generated more guilt than it took away.

For some reason my lines were usually the longest. Was I an easy mark? Or was I a bit more compassionate and understanding? At the time a large number of elderly people in the parish insisted on doing their confession in German They knew that I had grown up in the Holy Land and since many were "Holy Landers" they felt some sort of kinship (many of them were probably relatives). They'd learned their catechism and confession in German, and never changed. In fact the sins didn't change much either. They were probably the only sins they knew the German names for, so they confessed them.

The real workout came with the first Thursday of each month. Some Saint centuries ago started the practice of receiving Communion on the first Friday of each month with the promise that a person who did it nine First Fridays in a row would never die a sudden and un-provided death. For some inane reason, we'd traipse the 800 kids in the parish school through the lines and hear their confessions. This usually took the entire Thursday morning, which was my day off. I don't believe I ever heard a sin with the school children. The ridiculous idea of parading seven year olds through the box each month was particularly inane. In reality, it was another cog in a huge guilt machine and a waste of time.

In their catechism lessons the children learned that there were two kinds of sin: mortal, which would send you to hell, and venial which would send you to purgatory. The venial sins: a burst of temper or getting drunk, (though theologians never considered driving in that condition was more serious since they copied from earlier writers who thought about the subject long before there were cars). Children confessed disobeying their parents and people of all ages confessed missing their morning and evening prayers. I used to joke that if I had a nickel for every kid who confessed going to the bathroom outside I would be able to retire. When it came to youngsters going through the hormonal surges of adolescence, they were definitely in trouble with the Church. Every sexual thought or feeling was mortally sinful, especially if you enjoyed it. The same was true of women having hot flashes during menopause. Neither the theologians nor priests had any idea how to deal with these natural cycles or urges of life without imposing some guilt.

Somewhere along the line some theologian or pious writer posed the theory that there was some sort of "sacramental grace" associated with going to confession, whether you had a sin to confess or not. Children learned in their old Baltimore Catechism that a sacrament was "an outward sign instituted by Christ to give grace" I doubt if many people had the foggiest notion of what that meant, but they believed it gave them points in the great book kept by God. So the faithful trudged to church, stood in line and asked forgiveness to imaginary sins, or for sins long since forgiven, merely to obtain this nebulous "sacramental grace." This led to ridiculous situations where people would go to confession weekly and sometimes even daily to accumulate these "graces" whether there was a sin to confess or not, but there was this magical "grace" that would be recorded in your golden ledger in the sky.

A practical downside of this was the tremendous drain on priestly manpower. Saturday afternoons and evening, and often during the week, priests would sit in the dark box of the confessional and lines would form. Parishes were staffed to handle the number of confessions on Saturday while there was perhaps little else to do for the rest of the week. Priests held a little "counter" to record how many confessions they heard. At the end of the year a report was made to the bishop, who ultimately would send the numbers on to Rome on how many confessions were heard, how many communion wafers were used, how many baptisms, marriages, funerals. The numbers were used to determine the spiritual health of the parish. On average a priest would spend 20 to 25% of his time hearing confessions, a practice that probably had little effect on most people despite the dramatic scenes depicted in the movies.

Another side effect was what it did to people who availed themselves of confession. Was the guilt brought on regularly by confession a mentally healthy thing? Was it a contributing cause of mental illness? Certainly the exercise of dwelling on one's faults was not helpful to a person who had mental problems to begin with. The potential for abuse by the priest who used it as an instrument of control was indeed real. The biggest horror in the mind of many people was to be denied absolution in the confessional. Some priests would regularly refuse for various reasons, mainly because the person dared to disagree with the priest. Some of them took the words of the gospels literally "whose sins you have forgiven they are forgiven, whose sins you have retained, they are retained." The no-brainers were the people who were divorced and remarried or who insisted on continuing to practice birth control, which was the "sin de jour" of the 60's, or those who for some reason were in marriages that were not performed before a priest. If a person had no intention of changing, there would be no "absolution." I never found it in myself to come down hard on a person who confessed practicing birth control. I felt this was a decision left to the couple without the guilt of the church.

A false sense of "morality" came with the practice. At some time in their lives, children were given a prayer book that had an "examination of conscience" printed along with the directions for a good confession. Usually this was given to the child when they were preparing for their first confession and first communion, usually around age seven. What they learned then stayed with them into adulthood and few progressed in moral thinking beyond that point, so that if their lives included deeds or practices that were not included in the list of taboos in the prayer book, they were all right. Thus it was OK to discriminate against others because of the color of their skin, or to run sweatshops where workers were poorly paid and worked in unsafe conditions. It was all right to run a dishonest business, as long as you didn't actually "steal." There was no prohibition against pollution, while adultery and sexual thoughts were "verboten," while child abuse was sanctioned as a parental right to discipline.

Stories told by priests and nuns about the reprobate who made a deathbed confession and was "saved from hell" instilled the concept that no matter what you did in life, if you were fortunate enough to be able to get to confession before you died, you were assured heaven. Hospitals had priests either in residence or on call and when a patient was near death the priest would get the call to hear the person's last confession and give "Extreme Unction" as the anointing of the sick was called. In actual practice the deathbed confession was mainly a myth. In my experience, it never happened. I remember one Saturday morning being called to a home for an "emergency sick call." When I got there, there was no ambulance, the police were at the house, and so were the coroner and the undertaker. The man had hung himself from the doorframe perhaps a day or more ago. I was late for his deathbed confession, to be sure.

There were some wonderful Catholics who strove for personal holiness in their lives and gained comfort from the sacrament and the counsel they received from the priest who was able to take a few minutes with them. In practice, many Catholics fell between two extremes: the scrupulous who were filled with guilt and those who felt that as long as they could get to confession and get their sins forgiven, there was nothing wrong with their lives.

The problem, to be fair, was not unique to confession or to Catholics alone. From ancient times people have practiced rituals to appease the gods. These gave them a false sense of security in that the ritual somehow worked magic and protected them from the wrath of a vengeful god. As long as they performed the ritual, they were saved. The ancient Romans enslaved much of the ancient world and never seemed to feel any guilt because they erected temples to the gods wherever they went. Medieval princes kept serfs in poverty but clothed themselves in the prayers and chants of the monastery and cathedral. The explorers of Spain enslaved and plundered America but few rued the cruelty and injustice that came under the flag and cross of Christendom. Their priests heard their confessions and forgave their sins.

In the early days of the Church it was the practice that people who had fallen into disfavor with the Church make a public confession and ask forgiveness from the community. When and where the practice changed or evolved to the dark "boxes" that line the walls of every Catholic Church was never explored in my years in the seminary. There does not seem to be much evidence of the practice until at least the time of the Reformation and the Council of Trent that followed it.

However, the practice of the "confessional" was deeply engrained in the American Church at least until the Vatican Council. Church law required Catholics to confess their sins at least once a year. Those who had no sins to confess obeyed this law scrupulously, while I am sure the real sinners never bothered.

Priests encouraged monthly, even weekly confession. In the seminary we were expected to go to confession each week, and Saturday afternoons were set aside for confession, whether we had anything to confess or not.

I would often hear over two hundred confessions on a single Saturday afternoon and evening, often spending less than a minute with a person. It bothered me that we had to run such a "mill." No one ever wondered if there was any relationship between the numbers and any changes in the morals or virtuous lives of the people.

The opening lines people used were always the same…what they learned for their first confession "Bless me father for I have sinned. My last confession was…ago. I have…" and they mentioned their sins, real or imaginary. If it had been more than a month or two since the last confession, most priests would give a stern lecture about living in sin and the danger of hellfire. At the end, the person would say something like "for these and all my past sins, I humbly beg forgiveness and absolution."

At this point the priest might have questions or advice and would give a "penance" which usually consisted of saying a few "Hail Mary's" or if it was a serious offense, maybe even the rosary, which might take all of ten or fifteen minutes of a person's time. Then the priest would say the words of "absolution," in Latin up to a time in the late 60's when the vernacular was allowed, while the penitent would recite an "act of contrition" asking God's forgiveness. Theology of the time was that using the correct words was more important than whether or not there had been any change of heart. I used to wonder who determined what the exact words for the essential part of the sacraments should be and would it be valid if some other words happened to be used. Some priests had the words typed out on a card they read so they would not make an error, leaving the person with a sin unforgiven. The priest had the authority to forgive sins for God if he used the approved words designated by the Church as the words of absolution. I always hoped that God would agree with my decisions.

I'm not sure if it was the Vatican Council or an outbreak of common sense, but the institution of confession gradually changed from the "spiritual filling station" of the 50's and 60's. Is there less neurosis among elderly women and adolescent boys today as a result?

The Church guarded the secrecy of confession with the utmost vigor. If a priest was found to have violated the "seal of confession" he was suspended without question or recourse. In the seminary this was drilled into us as the worst possible violation that would not only be mortally sinful but would also bring the full wrath of the Church's disciplinary sanctions on the one who betrayed the seal of the confessional. I do not recall a single instance where any priest did violate this trust. However, there were times when priests, without naming names, certainly used the information gathered in the confessional in their sermons and instructions.

The flip side of secrecy was that it bound the priest but not the person making the confession. People would talk about what Father said to them in the confessional. Thus if a priest happened to take a more liberal view of human sexuality and would tell a person that they were not going to go to hell for fondling each other before marriage or practicing birth control to avoid having the 8th or 9th child, it was almost certain that the word would get around, and quite often the priest with the more open mind would be called on the carpet by someone: the pastor of the parish, neighboring priests, or the office of the bishop in some cases. So in practice most priests would simply go along with the strictest interpretation of morality or just say the words of absolution with no comment and tell the people "go in peace and God bless you."

Often the people we were dealing with had serious problems and needed help beyond the words of absolution in confession. Some, including myself, would recommend that the troubled person would seek help outside the confession box, but for the most part the priests would either give a word of encouragement or mild scolding and get on with the next one in line. We were simply not trained to even recognize mental illness or problems that required treatment. Combined with the anonymity of the person in the dark box, there was little opportunity to help even if we recognized it. Often I would want to give more than a simple pious platitude but was really torn, knowing that there was a long line waiting their turn, and if I took the time needed to give meaningful advice, the person would be embarrassed to walk out of the confessional. Everyone in line would wonder what awful thing this person must have done that took so long. In the end it was far easier to mumble the magic words of absolution and send them on their way, hoping that somehow their lives would change because of the encounter, which I am sure seldom happened.

Church law also taught that for a person who had an unforgiven "mortal" sin, it was also a mortal sin to receive any other sacrament as well. The "guilt machine" of the Church was fueled not only by the confessional but also from the pulpit and much of the liturgy itself. For example, one of the most frequently used "Mass" liturgies was the "Requiem" Mass for the dead. Many priests would use this liturgy for any date in the Church calendar that did not have its own specific Mass liturgy in honor of a particular Saint. Complete with black vestments, the tone was equally dark. Particularly guilt laden was the "Dies Irae" –a medieval poem inserted between the readings that depicted the horrors of the "last judgment" when even the saints would tremble in fear when called to task for the sins of their lives. I used to wonder if some of the Saints we revered would be sent to hell at that time, sort of a re-trial.

"Parish Missions," which were held at parishes every few years brought in outside priests who conducted an intense week of preaching and special services, similar to a revival. The preaching was long on guilt and the need for forgiveness and confession. If the parish priest sensed that his people didn't feel the appropriate level of guilt, he was certain to arrange for a parish mission.

The common teaching was that even when a sin was forgiven, God would still extract retribution and purification before a person could enter heaven. Thus the theory of "Purgatory" was taught as the temporary cleansing of the deceased before they could enter heaven. For some reason it never occurred to theologians that "time" ceased when a person died, since time is a measure of the rotation of the earth on its axis and its orbit around the sun. This "halfway house" of suffering and purification had little basis in theology or scripture. It was a "theological opinion" but loomed prominent in Catholic practice. So we recited prayers for the dead to be released from their sins, offered Masses for the repose of their souls and there were certain prayers and works to which Rome had attached "indulgences" to free people from the time in purgatory. Prayers and devotions would have a certain curious "indulgence" time attached to them. It could be "seven years and seven quarantines" whatever that meant or it could be a "plenary" indulgence, which would take away all the "temporary punishment" due to sins. Of course these didn't do a thing if the sin was one of those "mortal" ones.

For some reason the Church of Rome had forgotten that the Reformation began with a controversy over these "indulgences" when the preachers of Rome offered remission of punishment in exchange for a donation to the building of St. Peter's in Rome. The modern practice of donating a "stipend" of a few dollars and have the priest celebrate a Mass for that particular person is only slightly different. Centuries later the publishers of prayer books and devotional services would appeal to Rome to have their prayers sanctioned as giving generous "indulgences." I used to wonder who kept track of this all in Rome or in heaven.

In reality, the preoccupation with guilt and sin had less to do with behavior than it had to do with control. Priests controlled the lives of the penitent in the confessional and the church maintained attendance at Sunday Mass and the assorted devotions during the week to remove guilt or the retribution they feared God would extract for their misdeeds. Rome maintained discipline by categorizing violations of church law as sinful and required the priest in the confessional to obtain "faculties" or permission from higher church authority to forgive certain sins.

The categories of sins were another mystery. "Venial" sins would not condemn one to hell, but would certainly put one in purgatory. Mortal sins would put you in hell unless you got to confession or cared to risk a deathbed "act of contrition." God forbid if you should die instantly and not get a chance to make your peace with God by saying the magical words.

No one ever explained to me how one could decide if a sin was mortal or venial. There were a couple of rules everybody knew. For example, if it had anything to do with sex, even a fleeting pleasurable thought, that was mortal sin. It went back to the story of Adam and Eve, in the garden noticing after they had sinned that they were naked. I remember one professor in the seminary commenting that: "It wasn't the apple in the tree, it was the pair on the ground." The connection between anything of human love and reproduction and sin was deeply engrained in Catholic theology. Even the word "sex" is derived from the Latin "Sexto" – the Sixth Commandment in the Catholic enumeration.

Also considered a moral sin was anything that had to do with a Church law, such as missing Mass on Sunday, eating or drinking after midnight and going to communion, or eating meat on Friday. I never could understand how a loving God would condemn a hungry man to hell for all eternity for eating a hot dog on Friday. It was really about Church control over people's lives and conformity to the rules of Church. Of course, the party line on that was that it wasn't the hot dog, but the fact that one disobeyed the laws of the Church. I wondered what happened to all the people who went to hell for eating meat on Friday when the Church abolished that law after Vatican II? And what was it about anything sexual? Genesis clearly stated that the Lord created us male and female, and saw that this was good. How did it somehow become sordid and evil?

Venial sins included many infractions that in reality were not sins at all, such as omitting prayers at meals, a child stealing a piece of candy at the grocery, disobeying parents, and one of the favorites: going to the bathroom outdoors. When we heard the confessions of children, we were sure to get a few of these, unless it was a cold winter.

Since the Reformation, and perhaps even from the time of Aquinas in the thirteenth century, Catholic thinkers lived in dread fear of being condemned by Rome. So the safest route was merely repeating what had been written by someone earlier, whose work had been accepted. Thus if one theologian wrote that it was a mortal sin to eat a hot dog on Friday, those who wrote after him were sure to echo the sentiments. To be sure there was a great deal of Calvinism in the Church's approach to sexuality, namely that man was inherently evil and unworthy, a position that found favor again in the Victorian age through the teachings of a theologian named Jansen who reflected strict Calvinist thought. Since nearly all the Catholic theologians were celibate men, one can only wonder if their writings were a reflection of their own inability to deal with their own sexuality or of their lack of understanding of the love between man and woman and the God-given powers of attraction and pro-creation.

Few priests pondered the questions of morality. There were no simple answers to the complex questions of modern human life. In the confessional it was far simpler to listen and give the words of absolution rather than make any judgments, press the little button on the "counter" and wait for the next person in line. There was little time and little opportunity to do counseling when others waited in line and those in the pews would wonder why this person was taking so long. In a few short seconds there wasn't time to amend a tattered life, but there certainly was the risk of doing irreparable harm with ill chosen words. In the end it was easier to just say the "magic words" and keep the lines moving and hope that the people left with a feeling of relief from the burden of guilt that the Church laid on them.

Chapter Eight

Schneider Right - Schmitz Left

Kenosha was a new town to me and the assignment to St. Therese would prove pivotal in my life. I had no say in the assignment, just a letter from the Bishop noting the transfer from St. Mary's. The pastor, Fr. Vince, had founded the parish some years before on the south side of the city. In some ways, he was quite progressive. The church building was designed by one of the disciples of Frank Lloyd Wright and was built in an octagon with a gold colored roof that looked a bit like a spacecraft had landed on April Fool's day. And like Wright's other buildings, it came with a leaky roof. The parish had an eight-room school with the classrooms around the perimeter of the building. The basement hall was one of the premier locations for wedding receptions and parties, and the parish profited quite well from rentals. The parish not only rented the hall but also controlled the sale of beer for receptions, again with a nice profit.

The architecture of the church lent itself to some innovations. Acoustically I learned that I could walk up and down the middle aisle and be heard throughout the building without a microphone. So rather than stand at a pulpit beside the altar, I took to the aisles for my Sunday homilies. I would ask if anyone in the congregation had any questions or thoughts to share and we began a very good dialog during Sunday Masses. I viewed the Sunday sermon as an editorial, well chosen words to comment on current issues. The dialog format was the pre-cursor of the talk show. People would call the rectory to find out which Mass I was having and the church would be jammed with standing room only. People loved the more informal atmosphere and perhaps the content of my sermons. For some reason, they tried to avoid Vince.

The other acoustical quirk was the confessionals. They were on opposite sides of the building, next to the wall and had open ceilings. I could hear every word that Vince said in his box to whoever happened to be there. He had a raspy voice that carried, and he tended to speak loudly to give the impression of authority. Some of his comments were off the wall. I remember one night hearing him read out a poor soul. "You Pig" he said quite loudly. "Don't you ever do that again or you're going straight to hell." On other occasions I would hear him tell women that they had to obey their husbands or that birth-control of all kinds was forbidden by the Pope. I often wondered if the people in the pews could hear as well as I could everything that went on in the little box. I soon leaned to speak softly and watch my tongue.

When he started the parish, the first structure was a three-bedroom home on one corner of the property to serve as a rectory. In fact, the basement of the home served as a meeting room and for a while as the chapel until the church was built. Later, Sunday Mass was held in the chapel of a nearby nursing home. As the parish grew, Vince requested another priest for the parish, and he decided the best way to accommodate him would be to enclose the garage and make it an apartment for the associate. This meant there were separate entrances to the offices and living quarters of the pastor in the main house and the associate who lived in the apartment separated from the house by an enclosed breezeway. It was nice arrangement. I had an office, bedroom and bath, about par for the living arrangements of most assistant pastors. In fact a lot of rectories young priests lived in did not have a private bath.

With separate entrances, Vince thought it appropriate to have a sign in front directing callers to the proper entrances so neither would be bothered with the other's visitors. His office was to the right, mine to the left. Soon after I arrived a sign appeared in front of the building. FATHER SCHNEI-DER with an arrow in that direction with the word "right" inside the arrow. Below it was FATHER SCHMITZ with a similar arrow, and the word "left," inscribed inside the arrow. The word soon got out that we were probably the only church in the country that advertised theological positions.

I snapped a picture of it one day for posterity and to show to friends. One of them sent it to the National Catholic Reporter, which published it on the front page of the paper distributed nationally. To say the least, my days at St. Therese were numbered after that.

Sadly, the sign was accurate. Vince was lured into the deep end of conservatism, an avid reader of the "Wanderer" which was an ultra conservative paper published in Minnesota, and was on the mailing list of a number of right wing bulletins that flourished at the time. These included the Eagle Forum, the Veritas Forum, and the John Birch Society. Vince was convinced that the devil was behind the Vatican Council and that the Communists were infiltrating the church. He resisted the changes fiercely and was one of the last to offer the Latin Mass, which drew conservatives from all around the area. Later he became affiliated with a renegade group who had formed their own church and he said Mass in Latin according to the form of the Council of Trent, which that group contended was the only valid Mass. Vince became convinced that only a small remnant would remain faithful to the true Church and in the end would save the world from all this heresy. He was suspicious of me from the beginning.

At a meeting I was conducting, one of his "plants" asked me if I was a liberal or a conservative. I sensed I was being set up, so I replied "There are some people who are ignorant and call themselves conservatives and others who are irresponsible and are labeled liberals. I hope I don't fit into either of those categories." Vince berated me for telling people he was ignorant.

He would call parishioners and quiz them about what went on at various meetings, in the high school or elsewhere, and often twist what they said to what he wanted them to say. What they told him was entirely different than what he reported. It became a witch-hunt, looking for something about his fellow priests or the religious that he could criticize which would give him the assurance that he was still faithful to the "old time religion." He was famous for writing letters to the pastors of Kenosha complaining about something he heard from someone, often anonymously, or citing anonymous sources. Even after I left there he continued the letter writing campaign. The letters went to the head of the religious orders whose nuns taught in the schools, particularly at

St. Joe's High School. The sad part is that some people took him seriously.

We had an organization of priests in the county, and Vince was the president of the group. For some reason I got elected secretary and recorded the minutes and sent them to all the priests in the area along with a reminder for the next meeting. At one meeting Vince went on for about an hour about the terrible things that were happening in Kenosha, particularly at the Catholic High School, how the nuns were not wearing habits and going around in their short skirts and all sorts of terrible things. Some of the nuns lived apart from the school, sharing an apartment. He reported rumors that they were doing waitress work at one of the restaurants on weekends, and that the students at the high school were not required to attend daily Mass, and there were reports that the students were getting some kind of sex education. It went on for over an hour, with ramblings about rumors and how this was undermining the church in the area, and people were going to hell because of all this.

My dilemma was how do I put this into some form for the minutes and send them out? Since there was no agenda, no discussion, no business to tend to, I wondered about the value of the meeting and of future ones as long as he was in charge. So I sent out the minutes

The Kenosha County Priests Association met March 10, 1969 at St. James Parish. Why?"

I don't recall that the group ever met again.

One of my parish assignments was teaching religion at St. Joseph's High School with two classes in the morning. Teaching was fun, but the last thing the kids wanted to learn was more about their religion since by the time they got to high school most of them had tuned out the Church. But there were moments.

Fr. Leslie, the principal, would begin each day by reciting a morning prayer over the loudspeaker system, followed by the Pledge of Allegiance to the Flag and any announcements that needed to be made for the day. One particular morning he recited the prayer, then the pledge of allegiance, and a couple announcements.

Next we heard him screaming, "Those goddam sunabitchin nuns!"

He apparently was having some conflict with the nuns who staffed many of the teaching positions and who technically still owned the buildings. He'd forgotten to turn off the microphone before he vented his anger.

Among the priests in Kenosha, Father Bill was known as the "hard nose" that nobody seemed to like. Those of us who knew him from the seminary remembered that he always had a cotton ball in one of his ears, and was not known as the brightest candle in church. The pastor at St. Mary's, Fr. Ray, was a bear of a man to get along with. Gruff, reputed to have a drinking problem and unapproachable, he was known as a difficult assignment for the young priests who served under him. Few lasted more than a year or two. Fr. Bill seemed to thrive there, but nobody else seemed to like him.

We bowled in a Friday league and some of the group were quite fun loving. We knew that Fr. Bill couldn't handle his liquor, and many a night we were worried about his driving home after bowling, though the lanes were only a few blocks from the parish. One Friday somebody got the idea to have a little more fun than usual. Instead of only the 5th frame of each game as the beer frame, they designated the 3rd, 6th and 9th frames. And when Fr. Bill got his drink, there was a shot on the side for him. By the middle of the second game, someone had his car keys and offered to drive him home.

All went well and he agreed to it. The only problem was that the driver made a slight detour to Bruno's bar that featured nude dancers. Fr. Bill sat with the group and was sipping a beer, wearing his bowling shirt with "Fr. Bill" embroidered over the pocket. A young lady came on stage and started to dance, gyrating seductively to the music and she proceeded to wiggle her way out of her top, revealing more than average feminine charms. She then removed her skimpy panties as well, clad only in her earrings and shoes. At some point her eyes adjusted to the light and she spied Fr. Bill sitting in the front row, next to the stage.

"Fr. Bill," she screamed and ran off the stage. It was a girl from his parish. I don't know if he remembered the next morning, but the whole town knew about it.

Years later, Fr. Bill's dark side came to light as accusations of pedophilia surfaced. A reporter from a TV station confronted him at his parish in Sheboygan and on camera he admitted that the accusations were true. The clip aired on Milwaukee stations and all chance of denial was gone. He was sentenced to prison where he died a few years later of cancer.

It was another of the sad chapters in the relationships of priests to their young charges. The parish priest was generally respected and trusted by the people and many considered it an honor if a priest became friends with their son. It might spark a religious vocation in the young man or at least provide a positive role model. Unfortunately, the idol worship and trust were all too often fertile ground for the pedophile. It has proven costly for the Catholic Church, not only in untold millions paid in either damages or to silence victims but also in the destruction of trust in the minds of the faithful.

Fr. Jim who had been at St. James Parish for many years was retiring. He was one of the last of the stereotypical Irish priests, a winning smile, a great sense of humor and he loved life, and his parishioners loved him. Of course the parish had a going-away party for him and, being a good Irish priest, there was a cocktail party preceding the farewell dinner.

I was sipping a Manhattan when a little elderly woman from the parish about five feet from me collapsed on the floor, spilling her drink over the gym floor. I was tempted at first to begin lapping it up but on second thought put my drink down and rushed to her aid. One of the parishioners was a doctor and arrived at her side about the same time I did. He took her pulse and looked for signs of breathing while someone else was on the phone calling an ambulance.

I knew the woman, one of the little old ladies who found their second home around the Church and the parish rectory, so when I was visiting the hospital the next day I checked in on her. She was all right. They pumped her stomach and kept her for observation overnight. I asked her "Annie, what happened?"

"Father," she replied, "those drinks at the reception were so strong. I was watering mine down and it was still too strong."

I remembered pitchers of Manhattans and Martinis at the reception but no pitchers of water. What she was doing was watering her Manhattan down with a Martini. That'll get to you.

When I arrived at St. Therese in 1968, the parish had adopted a sister parish in the coal mining Appalachian area of Virginia. The parish was in a little mining town of St. Paul, with a mission church in nearby Lebanon, in the little neck of the state that borders West Virginia and Kentucky in the Clinch mountains. St. Therese parish had taken on a financial obligation to help support the struggling parishes.

St. Therese could easily do this. Shortly after the founding of the parish, a widow in Kenosha named the parish in her will, to receive the "residual" after all her relatives and other causes had received their specified inheritance. Little did she or anyone foresee that the stocks in her investment portfolio would mushroom and the parish received enough money to pay all its debts and have a pretty healthy surplus invested for future needs. So the parish adopted the churches in Virginia, committing to financial support for five years.

Fr. Vince and his cook, Dessie, had taken a trip to the area early in Spring and spent a few days in the mountains, discussing their needs and what we could do to help. One of the things they desperately needed was clothing for poor families. Used clothing, on the line of our St. Vincent de Paul stores was unknown but social workers talked of children who didn't go to school because they didn't have decent clothing to wear.

St. Paul, Virginia, was to have a sister community, named Minneapolis, on the opposite side of the Clinch River. It never materialized. They were to be the Twin Cities of Appalachia. The area was depressed, with the coalmines shutting down in favor of strip mines in the West. There were few jobs. The great society program hadn't done much for them. Vince posed the problem to me and asked what I thought. I suggested that we could probably get a clothing drive locally and if we could get someone to truck it out there, we'd be in business. All they had to do on their end was to find a place and each of the parish churches had a basement that would work for a clothing store.

A well placed story in the Kenosha News and a couple ads in parish bulletins and we were ready to go. People began bringing boxes and carloads of used clothing to the church basement. We soon had enough for a truckload – a forty-foot trailer filled to the top with used clothing, blankets, and the like.

The kids in the parish helped sort the clothing and boxed it all, and we found a parish member who owned a semi and another who volunteered to drive it. The truck was loaded and we proceeded to Virginia. I drove with a carload: two nuns from the parish and three kids who helped with the packing. With AAA maps, a camera and a lot of enthusiasm we were on our way. It was dark as we entered the mountains, thick with fog settling in the twisting roads, but we arrived in one piece.

The truck arrived before we did, and so we unloaded the boxes in the church basement. The truck found a load nearby to haul back to Wisconsin. After a good night's sleep and Mass in the parish church the next morning, we set out to find a place for a clothing store. The only building available was an old store that had been abandoned, with the back part of the building dangerously rotting away. But the front would do for a temporary site. The merchants in town were fearful that this would cut into their business, and were reluctant to have the used clothing store anywhere, and since they owned most of the real estate, they were not willing to create any competition. Once the store opened, that changed, and they found a better permanent building within months of opening. But to begin with, we strung wires from wall to wall and hung clothing as best we could. It was a start.

I got a good tour of the area from some of the locals. The area was a coal mining area, with the narrow valleys or "hollers" as they called them, snaking twenty miles or more like turkey feet back into the hills, where narrow streets were lined with homes nestled right against the hills. Most of the towns were originally "company towns" with the mining company owning the homes, the stores and everything else. In the 60's some of them were privately owned, while the company retained some, which were usually in disrepair. It seemed like many of the mining families were Italian immigrants, similar to the Italian community in Kenosha. During the early part of the century the mining companies would send their recruiters to New York to meet the immigrants as they got off the boats. They offered the men a job, a place to live, and a train ticket to get there, to a nice Italian community nestled in the beautiful hills of Virginia.

The mining companies owned the mines, the mineral rights to the land, the company stores, and the lives of the people who came there. As the miners worked the mines, little thought was given to safety or health. Life was harsh and often short. People remembered the days when trains shuttled back and forth up the hollers with carloads of coal behind a chugging steam engine. Nearly every week one of the cars would bear the body of a miner atop the load of coal, a victim of a cave-in, gas, or explosion up the line. Wages were low and people were poor.

Others lived back in the hills, often miles from the end of a road and who survived living off the land, with subsistence farming and a bit of moonshine. The social workers I met talked about them, families with children who did not come to school because they did not have proper clothing, or in some cases, even shoes. Homes were without electricity and had water from a dug well, often polluted by the mine tailings upstream or in the hills.

Fiercely independent, these were the people who would come to the clothing bank and at a cost of whatever they felt they could pay, they would get used clothing as good as the new items that they could not afford. We were careful to preserve their pride. They would not take a hand—out, but were open to buying at a reduced price. If they could not afford to pay, there was no charge, but an offer to have them work at the store in return. Many did.

The countryside was once beautiful, with mountains heavily wooded, wide vistas and spectacular views, quiet and peaceful. Then came coal- mines. Mountains were dotted with mine entrances and mine tailings rolling down to the valley floor. Open pit mines scarred wide areas polluting the waters of streams for miles in many cases with conveyors hauling coal miles over the wooded hills and trains shuttled back and forth up the narrow "hollers." Old timers talked about the times past when mine safety was nearly non-existent and cave-ins were common. They remembered days when the families would watch carefully when the coal cars arrived from the mines. Nearly every week one of the cars would have the body of a miner lying atop the coal, the victim of a mine accident. Even in the late 60's, women were not allowed in the mines. There was a long-standing superstition that it was bad luck if a woman entered a coalmine. (I suspect it was perpetuated by women who were smart enough to realize the dangers.)

Old company towns were a mixture of homes well kept and painted and derelicts that had either been abandoned or suffered severe neglect. Old appliances and furniture were usually stored somewhere on the property, often along with rusty cars that hadn't run for decades. The narrow streets were often unpaved and in wet weather nearly impassible as the streets also served as the storm sewers. The area was rich in coal but the wealth didn't make it to the people. The few who were fortunate to get jobs in the mines lived comfortably, but poverty was evident.

We were there for a week, and in evenings we heard stories of relatives who went off to the cities of the north in search of a better life, whether to Cleveland, Detroit or Chicago, where jobs for unskilled workers were available. They were not often suited for city life and the families told stories of heartbreak, broken marriages, drinking problems and unhappiness in the big city. Some who left tried to come back but found they no longer had much in common with the folk of the mountains and there were no jobs back home. Unable to adapt to the city, they were unable to fit in back home again. There were a few who were able to make it out and go to college, either in the area or somewhere else. They rarely returned to the mountains, except for funerals and family visits.

It was a culture shock for me: a different life, different values and a somewhat different religion. Even with the Italian heritage of many of the miners, Catholics were a minority and certainly not in the power elite. The mountain people often had a religion of their own, with tent churches set up and people would come from mines to hear the preacher vent his brand of Bible fundamentalism.

While we were there one of the local churches, which engaged in "snake handling," had a fatality. Jesus sent his disciples out to preach and told them not to fear, for even if they took up serpents, they would not be harmed. Well, these people took up rattlers and passed them around the congregation to prove their faith in Jesus and every now and then someone would get bit and in this case it was fatal. Local authorities banned it but there wasn't much they could do about it.

The communities were close knit, with everybody knowing everyone else, including the children and everybody's business. There was a simple openness, where you were always welcome. Few if any of the homes had locked doors. Honesty was prided as the essential virtue and if anybody was caught stealing, the thief might just as well leave town. People had long memories and this was one sin they would not forgive.

I often wondered how the communities have changed in the years since I was there. I wanted to return to see what has changed and what has remained the same. I suspect that they were able to attract industry with available labor and no unions, and educational opportunities probably became more available, but I am sure there are a lot of locals whom progress passed by and they remain off the beaten path of prosperity. What I remember was a beautiful country with charming, simple, honest folk, a people who had been exploited by the coal mining companies to warm the homes of the rest of the country and fill the pockets of the corporate stockholders with dividend.

Thirty-five years later I was traveling east and decided to visit the little mining town and see what had changed. Instead of the twisting two-lane road winding through the mountains, there was a four-lane highway filled with large coal trucks. When I got off the main road and into town, little had changed. I drove to the little Catholic Church and it hadn't changed a bit with its red brick front and cement block side and rear walls painted with aluminum paint, but when I drove around to the back, I noticed a building about 16 X 30 that now housed the clothing store. I met the people who carried on the mission we started some thirty-five years ago. They were open two days a week, and were serving over one hundred people each day they were open. The program had expanded from clothing to include food and other support for the needy. They were receiving donations of clothing from other areas of the country, mainly in the East, and received food both from government programs as well as from several local grocery stores. True to the philosophy we initiated, they still asked people to pay what they could depending on their means, preserving the pride and dignity of the poor, while at the same time providing funds that could be used for utilities, medical bills, or other expenses that the poor were not able to meet.

One year with Vince at St. Therese was about the limit of any sane person, and my predecessors had all left after one year. In discussions with others around town I knew the situation was hopeless. Classmates who taught at St. Joe's High School asked me if I would consider teaching there. I loved to teach, but there were some problems with that. Four priests lived in the house next to the school. The living quarters were far from the Ritz, and I wasn't sure I wanted to spend the entire day teaching the "party line." At the time the school did not have enthusiastic support from most of the priests in town; pastors were certain that the school was too liberal and probably heretical.

A friend of mine was chaplain at UWM and inquired if I would be interested in a position at UW-Parkside and other schools in the area. We talked, and I agreed to consider it. He was head of the campus chaplains for the diocese, and requested me for the position.

Never having been on a college campus other than the seminary, this was a learning experience for me. My introduction was a chaplain's school held at Harvard University during the early part of the summer. The diocese did not financially support the campus ministry very well, and while they were willing to pay the tuition for the school, I had to supply my own transportation. Since I couldn't afford air fare, I decided to drive to Boston.

The Boston area is a treasure trove of history. I came in a day early and strolled through Boston Commons, which was the first public park in the country, climbed the tower on Bunker Hill, which is actually on neighboring Breed's Hill, and visited "Old Ironsides" in the Boston Harbor.

Sunday was registration day and as I came across the bridge to Cambridge, I noticed the Cambridge Commons filled with people. There was a concert there every Sunday during the summer and, with a telephoto lens on my camera. I was able to capture the spirit of the 60's in one afternoon.

There was plenty to do in the area. One night we went to Anthony's Pier Four, one of the swank restaurants on the waterfront. The Boston group I was with told me to wear my Roman Collar because we would get special treatment. There was a long line when we arrived but when the head waiter spied the Roman Collar he said "right this way Father, your table's ready." We had a window table overlooking the water. It was a memorable dining experience.

Another night we took in the Boston Pops with Arthur Fiedler conducting. Rumor around town had it that when the orchestra played in the music hall Fiedler was distracted by the popping of champagne corks at the tables. He stopped the orchestra, turned to the audience and declared "we might as well call this orchestra the Boston Pops"

Another night we had tickets to Hamlet, in one of the most moving performances I have seen. The night before the actor playing the lead walked off the stage in the middle of the performance and only after minutes of cajoling by the director returned to finish the performance. He apparently felt the audience was not receptive to his artistry. The night we saw the play he was superb. He played Hamlet with more than a hint that the Dane was probably gay, and unsure of his male identity.

One weekend I spent up the North Bay, taking in Plymouth, Salem, Glouchester, and points north, finally ending up in southern Maine. The rugged coast was spectacular and the seafood on the pier, plucking a lobster from the bin on a boat that had just arrived, was superb. The second day we dug clams on the beach, and with a bucket steamed them right there, less than an hour from bay to belly.

We did a Cape Cod trip the next weekend, spending a bit of time on the beach and taking a tour of Provincetown at the tip of the cape. At that time it was an artist community, with little shops and casual life. The drive back was a traffic jam all the way back into Boston.

This was the summer of '69, and there was a great deal of turmoil on the university campuses. In fact, Harvard students had taken over the office of the president a few months before in protest of the Viet Nam war and other issues. The racial pot was still boiling in the Boston area. It was these issues that were the focus of the Campus Minister's school.

As I reflect on the Chaplain's School itself, I wonder why the content was so sketchy. True, there were social issues that had burst upon the college scene as the university was the strike point of what was happening in the world, as well it should be. The campus chaplain was often the lightning rod that attracted confrontation. For the first time in my life I came face to face with the ugly side of racism and the anger of the black community. We also received a heavy dose of opposition to the War in Viet Nam and the dangers of nuclear war and the destruction it would bring. Harvard was the center of radical activism in the months before when a group of students took over the office of the president of the university. I learned that most of the people in campus ministry tended to be quite liberal, even bordering on radical in some instances, while some of the "old timers" were the "good fellow priest" type who had carved out a parish of sorts on the college campus. But really, I wondered if there was any idea among the chaplains of the role of the Church on the secular campus. Did anyone know what we should be doing? I had my doubts there.

When I finally settled in at Parkside, I found myself wearing a lot of hats in addition to attempting to start a campus ministry on a commuter campus scattered over two counties. None of them were paid positions. I was area director of the CCD (religious education for the kids in public schools) and responsible for teacher training, and assisting the parishes in setting up their programs. My success with the program at St. Mary's in Fond du Lac put me in good stead in program development. I spent the summer prior to coming to Kenosha at a CCD (Confraternity of Christian Doctrine) school at Catholic University in Washington D.C. I had several articles published in national religious education periodicals on various aspects of our program. I was probably the only priest in the area with a reputation beyond the confines of the local parishes.

When the area coordinators of the diocese met, I found my opinions carried a lot of weight when I proposed that the children who did not attend the parish schools were getting only lip service while the bulk of the parish and diocesan resources were steered toward the parish schools. I proposed that a professional office of religious education be established that encompassed not only the children in the parish schools but worked with all the children regardless of what school they attended. The result was that an office of religious education was established and staffed. For the first year I edited (and wrote a good deal of) the CCD newsletter for the diocese.

On the local level, I taught courses one night a week for these teachers, preparing them for the task of teaching the children in their parishes. I found myself working with the area clergy of all denominations, served on the board of the area clergy association, and soon discovered that the Catholic priests had the least interest of anyone in what was happening on campus. On a diocesan level I was elected president of the campus ministers association, which included the priests who worked in campus ministry throughout the diocese. The only campus in the area that had resident students was Carthage College, which was a conservative Lutheran school. I would have Sunday Mass for the students there in a small chapel on campus. I was involved in weekend retreats for High School and college students and quite often some follow-up counseling of participants.

College students on the secular campus had problems with their faith because the local church was not perceived as credible with them. Apart from the usual questioning of youth on the college campus, there were problems with the Church itself in their minds. It was an age of social upheaval and ideological turmoil. It was at this time when the Catholic bishops in their annual meeting declared that it was not possible for anyone to be a conscientious objector to the war since we were fighting godless Communists. This was the year when the Pope made the pronouncement that anything other than abstinence was not a morally acceptable method of birth control. For the vast majority of couples in their child - bearing years, he might have saved the effort. It always amazed me that the Church taught that a person be allowed to follow his or her own conscience, except in matters of sexuality and birth control.

It was a challenge dealing with the academics. The climate of higher education is to explore and to question, while the posture of the Church indicated that the hierarchy had already determined what the answers were and that the only discussion needed was to study what the pope and bishops had said. Obviously this created conflicts between the students and their conservative families, and certainly with their ultra conservative churches. Pastors railed about the "liberals" on campus destroying the faith of their young members, when in reality it was the local churches that were not able to stand up to scrutiny and come away believable.

This was the year of demonstrations about issues ranging from the war in Viet Nam, to nuclear arms, to racial issues, to open housing, and the plight of migrant workers in the grape fields of California. If there were Catholics involved, I was asked to participate, usually as a speaker. It was interesting that none of the priests in the parishes were ever involved, and to my knowledge were never even approached. The people knew their priests. My own feelings were that the Church embraced people of all interests and points of view, not merely the ultra-conservatives and that true ministry needed to reach out to all. And frankly, I trusted myself to bring some semblance of sanity to the issues, something often lacking in those days. The chaplain at Dominican College in Racine and I clashed on tactics constantly. He would barge into the dining room and pour ketchup over all the grapes and lettuce in support of Cesar Chavez and the farm workers in California. Some of my friends in Milwaukee broke into the offices of the draft board and burned records, as if they would not be duplicated easily. Mike Cullen, an Irish native, was arrested for his part in the break in and was deported, while his wife and their children remained here. There is no doubt it was a troubling time, and quite often I found myself in the middle of the fray.

Of course, I was invited to sit in on planning meetings of various sorts. One of the most memorable was at Dominican College in Racine, which was having its problems recruiting students once Parkside was up and running. In an effort to boost enrollment, particularly among the young black high school graduates, someone decided that what they needed was a field house where they could play basketball. Talk about stereotyping! Of course the nuns, who still owned the buildings, wanted a fine arts and media center if they were going to build anything. The college had a lay president, who after months of planning held a meeting to unveil the ambitious building project. Someone asked the question about costs, and he gave a rather general answer as to the overall cost of the project. Finally one of the Dominican nuns asked: "Dr. Stevens, what are we going to do with our current deficit?"

His answer was classic: "Don't worry about the deficit, Sister, we have funds to cover that."

For the first several months of my assignment there, I lived at Dominican College, on the far north side of Racine in a rectory I shared with two aged Dominican priests who apparently had some duties with the convent next door, though I was at a loss to know what they actually did.

The problem was that the schools I served were in Kenosha, and there was no easy route through Racine without an hour's drive on narrow streets. I noticed a home for sale across the street from the Parkside Campus and suggested the diocese put in a bid on it. It was a nice three- bedroom home that they bought for about $25,000. About five years later they sold it for over $100,000. But for the remainder of my year there, this was home.

This was the year of the 4th Annual 29th Birthday Party. Karl Acker, a classmate, and I shared the same birthday. We decided to celebrate together for a change. We sent out a handful of invitations and told the people they could bring a friend and a bottle, and we hoped they wouldn't drink more than they brought. The little house was jammed from one end to the other throughout the night as people came and went. We never did get an accurate count, but we know it was over a hundred. The next morning we hauled the empties off to the town dump, completely filling the trunk of my Chevy with empties. Everyone had a good time.

Among the successes I had during my year there was that I cajoled the priests in Racine and Kenosha to have me preach at all the Masses on a Sunday about college students and the issues in their lives. Over the course of several months I managed to be in just about every parish in the two counties and perhaps delivered a message none of the people would have heard from their own parish priests about the issues that were dividing the country and impacting the beliefs of young people.

At issue was the Viet Nam war and the disillusionment of the young people not only with politics, but with the Church that despite the promises of the Vatican Council was retrenching into an authoritarian conservative posture that seemed out of step with the younger generation of Americans, few of whom bothered with Sunday Mass. Just a look over the congregation at a different parish each Sunday told the story: the bulk of the audience was elderly, with a scattering of young families with their children in tow.

This was quite a change from the Church we grew up with, or the model espoused in the seminary where everyone attended Mass on Sunday, and the Church was central in the lives of people from the cradle to the grave. It was a monolith crumbling, unable to deal with diversity or to relate to those who did not always agree with the strict dictums handed down from the pulpit, the bishops, or the Vatican. In Milwaukee, Jim Groppi was still leading the open housing marches and battling the segregation that kept blacks isolated in the poor neighborhoods in poor housing. A classmate of mine, Russ, was leading the bigots from the south side in opposition. Russ was probably not the brightest candle in the candelabra, so that just about any cause that gave him some recognition must have seemed attractive. Throughout the diocese, there was division. The pastors generally were vehement in their criticism of Groppi and the cause he espoused, and pressured the diocese to do something about him, while Jim had support from the younger priests who seemed to have more sensitive social consciences. Just the mention of the name Groppi evoked hatred in the Church nearly everywhere in the country. If you'd mention you were from Milwaukee and a priest, his name would spill out with some choice expletives. Was the Church in the area racist? The young were convinced it was.

Jim Groppi was an interesting person; very well liked in the seminary, an excellent athlete and good student, he spent his summers working for the Children's Outing Association that brought children from the inner city to a camping experience they'd never get otherwise. He was one of the kindest and most sensitive priests I knew and after ordination was assigned to a parish near his home, on Milwaukee's southeast side.

We worked together on a few occasions with the Young Christian Workers in the diocese. After a couple of years on the south side, he was transferred to St. Boniface, in the inner city on the north side of town. His ministry took on a more political and socially active tone and St. Boniface became the hub of social activism. Jim was quick to point out the injustice inherent in racism. People were poor or near poor simply because of the color of their skin. Children in the inner city received inferior education in obsolete and over-crowded schools, and most of the black residents were crowded into the decaying housing in the older sections of town, much of it owned by absentee landlords who extracted high returns for inferior housing to support their lifestyles in lily white suburbs.

Jim also noted that there was a power "elite" in the city centered around the local Eagles Club, which had a whites only policy. It was a hangout for politicians and judges as well as professionals from all walks of life. I remember even years later being approached to join the Eagles Club; part of the pitch was that I would be able to socialize with "my own kind." I didn't join.

Groppi gained fame when he challenged the city of Milwaukee to enact "open housing" legislation. The mayor at the time, Henry Meier, refused to consider it, saying it had to be a county or state issue. Meanwhile, realtors were refusing to show homes to black families in white areas, and on the fringes of the inner city realtors were engaged in "block busting" by selling a home to a black family in a white neighborhood and then spreading the panic in the area to get listings of the other homes in the block. Often the realtors bought the homes at a bargain, only to re-sell or rent them to a black family for a nice profit.

Groppi calculated his moves and began marches through the city at night asking for open housing. Each evening would start with a prayer service and instructions at St. Boniface, and the procession would head out. For the most part the marchers were peaceful but taunted by the whites along the way and often harassed by the police. The brilliance of the move was the fact that the city was forced to provide police protection along the route for crowd and traffic control. Since they never knew in advance which direction the group would march, they had to be prepared, which meant a lot of overtime pay for the officers. Groppi and his marchers were able to bring the city to the table because of the cost of policing the marches.

Milwaukee's open housing marches went on for months before legislation and ordinances were finally enacted making housing discrimination illegal. I doubt if Wisconsin, or the country for that matter, would have passed any open-housing legislation for years if it had not been for Jim Groppi and his "Commandos" bringing the city to its knees in the 1960's.

After the open housing issue passed, Jim was a man without a cause. He was the last white priest to serve in a leadership role in the black community. He tried to involve himself in the struggles in Northern Ireland, but was rebuffed. He left the active ministry, married, and attended law school for a while, but never graduated; and for the last years of his life drove a bus in the city, rising to become president of the Bus Drivers Union. He died of a brain tumor.

The "entitlement" of the incompetent in pastorates was widespread. In Kenosha and Racine most of them were unapproachable, comfortable in their rectories, doing little, unaware or unconcerned about the needs of their members, somewhat like a circus clown sitting on the hillside watching the circus train move on to the next town in the valley below. Life had passed many of them by. Some clung to the past, wanting to go back to the world and the Church of their childhood, some resembled the nobles of times past: apart from and aloof from their subjects. They seldom mingled with the common folk. Some were simply "over the hill" waiting out their time since there was no retirement plan that could support them in their old age and in most cases they could not provide for the housekeepers who had been their companions for decades.

There were other issues that bothered many young priests at the time. For example, the war in Viet Nam was viewed by many of the more liberal priests as immoral, and on the college campus was a volatile issue, particularly among those who might be subject to the draft. In the midst of the debate, the bishops in their annual meeting announced that a Catholic could not in good conscience object to the war.

It was also the same time when Pope Paul VI, who had appointed an international commission of experts in medicine, theology, as well as lay men and women to study the question of birth control. After several years of study, the Vatican ignored their recommendations, and reiterated what Pius XI had written some thirty years before: that birth control violated the "natural law." They took the most conservative position possible and ignored advances in medicine as well as growing concern about rampant population growth and the ability to support that growth in many countries of the world.

Cited in the document was the story of Onan in the book of Genesis, as the biblical foundation of the argument. It was a stretch at best, and the position represented the most conservative position possible, and ignored advances in medicine as well as growing concern about rampant population growth and the ability to support that growth in many countries of the world. For the most part, all but the most conservative Catholics did not agree with the Encyclical and ignored it. Priests were expected to support it and preach about it from the pulpit.

The argument of Onan completely missed the point and was an example of "text- proofing" in which a person grasps at a line from Scripture to prove a position he already holds. Onan, under Mosaic Law, was required to have intercourse with his deceased brother's widow, so that she could bear children who would inherit the lands of her deceased husband. Onan withdrew and "spilled his seed upon the ground." Onan was punished because "he did a detestable thing." The detestable thing was his treatment of the "law of the Levirate." If she had children, the lands would go to those children. But if she had no children, the land would go to Onan, the next of kin to his brother. It was avarice and land that was at stake.

At any rate, the question of birth control, particularly since the invention of the birth control pill, was a divisive issue. The Vatican argument was that it violated "natural law" that nebulous unwritten law that they seemed to pull out when it suited their purpose. The argument went that the pill altered a natural body function. I guess if we applied that logically every pill or medication from an aspirin on would violate the natural law.

Many otherwise upright Catholics were refused absolution and sacraments over this alone. It certainly drove many from the Church. It created a dilemma for the priests: adhere to the strict policy of Rome and alienate the majority of Catholics in the child- bearing years, or risk censure for disagreeing with the party line. In all other matters, the Church taught that one was to follow his own conscience but in this issue, the bishops and the pope stated that the issue was closed, and that one could not follow his or her own conscience, but was to adhere to the letter of the law. Most did not.

There was a progressive momentum created by the Vatican Council, and the younger priests embraced the changes that hopefully made the Church more responsive to the needs of the people. However, there was another tide moving in the opposite direction: the growing conservatism within the Church. It seemed that the conservatives, or probably more accurately, the submissive, were warmly welcomed in the Church but the liberals were outcasts in all but a handful of parishes throughout the diocese. It is unfortunate that there was not room in the Church for any but a narrow conservative point of view. It was obvious that the Church was losing a good portion of its people. Looking over the congregation at Sunday Mass often told the story. There were few young Catholics in attendance. We had lost a generation.

As the priest on campus I was at the cutting edge of all this, and at any gathering on campus where I was known, I was expected to defend the position of the Church, or at least to try to explain it. I knew that to be true to myself, I could not in conscience preach the "party line" without reservations. I knew that I could not last long on the college scene, caught between my conscience, the academia, and the state of the local church. I could talk about a modern church responsive to the modern world, but when I looked at the local parishes around me, it simply wasn't happening. I thought of asking for reassignment back to parish work, and the thought of another roll of the dice and some of the potential openings brought a shiver to my spine. I knew I could never go back to the dull routine of hours of children's confessions, supervising activities for high school students, and living in a rectory with another frightened or sullen old priest or even worse an autocrat who was more intent on defending his turf than serving the needs of the parish or one who felt his purpose was to enjoy the leisure and comfort afforded the pastor while keeping a tight rein on the younger priest who were entrusted to his care. My life was a one-way street, and there was no turning around.

A group of young priests in the area would usually gather for lunch or dinner on a regular basis. We shared our ideas, our concerns, and our frustrations. Two themes were nearly always echoed: personal honesty in preaching something we personally could not support, and our concern that the Church was losing some of its finest priests. Fully half of the men in my ordination class had left the active ministry within ten years of ordination.

I remember one of my classmates didn't even make it through the summer. He was accused of fooling around with the altar boys at his first assignment and was gone within a few weeks. Nobody in our class ever heard from him again. We suspect he was transferred to another diocese quietly.

Also a topic of concern was the priests who staffed the southern part of the diocese. It was an interesting lot. Several had drinking problems, for which there was little or no help afforded other than transfer to another assignment. A number had discreet but known affairs with women of the parish, their housekeepers, or women known from a former assignment. A number were known to be openly gay but were able to keep it quiet for the most part. A few were trapped in inner city parishes and wondered what had happened to the elite parish that once was but was no more.

Often within the group there was someone who knew these priests who, when as young assistants in their parishes they were filled with enthusiasm and loved by the people; the priests who were now the object of our criticism. Nearly all this group who met on a regular basis were the "younger" priests in the area. Apparently these two counties were not considered prime assignments for few of the "older" assistants served there. We noted a certain cynicism among the older assistants in the diocese. We wondered what happened to their idealism, to their zeal, even to their values.

I remember one rather interesting debate about what the Church and priesthood would look like in the future. We all agreed that it would be different from the traditional parish churches we grew up with. The vast majority of the people who were showing up for Sunday Mass were elderly. They attended either out of habit or that feeling of guilt arising from the Church law that required them to attend Mass on every Sunday and Holy Day. The insidious guilt machine kept them coming and gave reason for the existence of the church, namely to make things aright with God and remove the threat of divine wrath. Perhaps to be fair, different tactics are used by other denominations, but for the same goals. Many churches try to get everyone involved in something, whether choir, Bible study, fund raising, or some other involvement that requires their attendance on a regular basis.

During the 60's there was a Pentecostal movement in the Catholic Church, often with exchanges between some of the Pentecostal Protestants and Catholics, and it seemed to center around the workings of the Holy Spirit. One priest I knew was heavily into this sort of thing. People would gather for their prayer meetings and somebody would begin "speaking in tongues" – mindless mumbling it sounded to me. People would lay their hands on individuals and pray over them to receive the Spirit and experience great joy. I went to a couple of these meetings out of curiosity and for some reason nothing ever happened to me. For that matter, I didn't notice much going on with the others in the group either, except that they liked to sing and seemed to get happy when they did. I hardly thought this would be the future of the Church.

What role would there be for the Church in the future? About all we could agree on was that there will always be a ministry for Baptisms, Marriages and Funerals. The traditional ministry of the parish priest would be a thing of the past. Catholic Schools were closing for lack of nuns to supply the cheap staffing, enrollment in the seminaries plummeted, and we were losing our finest young priests at an alarming rate.

I remembered going to the Redemptorist retreat house, west of Milwaukee, for my annual priest's retreat and leaving after one day. I could not tell which sickened me more; the platitudes and guilt trips spewed out by the retreat master or the other priests who were making the retreat and apparently accepting all without question or any shadow of a doubt as if this would recharge the emptiness of their lives.

As I drove away I knew that I had little in common with either. When I looked around the room the first day, I saw myself in ten or fifteen or twenty years, going through the motions, mindlessly blabbering the same old line to the people, moralistic to everyone but myself, bitter on life, and seeking refuge in a bottle, or in the words of the Beatles song…"living alone, within a room, within himself." I knew from living alone for a year that loneliness was more than being without human companionship, it was facing the world without the support that we all so desperately need. I realized one can be lonely in a crowded room when one had nothing in common with those around him, the way I felt at the retreat with the gathering of priests.

I knew as I drove out the tree-lined drive to the highway that it was not a question of if, it was a question of when I would leave the active ministry. I was not the first, nor the last. But we all went through the same agony of decision. When it became more painful to remain than to leave, the decision was inevitable.

The first emotion that I had to deal with was that of guilt. Priests were admired and loved by their families, particularly by parents and brothers and sisters. Many of us still had the imprint of our mother's hand impressed on our backs, going back to seminary days. How would they deal with it? Would they feel betrayed? Was this another guilt machine? Eventually I knew I would have to talk to my family, particularly my dad, and I was grateful dad was kind and understanding, so I had no fear. I wondered about the rest of my family. How would they react? Would the wounds heal? How soon?

A second practical consideration was one of finances. By any measurement, I was poor. Seven years of trying to cope on $50 per month plus the meager stipends had left me with nothing in reserve. My wardrobe was limited and near the end of its useful life. I had a car on a lease. My entire worldly possessions I could haul away in the trunk of my car. I took the exam for an insurance license passed it with flying colors, and had a job selling life insurance. I had timed my departure at the end of May, and would keep my decision as quiet as possible until then.

I finished my commitment and remained at Parkside until the end of May. In fact, I had the afternoon Mass at one of the parishes on Sunday and went home, took off my Roman collar, lit a fire in the back yard and burned it. I still look back at that year as one of growth and enlightenment, as well as painful parting. I was thrust into a position for which I had no preparation, precious little support from the local parishes, and a mountain of criticism from some of the pastors who had lost touch with their flocks. I worked hard, took some risks, and tried to help the local parishes as best I could. When I packed up my meager belongings and left the house on the edge of the campus, I paused to wonder: "What was it that I was here to do? Did anyone know? Did anyone care? Did anybody value the work I had done, or even appreciate it? Or was this one of those positions that looked good in the directory?"

A friend of mine Dave left the active ministry some time after I did, after being transferred from Fond du Lac to a parish in Milwaukee. Dave had been the only assistant pastor Ray had at Sacred Heart parish; the two got on well, and Dave was extremely well liked in town. Like every young priest at the time, he was transferred to another assignment after seven years. Dave came to the same painful decision I had. When Dave told Ray that he was leaving the active ministry and planning to get married Ray's first question was "Did you go through the formal process to get your dispensations?"

This was the typical legalistic response so readily given. The most important issue was that everything be done according to the detailed rules of the Vatican. No one seemed to be concerned that the Church was losing some of its finest priests. In fact the Church treated the men and women who left religious life rather shabbily. There was no one who stopped to say thanks for years of dedicated service, usually the best years of the lives of these men and women. In fact, those who left the priesthood in the Milwaukee diocese did not even get a return of their contribution to the "St. Michael's Priest Fund," which was a sort of retirement fund for priests that each priest had to personally contribute, matched by the parishes. After years or haggling over the issue, with threatened lawsuits, some of the men did receive something. I never did. A classmate from another diocese spent thirty-eight years in service to the diocese. When he left they returned his contribution to the retirement fund. No interest, no pension, nor portion of what he deserved. Down to the penny, he received only the money he had put into the plan.

After our marriage, I must admit, I did not make many contacts with the people in the parishes I had served for a long time. The reason was a personal one. It might have been easy, at least for curiosity sake, for people to welcome us to their homes. But we had received more than a little dose of hostility from others, and the sting hurt. I realized that my life and marriage would present a dilemma for many and we would be viewed as a curiosity. On the one hand was their faith and the Church, and on the other their friendship and respect for the man who had once been their beloved priest.

I did not want to create a problem for people who still had a faith that was an important part of their lives. My own integrity told me that mine was a personal decision and I did not want it to become the problem for anyone else. At the time there was still a great deal of stigma attached to anyone leaving the active ministry. There were many who would have had a hard time dealing with it. On the other, repeating my apologia over and over served no purpose, and it was tedious for both of us. We simply wanted to get on with our lives.

What is interesting now is that after all these years, when I meet parish members, of relatives at occasions such as marriage, funerals or other gatherings, I am shown a certain respect and friendship. It is gratifying to know that time heals wounds and that they remember the good that I did and one constant refrain is that I was well liked and served the people and the Church far better than most of those who followed in my footsteps.

I often wonder if I had remained in the active ministry would I have turned out like the old men I find reason to criticize? Would the battles have left their scars and turned me into a bitter old man? Would I have turned to drink in my loneliness? Could I have survived merely going through the motions of the ministry? I know this, that in the years since I burned my "Roman Collar" the last day of May in 1970, I have never second-guessed that decision. I have never had a desire to return to the active ministry. Life is a one-way street and when you try to back up, even if you can, nothing good ever happens.

Contacts with former classmates have been very sparse in the years since 1970. The first few years a handful of friends stayed in contact. The last phone call from a seminary classmate was from one trying to get me to sell Amway. For the past several years I receive a letter inviting me to a class reunion during the summer. I'm not sure that I have the stomach for a banquet of nostalgia peppered with guilt. Each Christmas I now receive a form letter from a classmate in a small parish in rural Nebraska telling about the new roof on the rectory, or the rolls of sod on the parish lawn. On the other hand, I have not made efforts to reach out to former classmates either. We shared some years together but probably have little in common any more. Several priests who left the active ministry sought out careers similar to part of their pastoral duties. Some went into social work, a couple into counseling, a number worked for non-profit groups such as United Way, and a few returned to parishes to head up the religious education programs. One I know worked as custodian in a parish headed by someone a year ahead of him in the seminary. While some distinguished themselves in their second careers, many found that the seminary training left them ill prepared to enter the world without the Roman collar. Not all married, and a few returned to the active ministry. One common denominator is that the Church treated them as second-class citizens for the most part. None of us received any compensation from the retirement funds, even though we had served the Church for many years. If there is a tragedy it has to be that the Church lost some of its finest priests and religious who if given half a chance could have been valuable additions to a parish staff that is strained by the lack of available priests.

Chapter Nine

Learning to Love

Romantics sing of "falling in love" but "learning to love" is a more accurate description for it is a process of growth and development of the ability to love and be receptive to the love of another.

Entering the seminary at a young age, from a family of conservative innocence, the isolation of years in the seminary was hardly conducive to developing the ability to enter into healthy relationships with the opposite gender. In fact one might argue that the opposite was true. Before every vacation in the seminary we were sure to be lectured on the "dangers of losing one's vocation" – that special calling to the priesthood. Obviously, since celibacy was a pre-requisite, any relationship with a woman was a threat and danger to be avoided. It is interesting that we never heard a word about the dangers of homosexual relationships or pedophilia. In fact the "brotherhood of priests" was considered a virtue. Female contacts for most of us were limited to family members, nuns, relatives and parish members who tended to put the seminarian on a pedestal to be respected from afar.

Upon my ordination, my first assignment at St. Mary's certainly put my life in a fishbowl. Being in front of a thousand or more people each Sunday at Mass meant there was hardly a place in town I could go without being recognized by someone, whether it was to take in a movie, have a meal in a restaurant or a drink in a bar, tongues were sure to wag. With so many people it was more likely someone would recognize me than the other way around, and that could be embarrassing. Lingering in the back of my mind during my years in Fond du Lac was the knowledge that what I did would filter back to members of my family, to parishioners I worked with, or to the ever-present watchful eye of the pastor, or the senior associate who felt it was his duty to make certain that I was a paragon of virtue. Everything I did around the parish or around town or what I said from the pulpit or even in the privacy of the confessional was certain to be spread on the community grapevine.

The priests I served with generally shared that fishbowl feeling, particularly young priests in small towns. On their weekly day off they left town, either to spend the day with family, or if they wanted to take in a movie or have a drink, it was out of town. Two of the pastors in Fond du Lac routinely took three or four days a month in Chicago, either at the racetrack or at a downtown hotel for a few days.

There was the image of the priest that had to be upheld at all costs. No matter what his faults, he was expected to present an image above reproach when in the public eye or with members of the community in which he served. In fact, the bishops routinely tried to cover up the wrong doings of their priests with the police and the judges who were all too willing to drop charges of driving under the influence as well as sexual allegations to preserve the image of the clergy as being above reproach. The reality was something different.

When priests in the area gathered for parish celebrations such as the visit of the bishop for Confirmations, it was a different matter. In the closed confines of the parish rectory the liquor flowed freely (usually at parish expense) and there were often high stakes poker games that went well into the night. I remember priests openly cheating at poker, and after seeing their dishonesty I vowed never to get into a game with them. I remember on more than one occasion wondering how some of the priests were able to drive home after the celebrations. One night at St. Mary's we spent about an hour trying to find the car of a priest from Milwaukee who couldn't remember where he had parked. He was in no shape to drive. I didn't want him to get behind the wheel of his car, but Hank and Roger were all too willing to be rid of him. I worried that we would read in the paper the next day that he had crashed on the way home, killing some innocent family on the way.

My parish duties brought me in contact with many women of the parish. I worked with the women who taught the religion classes for children who attended public schools. I served on the board of directors for the local Girl Scout council and I was active with married couples in the Christian Family Movement, but all these contacts were impersonal, playing the role of the priest, the mentor.

When I arrived at St. Therese, I was put in charge of staffing the CCD program for the children who attended public schools. We had a section for the high school students on Monday evenings, and the grade school age children came on Saturday mornings. Being new I town, it was a problem to staff the program at first. Sister Dolores who helped with the program and was principal of the parish school, recruited some of the teachers, among them a nun from St. Joe's high school, Jo Ann Frick.

Jo Ann was a first-year teacher, a member of a group who chose to live away from the high school, in two duplex apartment buildings on Kenosha's south side. This was quite a departure from the usual housing for nuns, which was the convent on top floor of the school building at St. Joe's. Certainly the living arrangement was far better for them, though it soon came under criticism from the conservatives in town, especially since they did not all wear the "black and white" traditional habits and live under strictly controlled conditions and some wondered if they were observing all their religious practices as they did in the convents.

I taught religion classes at St. Joe's high School every day, having the last two hours before lunch. I soon got acquainted with the staff at the school and in my role as area CCD coordinator, I began conducting classes at the school in the evenings for religion teachers around town. I remember teaching a class on St. Paul's letters, and another on audio-visual techniques and presentation. They were quite well received.

Jo Ann and I got acquainted through her work at the parish and a friendship developed, not only with her, but with all the nuns who were living in the two apartments. Apart from going to Gurnee to the Shakey's Pizza Place, which had a spectacular sing along with an old man on piano and a blind banjo player, we really did not socialize much. I had a pretty heavy schedule at the parish, and they were busy teaching, correcting papers and preparing for the next classes.

In June, I was assigned as chaplain at UW-Parkside and would be leaving St. Therese. I had also been asked if I wanted to teach at St. Joe's, since there was an opening there. The Parkside assignment was interesting. I had no place to live and only a meager income from the diocese that barely covered my expenses. I finally settled in with the Dominican priests at the rectory of Dominican College in Racine. The college had built a large rectory for the priests who were expected to staff the college. In reality there were two old Dominicans, who didn't do much of anything as far as I could see, and the rest of the building was empty, so the college was happy to have the place occupied. (There was a resident chaplain from another order who lived in one of the dorms at the college.)

Jo Ann and I did maintain contact, if nothing more than a silly little card now and then. I spent the summer first at Harvard for a chaplain's school, and then taking a three- week vacation through the Canadian Rockies and down the West Coast into San Francisco, Reno and Las Vegas. There were four of us, Karl Acker, a classmate, Bob, a librarian, and Bill who worked at American Motors. We bowled on the same team on Friday Nights.

The vacation was a dream trip through some of the most beautiful scenery in the world. We drove across the Canadian prairie and through the Canadian Rockies, into Vancouver, Seattle, and down the west coast to San Francisco, Reno, and Las Vegas.

I called my friend Frank Pickart from San Francisco and told him we'd be in town on Monday night. I asked if he could get us a place to stay and tickets to the Lido. That was the only totally nude show in the country at the time. We got to the hotel where the show was early, I played a few slots and I found a man wandering around outside the lounge door with a clipboard. A couple of bucks in his hand and our name had a checkmark in front of it. Our table abutted the stage. Fr.

Karl was one of the more conservative, if not sheltered classmates from the seminary. He still wore white socks even with his black priestly garb. I am sure he had never seen a risqué show. The curtain went up and beautiful nude women danced across the stage, came out of the floor and down from the ceiling. The look on his face was worth the trip. I don't know if he ever forgave me for that one.

One might think that learning to love another person is easy, but we faced numerous obstacles. The first, obviously, was that if we were seen publicly around town where both of us were well known, tongues would begin to wag. We both had responsibilities to our positions that we did not want to jeopardize and we didn't need the grief that was sure to come if our love was discovered. So if we wanted to get away anywhere, we needed to get out of town, if it were for a movie, a dinner, or just a pizza and a little time to talk.

Another hurdle to overcome lay within ourselves. In my case, entering the seminary early in adolescence, I had hardly experienced anything of a relationship with women beyond the interactions in grade school classes under the watchful eye of the nuns. Our family did not openly show affections. I don't remember ever seeing mom and dad hug or kiss. Open showing of affection might have been there for little children but certainly not as we got older, vanishing completely by the time we entered adolescence. The years of seminary training surely eroded my abilities to be emotionally attracted to a woman, or to give and receive love. In fact our training was such that our instinctive reaction to any woman showing interest was to view it as a threat to our virtue, and rebuff as quickly and firmly as possible. Propriety was valued above all else.

I remember one of the instructors at the seminary was asked by a classmate when it was appropriate for a priest not to wear his Roman Collar. The Monsignor, replied that if you were going anywhere where you did not want to wear your Roman Collar, then you probably should not go there. The proper priest "never took off his collar" to become like the rest of men.

My years in Fond du Lac were under the watchful eye of Hank (and Susie) and for the first year the other assistant, Roger. The social lives of the priests, in their minds, was one and the same as their priestly role. Even in purely social settings, we were expected to keep our guard up lest we bring scandal to the parish and the Church. Since most of my social contacts were people who were active in parish organizations, there were few if any secrets. Any miscues traveled through the grapevine to priests throughout the area. Add to this the fact that my family and relatives lived in the area, many of them members of the parish, nearly all the socializing that I did during those years was with relatives or people who were active in parish organizations.

Fond du Lac was something of an "outpost" for the priests of the diocese and we seldom socialized with classmates or friends from other parts of the diocese. It was a matter of matching days off and often it meant driving a distance to meet. There were only a few in the city who were compatible. Dave and I bowled together in a Friday Night league, and I would golf a few times during the summer with Fr. Don, and the year Fr. Jim was at St. Mary's we'd golf and perhaps take a walk at night together but we really never felt comfortable dropping by another assistant in town for a drink, a few hands of cards, or just to shoot the breeze for a while. The assistant's rooms in rectories around town were generally small, and afforded precious little privacy.

I remember one Good Friday when Don, who was then at St. Pat's a few blocks away stopped by for a drink. We talked about going golfing early on Saturday morning. There wasn't much doing for either of us until the afternoon with confessions, and then the Easter Vigil at night. So we agreed we'd go out and play nine holes of golf in the morning. We planned to get there about 7:00 and that would get us back early enough. I told him I would call him in the morning.

My alarm went off at 6:00 so I picked up the phone and woke him up. I showered and dressed, and only when I headed out the door did I realize it was pouring rain. I drove to St. Pat's, and Don came out, and told me that come Hell or high water, I was going to play nine holes of golf in this stuff, even if he just sat in the car and laughed at me.

All the way to the golf course, about a twenty-minute drive, rain came down in torrents. We drove into the parking lot of the course and the rain stopped. We teed off and played nine holes. Just as we were putting our clubs back in the car the rain resumed, and it poured for the entire day. Who was in charge of the weather that day, Don or I? We were good friends then, but when I was transferred to Kenosha we never met again. Some of us seldom made lasting friendships. The need for human companionship seemed to be foreign to the priest who was to seek solace in prayer and his ministry.

I look back at those years of isolation and wonder why none of us reached out. There simply wasn't the camaraderie one would expect from people who shared a lot of the same professional problems and goals. I knew Roger at St. Mary's was a loner who spent every one of his days off as well as his vacations with his parents. I don't recall any of his priest friends coming to visit. Hank had few friends who stopped by, but every month he and Ray Fox would take a trip to Chicago for a few days, sometimes with one or the other of the more affluent men of the parish. Usually this included some days at the racetrack during the racing season.

Some priests, like Fr. Jerry, seemed to attach themselves to a family like leeches, showing up at the doorstep of the family several times a week. I had my friends in the parish, but never quite felt like they should "adopt" me. I learned years later of the pattern of pedophiles among priests and one common trait was that they seemed to have the ability to get very close to the families of their victims. It was usually considered flattering for a good Catholic family to have one of the priests as their personal friend. At any rate, though I enjoyed the company of parish-ioners, there was never a time when I could let my guard down and be anything other than the parish priest who was expected to comport him-self above reproach. It was much easier to put up an emotional wall. A wall that shielded me from the outside but also kept me a prisoner inside my own repressed emotions.

The move to Kenosha was a change. I spent a good part of the summer at Catholic University in Washington DC working with peers in religious education in the summer workshop, which allowed a great deal of inter-change with men and women from all over the country. There was a good mixture of priests, nuns and laymen and women in the group. In discussion groups, workshops, and after class activities, we tended to be far freer than we were at home. Being in a group of strangers meant we didn't need to put on the "official" posture and could relax with one another without worry that rumors would drift back to the parish or family. The workshop was a growing experience in that regard.

I began to realize how sheltered I had been and wondered why. It was a new experience to interact as a person rather than as a priest with a Roman collar. We spent time touring the city on weekends and participated in one of the largest demonstrations in history, the final days of the Poor People's March that had began months before with plywood tents erected in the park on the Mall as a protest to the conditions that minorities were forced to live under because of the color of their skin.

Having grown up in a whites only community (Fond du Lac had a city ordinance that forbade a black person from staying overnight in town, as did many cities in the area) my contact with people other than whites was very limited. Coming to Washington for the first time, I experienced a black majority in the population and saw first hand urban poverty that was evident, as were the scars of burned out buildings from the riots of the 60's, particularly the unrest that followed the death of Martin Luther King a few months before. The National Guard was stationed in the city in full uniform, and for the first time I smelled the sharp odor of tear gas as we drove through the city one night.

When I arrived at St. Therese, there was a freedom that I had never experienced in Fond du Lac. Vince and I had separate entrances, with my apartment separated from the main house. For the first time since I left home for the seminary, I could come and go according to my schedule and didn't need the permission of anyone.

Teaching at St. Joe's high school brought me in contact with the women religious who taught there. They were a bit different from the nuns I had grown up with, or for that matter those I was acquainted with in Fond du Lac. They were modern in their dress and modern in their ideas. Gone was the long black robe and complicated head dress and all that. Some would wear a simple black veil with a white headband and a "Tau" cross that was the symbol of the order. What made this interesting was the fact that all the kids at St. Joe's wore uniforms, while the nuns who taught them were wearing whatever was appropriate to them. This group of women was interested in the world around them. Their order at the time was undergoing an internal transformation, trying to develop an idea of their mission in the modern world apart from providing reliable and cheap labor to the Catholic schools.

This obviously didn't sit well with some of the conservative priests in town, particularly Vince who wrote a letter to each of the pastors in town condemning these nuns and their "liberal" lifestyle. Among other things he accused them of wearing "mini-skirts (he seemed to have a thing about them) and even stated that a group of them were working as waitresses at one of the finer restaurants on weekends. When the priests of the area met for one of their monthly meetings, Vince brought the subject up, and I exposed his lie about the waitress thing.

One of the group played the organ at St. Therese on Sundays, and some of the others taught in our CCD program at the parish. I had developed a slide/audio presentation for use in one of the high school CCD programs to promote discussion on the role of the Church in the modern world and in the lives of people. I used it with the teacher-training program with great success. In fact, the Order of nuns used it for several of their meetings as an opening presentation to their group discussions on the mission and role of the Church and their Order in the modern world.

Friendships developed, particularly with Jo Ann. She was working on one of the committees of the order that was trying to define its mission. With her writing talents, she worked on one of the publications groups and needed some photos to use. We spent a few Sunday afternoons taking pictures at various locations. On a few occasions I would skip my Friday night bowling and we'd head to Gurnee for a pizza.

When I was appointed chaplain at Parkside, Jerry Weber, a priest who was one of three heading up the CCD program in the diocese and myself lived in the rectory of Dominican College. It was ideal from the standpoint that we were free to come and go as we wanted and if we needed a meal, we could always slip next door to the convent. Jerry and I were friends. In fact I was somewhat instrumental in getting the CCD program staffed with some full time people. Before that, the task was given to a priest at the seminary and not very much happened. It seemed the Church was more interested in committing its resources in the parish schools and could actually care less about the kids who attended public schools. I lived in Racine for several months until I was able to purchase a house across the street from the Parkside campus.

When school started, I would have Mass for the students at Carthage College, a Lutheran School, in their tiny little chapel on campus. There were only a few Catholics there on a weekend, judging from the number who would show up for Mass. I invited the nuns from St. Joe's who were pretty well turned off by all the parishes in town, to join us at Carthage for Mass on Sunday's. A small group came and we'd often have brunch at my house nearby. If the weather was right, we'd take a walk in Petrifying Springs park nearby, which was outstanding in the fall colors.

I would often take the early Sunday Masses at one of the parishes, or the Sunday evening one, which a few of them had. One of the regular stops was at St. James, where my friend Roy was the assistant. Roy's parents had a cottage on a lake near East Troy, and invited us out one evening in October. We cooked burgers and whatever on the grill, and sat around and talked. Everybody wanted to go for a walk after we ate and Jo Ann paired up with me and we wandered away from the rest of the group. It was then that she told me for the first time that she loved me. It was a tense moment as we walked in silence but we both knew that our lives would change, since I felt the same way about her but did not know how to express it or even to sort out what this was all about.

Our contacts became more frequent after that. We'd talk on the phone or drop notes or cards in the mail to each other. I learned that I had a talent for writing poetry, Some of them, she discovered hidden in a trunk in the basement and gave them to me for my birthday. I have included them at the end of the book.

We began spending more time together, often taking a walk along the beaches south of Kenosha where we could sit on the beach and watch the waves, or head south of the border for a meal or a pizza. Both of us needed to learn to be comfortable with each other. Convent and seminary training did not include showing or receiving affection. In fact, any physical or emotional contact was considered a threat. I remember clearly Thanksgiving that year. For some reason we were both in town. I had just returned from deer hunting and had agreed to speak at something or the other on Friday, and had committed to speaking at all the Masses at one of the big parishes in Racine on Saturday and Sunday.

Jo Ann invited me over for Thanksgiving dinner. I will never forget the kiss at the door when I arrived. It was the first passionate kiss in my life. It was wonderful and exciting and beautiful. There was no doubt we were in love but it was somewhat tricky to keep our love secret. We apparently did a pretty good job since even the women she was living with had no idea. Of course, they were involved with their own lives and men, and were trying to keep their affairs secret from Jo Ann. Little did they know!

During the early winter I had a few friends from St. Therese parish over along with a group of nuns including the group Jo Ann lived with. One of the people from St. Therese mentioned to Fr. Vince that they had been out to see me, and he quizzed her at great length. Vince then wrote his own version of it and sent a letter to the head of the religious order and a copy to every pastor in town, mentioning that one of his parishioners was scandalized at what was happening at the Campus Ministry. He mentioned the "young nuns parading around in their miniskirts." He obviously had a problem.

When I heard about it I was livid. I called and spoke to the head of the Order, who was more willing to accept Vince's version than what had actually happened. I fired off a letter to each of the pastors exposing Vince's version. I found out that most of them didn't take him seriously anyway. I also made a complaint to the diocese asking that they reprimand Schneider for his malicious slander. They never even bothered to reply to my complaint.

Two things resulted from the incident: one was the realization that the diocese and the religious orders cared little about their people, at least not to the extent of trying to defend them against people like Vince. The second result was that this apparently was the final breach of trust and hastened my decision to leave the active ministry.

Unknown to me, the incident had the same effect on Jo Ann, and two of her friends and their decisions were made about the same time.

My meeting with the bishop was a disaster. He had no personal interest in me and did not in any way ask me to reconsider my decision, nor what brought me to this point. He was more interested in how the Catholic Directory would list my name than in the fact that one of his priests was asking to be relieved of his duties. I received no words of empathy, no offer of support, financial or otherwise and we parted without a handshake.

When my anger subsided a bit I called Jo Ann and asked if she would like to go out for a walk along the lake. We stood on the sand watching the waves, really a pretty sight with the sun at our backs. I told her at that time that I was going to be taking a leave of absence at the end of May and had been studying for my insurance license. After a long talk I asked her if she would consider marrying me some time in the future. She didn't hesitate and said yes.

I still remember the wonderful rush of happiness when we were together, whether it was sharing a pizza, taking a walk in the woods or watching the waves crash upon the shore at the beach. We were in love, we were happy as only lovers can be. We knew we had a long path ahead of us. We needed to learn to become intimate, to share with each other, to trust, to give and accept love, to take responsibility for our love and for each other. There were many things our lives in the convent and seminary had kept from us and we would now have to learn in patient understanding.

It was a beautiful time: it was a frightening time. We had no money, I had the promise of a job, we had no place to live, no furniture, very little clothing. It was insane.

Jo Ann told me that she had a job for the summer in Omaha, working for the parks department running a summer camp in that city. She would stay with her brother Mike during that time. She'd be back some time early August.

I continued on my job at the University and fulfilled all my other jobs until the end of May. In fact on the last Sunday in May I preached at all five Masses at a Church in Racine, and then returned to Kenosha for the evening Mass at St. Thomas. To my knowledge no one in either city was aware that this would be my last day. As I drove home I wondered if they had known would anyone have cared.

A friend of mine, Don, who was in the life insurance business, lived alone in a house on the north side of town. He asked me if I would like to move in with him for the time being and share the rent. It was an OK move. I didn't have a lot of furniture. In fact, about all I had was a bed, a few clothes and personal belongings and a small library of books on theology and religious education.

For perhaps the first time in my life, I truly missed someone. I missed Jo Ann. Frequent cards and notes didn't quite replace the person I so dearly loved. We agreed that I would come to Omaha over the 4th of July. Don took me to O'Hare and agreed to pick me up again a few days later. JoAnn met me at the airport in Omaha along with her brother Mike, who informed me that they were going to be away for the weekend so we'd have the house to ourselves. I suspect it was intentional on his part and have been grateful to him ever since.

We had a beautiful weekend and set a wedding date at the end of August. The question was where and how. A friend was leaving Kenosha and his apartment on the lake was available. I talked to the landlord and we agreed to take over the lease. It was a nice place, and I could move in the first of August. We decided to get married there, inviting only close friends and family. A friend of mine agreed to perform the ceremony, and some friends in Racine offered their place for a reception. On August 29th, we were married in the living room of our apartment.

One facet of our wedding was puzzling. Jo Ann's family were all in attendance, but for my family, it was a different story. My Dad was happy to attend, as well as my sisters, Alice and Dottie and their husbands. Bert and his wife attended, Lil and Jim were caring for their daughter Linda who was seriously ill, but the rest were notably absent. It would take time before they were willing to accept us as a couple.

Jo Ann had applied for a teaching job at one of the Catholic schools in town, and they turned her application down since the word had gotten around that we were getting married. I learned from a friend that

Racine was looking for teachers, and Jo Ann went there for an interview and was hired on the spot. Of course the school year started in August, so we had only a short honeymoon: an over-night stay in a motel in Illinois and a stroll in downtown Chicago the next day. Monday we were both back to work.

However, the next weekend we took a trip to Niagara Falls over the Labor Day Weekend. We had a great time and for some wacky reason decided to take a helicopter flight over the falls. Jo Ann had never been in a plane before and here she was in this "bubble" with open sides, soaring over the river and waterfalls. She was terrified. She's a white-knuckle flier to this day.

Living together and growing in love is a challenge, but a rewarding one. It was certainly a learning experience for each of us. We were quick to support, and to console, to help and very hesitant to criticize. We learned to care for each other and were interested in each other's growth as a person as well as in our careers. At the same time we became not only tolerant but understanding of our shortcomings and moods. We were careful to nurture the love that we so cherished, to care for it and help it grow.

It is interesting in retrospect that our family and friends have admired our relationship. Even if we tried, I'm sure that if we complained to any of them about our spouse, we'd hardly get a sympathetic ear. Not that our love hasn't gone through some painful times, but there was never a question of the depth and durability of our love.

Perhaps the most painful in the early years was Jo Ann's pregnancy in 1973. We were excited to be parents. We took a vacation in Colorado to visit her brother Mike. At the time he was working for a company that had a cabin high in the mountains near Dillon. He made arrangements that we could use the place and they would join us on the weekend. Saturday Jo Ann began bleeding, and was terrified. We found a doctor in one of the resort towns who gave her a shot and said "good luck." The pain and bleeding continued. We traveled back to Greeley and admitted Jo Ann to the hospital where she had a miscarriage. It was a sad and quiet drive back home after that, as we both learned another facet of our love, the ability to console, to pick up the pieces and try again. We both felt the pain of loss and shattered dreams, and leaned on each other for strength. Only later did we learn that miscarriage was quite common with women who had been on birth control pills.

Apparently the shot the doctor at the resort had administered had some long-term effects, and it was a year later that Jo Ann finally became pregnant again. Carefully we guarded our hopes and enthusiasm, not wanting to deeply hurt again. The experience left me with a nagging thought of how insensitive and inadequate I had been in consoling those in my parish work who had gone through the same loss as we had. However everything was progressing smoothly. We attended the pre-natal classes at the hospital in Cudahy. I remember the session where a woman talked about the benefits of breast-feeding which was for some odd reason not as common then as it is today. The woman talked for about an hour on the nutrition in breast milk, the physical and psychological effects it has on the mother, the convenience and cost and whatnot.

I nearly got thrown out when I summarized it for her. "It's better for the baby, better for the mother, more convenient, cheaper, and it comes in such beautiful containers." We bought baby clothes, and things, and I even built a cradle for our expected arrival. It was a wonderful time. At the same time it was a bit fearful, filled with a world of what if.

I remember the early morning when Jo Ann went into labor, and we drove to the hospital. The labor continued for hours, the baby was not in a hurry to join us in the outside world. They did an ultra sound, the first one that the hospital had done with its new machine and it soon became apparent that the baby was larger than the opening that it was supposed to go through.

Late in the afternoon Dr. Fons appeared. He was a huge man, but a good obstetrician. He informed us that he'd have to do a "C Section" and he wanted to get it done soon, since he was leaving town the next morning on vacation. About 5:30 David entered the world, twenty-three inches long and weighing nearly nine pounds. When I first saw him he had a little band-aid on his rump. The doctor had been a bit too hasty with the scalpel.

It is an incredible joy to see your own child for the first time, almost afraid to hold that fragile little body. I remember staring in wonder as he slept in that little cradle I had built for him. The awe hardly diminished over the next several years as each day, each week, each month brought some new cause of excitement from that first smile, to the first incoherent babble, the first hesitant attempts at crawling, the first words; it was a beautiful experience.

I got in trouble at the hospital with my smart mouth. A good part of the pre-natal classes was training for assistance in the delivery room. When David was born by C- section, I was sitting in the waiting room. They didn't want husbands in the operating room at that time. A couple of days after David was born, the nurse who headed the program stopped in Jo Ann's room, and I asked her if we should be getting a refund since I didn't get to be in the delivery room and that seemed to be a good portion of the course. The poor nurse stuttered a bit about all the wonderful things we learned about nutrition and the like. It was only when I started laughing that she realized I was pulling her leg.

We bought a home shortly after he was born, our first, on the northwest side of Milwaukee. We'd move in June. When we had lived in the apartment, we hardly got to know anyone else in the building but as soon as we moved to a house, we got acquainted with our neighbors and people in the area quickly.

One of our neighbors, Lester, asked me if we were going to take the wall paper down in the bathroom. I thought a bit and asked him why he was interested. He told me that under the wallpaper was a mural painted by the man who built the house, and that it was a scene of nude women. Well, I didn't like that old wallpaper anyway. Lester volunteered to help wash the glue off the walls.

Across the alley lived another interesting family. Artie was a tall kid in his twenties, mentally handicapped, who worked for Goodwill Industries. For some reason Artie wandered outside most of the time. A harmless fellow, he got to know everybody in the neighborhood. We all looked out for him. His dad Virgil worked at a factory in Oak Creek and took as much overtime as it was possible for him to get. When he was home he spent most of his time in his garage across the alley. He was a typical Milwaukee redneck who harbored some deep-seated racism. I

238

remember a few years later when we had that house up for sale that an Afro American agent in an insurance class I was teaching stopped by. We thought we'd have a bit of fun, so I showed Willie around the house, opened the garage door and showed him that the lawnmower worked and all that. All the time Virgil is keeping a close eye on us. Willie and I shook hands and he left. Virgil immediately charged across the alley to ask if that was the guy buying our house.

Another family up the block had a boy about David's age and the moms would get together with the kids. Margie's husband was one who never remembered birthdays and the like. One Valentine's Day, Margie ordered a dozen roses to be delivered from a local florist. It drove her husband crazy. She wouldn't tell him where they came from. We moved before we learned if she got anything the next year.

When David was about a year old, we were sure we wanted another child, and Jo Ann was pregnant again. The doctor had already told us that delivery would be by C- section, and we had set a date. I even made a few bets with some of the people in the agency that our baby would be born on a specific date. I should have known better. Rebecca came about two weeks earlier than predicted.

When we arrived at the hospital in Menomonee Falls in the middle of the night, we found the place dark. They were in the middle of a construction project and at night they operated on emergency power while the crews worked. So down the darkened corridors to the OB section we went. The nurse on duty was the wife of one of my agents and made sure that I had a comfortable couch to nap on while we waited for things to develop. As they wheeled Jo Ann into the operating room, she asked where I was. The nurses told her that I was sleeping. She told them in no uncertain terms to wake me up.

Rebecca was a little bundle of joy, but had her problems. Being a bit premature, she was jaundiced, but that was handled easily with the "bilirubin" light. As much as David was a peaceful child, she was the opposite. We soon noted that she had crossed eyes, a condition called bilateral strabismus. She seemed to cry constantly. Two things were bothering her: she couldn't see anything clearly and she had a bundle of allergies, including an allergic reaction to her mother's milk.

At about eight months old, after attempts to straighten her eyes with a series of eye patches failed, we had surgery to correct the condition. It was successful, and when she came home her personality changed from the cranky baby to a pleasant and delightful little charmer.

Meanwhile our love had taken a new dimension. From caring for and about each other, we had two children to care for. We delighted in walks through the zoo on Sunday mornings when it was free for Milwaukee residents. We carefully nurtured the young lives, trying to give them experiences and opportunities for their little minds to explore the world around them. They loved to have someone sit and read to them. I remember the Saturday trips to the library where we would take a crate along to fill with books they picked out in the children's section. The next week we'd take them back and get another crate full. We shared the joys and responsibilities of parenting.

We moved to Brookfield in the fall of 1978. There were several reasons for our move. Our children would be entering school in a couple of years, and the Milwaukee schools were going through dramatic changes. They began bussing kids from different parts of the city to schools in our neighborhood, while some of the kids in our area were put on busses to schools elsewhere. We wanted a bit more space than was afforded on our busy street with a tiny back yard that opened to the proverbial Milwaukee alley. Besides that, Milwaukee taxes were climbing rapidly and with a changing neighborhood, we thought it was best to get out while we could still get a good value for our home. It was a good decision. Our neighbors who sold their home fourteen years later got less for theirs than we did, and they had a bigger home.

We put in an offer on a lot near the village of North Lake in Waukesha County, hoping to build a home on it. Unfortunately, or fortunately, the lot would not pass the perk test, so the only way we could build on it would be with a mound system or holding tank for waste and that was an iffy proposition. We felt badly about it because the lot we wanted had a good open space leading down to the creek that fed North Lake. It was an idyllic setting. But it was not to be. I drove through the area a couple years later, and that lot is still vacant, but the houses in the subdivision are huge, and I'm not sure we would have felt comfortable there in retrospect.

We spent most Sunday's doing the "open house" routine, and found one in Brookfield that was pretty well within our price range, had a large lot but needed some work. It came with a round pool in the back yard, with a deck and room for a garden. We put our own house on the market and put in an offer contingent on selling the one we had. Both deals went through and we moved in September. Brookfield would be where our children would find their lives, go to school, make friends and have their first jobs. It was a place we would call home though to a large extent our values and life-style never did quite reflect those of the yuppie suburbs.

Watching the personalities of our children unfold like the petals of a beautiful flower was an exciting experience. The early development, that first smile, the first incoherent babble that seems to have a pattern, learning to creep, to walk, to speak in ever more complex forms, it was all a miracle of life.

From an early age we tried to expose our children to a variety of learning experiences. I remember the tumbling classes in which David merely sat on the mat and watched the others. Rebecca was never a threat for a perfect ten in the Olympics either. Their talents lie elsewhere.

Our Christmas traditions included an evening of Christmas caroling around the neighborhood, usually with a couple of their friends for the evening. I remember one year it started snowing big flakes while we were out. It seemed like a Norman Rockwell scene as we caroled up and down the street. David's friend, Richie, knew all the verses to just about every Christmas Carol we sang that year.

David joined the Cub Scouts in third grade. I remember a call from the Scoutmaster asking if I would go along on a camp out. He mentioned the park in Waukesha. I asked if there was a Holiday Inn nearby. There was a long pause and he finally said "No." We spent some interesting times with the Scouts, in tents battling mosquitoes at camp, in rain, mud and cold. We canoed some of Wisconsin's most scenic rivers and we always seemed to be the lead canoe in the flotilla. Memories of swamping a canoe in the Boundary Waters on the border with Canada are priceless. We had a canoe that was a bit overloaded and took on a couple of waves in about sixty feet of water. The canoe caught the next wave and we were in the water about a hundred yards from shore. We swam around and caught all the gear and headed toward shore. When the rest of the troop came back found us, we had stripped down to our underwear and hung our clothes on a rope hung between two trees.

We camped in the Mountains of Colorado. Driving through Colorado the boys spotted a sign for a "topless" donut shop called "Debbie Does Donuts." Despite pleas from the boys, we decided to stop at Mc Donald's instead. The camp was located in the mountains of northern Colorado, so we had our share of rock climbing even going to and from the dining room which was quite a hike downhill from our camp. One of the staff members was a blacksmith who set up shop in an old shed left over from when the camp was a working cattle ranch. He lived in a tepee during the summer and had a beard that came halfway to his waist. Somehow word got around that he was living proof that the Indians made love to buffalo.

David attended the international Scout Jamboree in Virginia one year, returning with a load of memories of camp and Washington DC. We had some interesting times Scouting. He ended his scouting career two merit badges short of his Eagle Scout ranking. We got a new scout-master about that time who was a fundamentalist Lutheran and believed that scouting was a program of the church. It was about the same time that the Boy Scouts began open discrimination against gay men as scout leaders. It was here that David's principles presented a roadblock. First of all, he didn't like the brand of religion that the scoutmaster wanted to instill in each of the scouts; and secondly, his sense of tolerance would not abide the scouting movement's intolerance and bigotry. While I would have liked him to be an Eagle Scout, I had to agree with his adherence to principles.

His high school Spanish class sponsored a summer tour of Spain. David became the world traveler, coming back with a suitcase filled with Spanish wine, a ton of pictures and memories to last a lifetime.

He became the first National Merit Scholar in the school system who did not at the same time make the honor role. He was a child who was not going to let homework and class interfere with his education.

For many years at parent-teacher conferences we heard the same tale. David would be getting an "A" in the course if he did the homework. I think we asked every teacher he ever had if David knew the material and could apply it. Of course! We then asked what the object of the course was, to obtain knowledge and skills, or to do homework.

College visits were indeed an experience that every child and every set of parents should have. We looked at several schools, with varying interest, and certainly were able to write off many of them after even a cursory visit. He finally settled on the University of Minnesota at Morris in the southwestern part of that state. Being a National Merit Scholar, Minnesota offered a four-year scholarship and the school was a small liberal arts university that provided smaller classes and greater opportunity for faculty-student interaction.

He was able to spend a semester in Italy under a foreign study program, working in a high school as a teaching assistant in English in Villa Franca, Italy, one of the towns near Verona. His then-fiancé Meg held a similar position in Verona. They started out for Italy about a month early, spending some time in France and Spain. Their immersion into Italian culture was priceless.

Their wedding was a classic celebration. The ceremony and reception were held in the historic courthouse in Stillwater, Minnesota, a gorgeous and ornate structure that dates from the lumber-baron era along the St. Croix River. Meg's heritage is Scottish, so the men in her family all wore kilts.

Rebecca and I scouted the area for a place to host a groom's dinner since there would be quite a number of relatives from out of town coming to Stillwater. Meg's parents offered to let us use their home, a beautiful Victorian house atop one of the bluffs overlooking the river. We found a German restaurant that would supply the food and began to put things in place. The food was delicious, and as usual we had far too much. Meg's dad and I collaborated on a slide show of Meg and Dave from their childhood years up to recent photos.

On Friday afternoon we had the rehearsal at the courthouse. Meg's brother Andy plays the bagpipes and led the procession in and out of the ceremony. He commented that he only knew two songs, and Jo Ann told him that this would be enough: One coming in and another going out. Rebecca provided a violin selection and one of Meg's friends graced the occasion with a flute solo. It was memorable and beautiful.

Rebecca's childhood was more problematic than David's. She required two surgeries to correct her eyes, after trying to straighten them with patches failed. After the first surgery her disposition changed dramatically. We had no idea that the poor little thing couldn't see clearly.

After several trips to pediatricians, we finally got an appointment with an allergist who ran her through a series of tests. We learned that she had allergies to a number of foods and environmental things. It was amazing that even as a toddler she learned quickly what foods she could have and what she could not. Most of the "treats" that were served to her classmates at school for birthdays or at parties with her friends, were on her list of allergens.

She seemed to have been a "daddy's girl" from an early age. During her early years I traveled quite a bit for my job, and when I was gone she was a very unhappy child who moped around the house asking, "When's my daddy coming home?" We enjoyed each other's company a great deal. Each night she wanted her dad to tell her a story for a "tuck in." I made up a few tales about life in the old days with a little boy named "Bullwinkel" and various other characters such as Petunia, Blondie, Baldy and Beer Belly. The gig was up though when Rebecca was telling some of the stories to my sister who recognized the characters as my brothers and sisters and life on the farm when I was a little kid. They were great stories though.

Rebecca took up the violin in third grade. Her teacher required that a parent learn the instrument and help the child practice at home. I went to the lessons with Rebecca. After the second or third one, Mr. Meyer told me that I didn't have to come any more. I guess that meant that Rebecca was learning far faster than I was. He could at least have put me in the remedial group.

As she progressed, we found Mr. Bjorkland for private lessons. She blossomed quickly and was probably the best student he ever had. Under his guidance she played for church services at his church on several occasions. The music was great but the downside was that we had to sit through a horrible Sunday service with Pastor Dale. It accomplished two things: Rebecca got experience performing before a group, and we all came away wondering why anyone would continue to subject themselves to the inane services on Sundays. About all I could think of was that they did attract some good musicians, since the choir director and organist were affiliated with the Symphony.

Rebecca's musical resume was extensive during her Middle and High School Years. Milwaukee Youth Symphony Orchestra, Concord Chamber Orchestra, Milwaukee Symphony Concerto competition, Interlochen Summer Music Camp, Carroll College Orchestra, Honors Orchestra, and in her senior year playing with the University of Milwaukee Orchestra, where she spent half her high school day taking courses in the music department.

Her senior concert in high school gave her the opportunity to show-case her talents with a solo that ranked with the best performance by a violinist at the school. She received an enthusiastic standing ovation from the crowd and a face full of tears of pride from her mom.

After visiting a few colleges, she settled on the University of Wisconsin at Madison for her college, graduating with a major in math. Taking a bit of time away from school, working at various jobs, she applied to a number of schools for a Ph.D. Program in math. She was accepted at the University of Virginia, they awarded her a scholarship with a stipend and a Teaching Assistant position.

We've had a tradition of surprise birthday parties in our family and circle of friends, so the first summer we were in Brookfield the kids and I planned a surprise party for Jo Ann. We managed to get the invitations out, buy the food and have all the preparations made without her suspecting a thing. Her first hint that something was going on was seeing her dad drive up. We even had a special cake made with the inscription "Happy Birthday Jo Ann. Age equals Bra Size." We never did quite figure out what either number was that day. But with family and friends, we had a wonderful party.

Having been out of teaching since just before David was born, Jo Ann wanted to go back to school to get her Master's Degree. I thought it was a great idea and she was accepted at UWM. It meant that for the next couple of years she'd be taking some afternoon and evening classes a couple times a week. She was a serious student, often enduring intolerable and inept professors along the way but she was there to learn in spite of them or with them. We were proud when she was awarded her Masters Degree, and again had a good celebration to mark the occasion. We were able to surprise her a second time.

While the kids were in school, I generally got the job to make their lunches in the morning. Usually I would take a slip of paper and drop a note in the brown lunch bag for the day. Generally they were somewhat lame puns, but what can you expect at 6:00 in the morning. There were some times though when the writings were a bit more worthy of the author, like the one on Rebecca's Sixteenth birthday.

To Rebecca at Sixteen

I can drive

Wear make up and heels

Boys notice me – sometimes

And I get annoyed and embarrassed

When they do – or at least pretend

I think that's what I'm supposed to do

I have hopes and reams

And the ability to make those dreams come true

I have pride in who I am and what I've done

And I'm hurt when others put me down

There is a person inside me

Beginning to come out

I'm not always sure of who that will be

It frightens me sometimes

At other times I can't wait

So see if that person is the one in my dreams

I hope so – or even better

Happy Birthday, Rebecca. Enjoy 16

   Love, Dad

Jo Ann started working full time at Alverno College as the assistant to the Academic Vice President. As the college grew, her responsibilities grew; and before long she was involved in just about every aspect of the institution. Through it all she made friends of people throughout the world who came to Alverno for workshops or whose schools used some of the faculty of Alverno for workshops in their own schools. In some ways her job at times seemed to consume her, with the turf wars and politics that seem to emerge in every work place.

In November of 1998, she went to her gynecologist for an exam, noticing that she had been spotting and perhaps needed to adjust the hormone replacement she was on. The doctor decided to do an ultra-sound, and it showed a tumor on the fallopian tube. They scheduled surgery for Monday morning. It was a tense weekend. Jo Ann was fearful, she told me that she just knew that it was malignant.

I met the surgeon after the operation and talked to him at the elevator. He was brief. The tumor was malignant, and it had spread to the ovary and the omentum, the lining of the abdomen. It was a stage-three cancer. He stated that he thought he had been able to get all of it, and she should make a full recovery. The news was devastating. I knew more than ever that she would need the support of my love. We would be in for some difficult times. I called Rebecca in Madison to tell her the news. The first words out of her mouth were "Pick me up at the bus station at 2:15."

We all knew that this type of cancer is dangerous, that the survival rate is not encouraging, but that we would make the best of what we had left of our lives together. A couple of days after surgery she started chemotherapy in the hospital. For some reason her blood pressure dropped precipitously while they were pumping the taxol into her, a rare, but dangerous reaction. They stopped the taxol for a while, then resumed it at a much slower pace. A few days later she was able to come home. As if the disease were not devastating enough, the treatment is brutal in its effects on the body. The fatigue, the nausea, the pain is debilitating, and just about when Jo Ann was up to feeling somewhat better it was time for another treatment. The hair loss connected with most of the chemo treatments is demoralizing. Jo Ann decided against trying to wear a wig, and seeing other women around the hospital with ill-fitting wigs, I agreed with her. She wore hats for a while, partially to keep her head warm. Between the bouts with chemo she continued to work at Alverno and shocked everyone one day when she showed up hairless, and without her hats. I wondered how she could manage to continue to work, coming home exhausted.

There were regular trips to the hospital for chemo with a series of in-patient treatments. I remember being there New Year's Eve that year. I informed the nurses that at five minutes to twelve the taxol bottle comes down and I was going to put a bottle of champagne up there in its place. They watched me carefully. I had made some cookies for the nurses for New Year's Eve. I made a batch of gingerbreads cut in the shape of little elephants. I frosted them with pink frosting. Jo Ann loved elephants. She once told me that elephants are very intelligent, never forget their friends and have remarkable love for their family. She had a collection of hundreds of elephant figurines and an equal number of jewelry pieces with elephants.

At the end of January or early February when we were back at the hospital, Jo Ann's sister Kathy came up to visit. She walked up to the nurses station and said she was Jo Ann's sister, and wondered what room she was in. A nurse spied the shopping bag that she was carrying and asked

"Did you bring cookies?"

By March the blood tests showed that the tumor tracers (CA 125) were back in normal range. We were hopeful and elated. Perhaps we'd get this licked yet. At least we had hope. Yet under all the stiff upper lip, the reality of cancer and the rates of survival for this type of cancer loomed menacingly in our minds like the black storm clouds on the horizon.

We were at the theater one night with our friends Lyn and Bill and I told them of my idea of having a surprise party for Jo Ann, sort of a celebration of life, and we would invite her family and friends. They both blurted out, "Have it at our place and it will be a complete surprise."

We worked out the details, and Bill was able to procure a lamb to roast. Meanwhile, to throw Jo Ann off the trail, Lyn sent her an invitation to her own retirement party from teaching. We picked Memorial Day, and the weather was beautiful. Jo Ann had me make a dessert to take along to Lyn's party. With their large rural lot they were able to hide all the cars behind the shed, so when we drove up we didn't see a thing. When we came around the house in the driveway, Jo Ann spied David standing there with his camera. She was completely surprised.

We asked that there be no gifts, but that Jo Ann would appreciate a flower she could plant in her garden. It was the beginning of her flower gardens that have brought her so much pleasure through these trying years. It was a happy occasion that celebrated a courageous battle by a wonderful woman. It was a complete success, except that we had far too much food and beverages left over. Fortunately, the beer didn't spoil.

It was a couple of weeks later when we returned to the doctor for additional blood tests and discovered that the cancer had indeed returned. It was devastating, not only that there had been a recurrence but that it had been so soon. The chances of long-term remission are proportionate to the time between symptoms. It had been only a few months. Not a good omen.

The second round of treatment was another kind of chemo infused as in-patient again the hospital. I remember when we were about to leave the hospital on Friday, Jo Ann began vomiting. She spent most of Saturday in bed, not able to keep anything down, and vomiting. We hoped it would subside. Sunday afternoon she got up to go to the bathroom, and fainted in the bathroom. Somehow she got back to the bedroom, and fainted again, falling into the mirrored closet door, shattering the glass. She was out cold for a few minutes, and I wasn't sure she was going to pull out of it. Her eyes rolled back and her breathing was a raspy snore.

When she finally came to, I was already on the phone to the hospital, telling them that I was bringing her in. At the moment, Jo Ann thought she would be all right, but I insisted that we go back to the hospital. By the time we got her in the hospital and up to the room she was fainting again, not even able to sit upright. The diagnosis: atrial fibrillation. Being a weekend, the only help around on Sunday afternoon were the residents or "baby doc's" as we liked to call them. They took all kinds of tests and came up with nothing. To monitor her more carefully, they moved Jo Ann to the intensive care unit for bone marrow patients. A male nurse was on call that night and talked to the doctors, who were ready to use electric defibrilators to try to stabilize her heartbeat, that they should put her on IV fluids and keep an eye on her.

For several hours Jo Ann was restless, her heartbeat irregular. About 3:00 AM she stirred and coughed from deep down in her lungs. Her heartbeat returned to normal, and she was on her way to recovery. This side effect of the chemo she had received bothers less than one person in two hundred, but if you're that person, it's a 100% problem. That was the case with Jo Ann.

As I went home later that morning, I began to realize how close to death she had actually come that day. If she had been alone, she would never have gotten to help in time. Death loomed larger in the background from that day on. It was always on our minds, though we seldom spoke about it.

A few months before we began this saga with cancer, I was approached through the Knights of Columbus to host a benefit event to help a little thirteen year old girl who had serious medical problems. Born to a diabetic mother, she developed juvenile arthritis. The doctors attempted to stabilize her tiny spine by inserting pins in the vertebrae. Something went wrong and she was paralyzed from the waist down. Even her bladder and bowel were affected. I agreed to emcee the event, which soon got happily out of control. A swing band of college students heard about it and offered to come to provide entertainment. Then we heard from another band that wanted to do the same, so we had two bands providing music. We served a spaghetti dinner and had a room full of donated items for a silent auction. It was very successful, and we raised enough money to buy her a new wheel chair, a chair lift for the family van, and helped pay some of her medical bills.

A few weeks later I got a call from a woman I had met through the event. She told her story and asked for my help in putting together a project she'd been working on for years. She told her story. At age twenty-eight, she had just given birth to her daughter and was having problems in her recovery from childbirth. After several medical tests, she discovered she had MS, a progressive debilitating disease. When her then husband learned of this, he left. At age twenty-eight she had a new child, a terminal disease, and a husband who walked out on her.

Rather than despair, she somehow pulled together the strength to look for answers, corresponding with people from Senators and celebrities to neighbors and relatives who had faced serious illness in their lives. She wanted to know how they coped. Together we sifted through a mountain of correspondence, and gradually some common themes emerged.

The first theme was love. Most of the writers called it empathy, but it soon became obvious that empathy wasn't strong enough. Being sick is terribly lonely and frightening. It is easier to bear the burden if there is someone to share it, someone who truly loves you, whether this is expressed in a back rub, just holding a hand, of simply being there, the element of love is crucial.

The second theme that came through was hope. Not the expectation of some miracle cure or wonder drug that would take away all disease and pain, but rather that there is still a great deal of life to live and love to give. Time after time we learned that many people do their finest human things after they had been diagnosed with a terminal illness. Things like building or rebuilding relationships, understanding what is important in life, and often writing beautiful insights into life on the edge while coping with disease. Yes, it is important to believe that the medical treatment will have some beneficial effect, but more important is the knowledge that there is still much of life to live.

The third element was a bit more difficult to define. It is perspective. There will be good days and bad days and the final illness of most of our lives is only a small portion of our lives. We are all terminal when you think of it. Keeping things in perspective helps avoid the illness from completely consuming us. Granted, it is sometimes difficult when you realize that the disease is always there, always gnawing away at our lives.

The final element is a sense of humor. Life, particularly when seriously ill, is serious enough and we don't need to take ourselves seriously. Being able to laugh at ourselves has been clinically proven to ease pain and promote healing. It may be as simple as a friendly smile, a twist of phrase, a ridiculous situation that makes us forget for a moment the pain we suffer.

We eventually printed a booklet that illustrated these traits. In fact most of the cartoons in the humor section arose out of my conversations with the cartoonist. Little did I realize that when the booklet rolled off the press that I would be one of the first who would have to put it into practice in my own life. The ink was hardly dry when Jo Ann was diagnosed with cancer.

I know that what the booklet contains has validity. The love between Jo Ann and myself certainly deepened. It became far more sensitive and caring. Her relationship with Rebecca, which was a bit strained at times during high school and college matured into a beautiful mother-daughter love that they clearly enjoyed each others company. She became closer to David than she perhaps ever was. She valued the love of her friends and family much more than she ever seemed to have time for in the past. As a family we embodied a sense of hope, in that we have come to realize a dimension of our lives that includes taking time to enjoy the things that are most important to us. Even with the disease ever in the back of our minds, we were able to keep things in perspective, that this was only a part of our lives and we could not succumb to being pre-occupied by it.

Sometime during the second year of her treatment Jo Ann developed a friendship with Joanna Spiro that has been a godsend. Joanna is a very bright, caring woman who has lived with medical problems for most of her life. She understood Jo Ann's fears and moments of depression and was quick to offer her love and support. Her wild sense of humor brought a chuckle even in the darkest moments, while her strong love gave needed support. What is interesting that they leaned on each other for advice, or merely to have another person who could understand.

Over thirty years of love, and they have been thirty years of growth. I feel that I am a far better person because of the love I shared with Jo Ann. For that I am grateful. We once had visions of growing old together, enjoying a leisurely retirement doing many of the things that we never seemed to have time for. Perhaps that will never be, but we've had a beautiful love, one that enriched our lives immeasurably.

One of our neighbors, in the process of going through his second divorce asked me how we did it. I told him that I really don't know much about love and marriage. I'd been in love with only one woman in my life and been married to her for over thirty years.

The saga of Jo Ann's battle with cancer, her reaching out over the internet to women around the world to console, encourage, comfort and advise is another volume in itself. Even in her last months, when she knew her days were numbered, she thought first of the effect that her disease was having on her family as she continued her courageous fight.

We were fortunate to have some of the finest and most gentle care anyone would expect throughout her illness. When her blood tests showed her cancer was progressing, and that her body could not endure any more chemo, I remember that her doctor embraced her warmly. Not a word was said. There are times when a hug communicates what cannot be put into words. As her doctor turned away I saw tears flowing down her cheeks. I had never seen a doctor cry before.

Hospice and home health care for two months helped ease the final difficult times. Through it all, they were able to manage the pain and provide some comfort in her final days. She remained alert and coherent right unto the end.

She had often said that when her death came, she wanted to die at home, in her own bed, in the arms of the man she loved. The night before she died she asked to sleep in her own bed rather than in the hospital bed she'd used for nearly two months. At 8:00 PM and again around midnight, I called the hospice nurse, fearing the end was near. Finally about 5:00 AM Jo Ann woke me and asked me to help her sit up. She was having trouble breathing, even with the oxygen. She sat up for a few minutes at the edge of the bed, and then asked me to help her lie down again.

I held her and told her "It's OK honey, you can go, but just remember that I love you." She got a little smile on her lips and a twinkle in her eyes, and replied "I love you too." Those were her last words, and her final breath.

Chapter Ten

School Board

When our children were in elementary school, I got involved with their school activities. I attended the parents breakfasts, open house, parent-teacher conferences and was involved with the scouting groups, as well as sports. I went to a few PTA meetings and soon found myself an officer in that organization.

During the 1980's we experienced a decline in student population, beginning with the elementary schools and working upward. We simply had a surplus of operating schools, and some would have to be consolidated or closed. Naturally everyone wanted to preserve the school their children were attending. There were numerous school board forums and meetings and the like, and after listening to the endless babble of parents, I began to open my mouth, and it wasn't long before I had a following.

The first round of consolidations spared the school our children attended, but we all knew there would be another as enrollments continued to decline. I worked on one of the committees to seek alternatives, and we consolidated two small schools into a larger vacant building for a great school. The next big issue was trying to equalize enrollment at our two high schools. Our children would have been re-districted into the high school on the other side of town, driving past one high school to get to one two miles further away. With some support from neighbors we confronted the administration, showing that their census data was flawed and offered more accurate numbers that would better equalize the enrollment. We won the battle, and the School Board and Administration agreed with our argument.

The President of the Board choose not to run for re-election, and after the meeting at which she announced her decision she took me aside and said "You're running for the Board, John."

I won the election for a three-year term, which were probably the watershed years for the district. We hired a new curriculum coordinator and we started improving the curriculum from kindergarten through AP courses in high school.

At my first meeting as a Board Member we had a presentation on the district's health insurance program, with excessive premiums that were getting even higher. I shocked the consultant who was trying to justify the rate increases with a few well placed questions, and then I made a motion that the District seek to self-insure its health and dental insurance plans. We saved about a half million dollars the first year alone.

At one of the high schools we instituted a "Learning Center" where students could go for that extra help they needed, whether it was tutoring for slower students or helping a top level student design a science project or outline a research paper. It was an almost immediate success, and there was never a shortage of teachers and students who wanted to get involved.

I was probably the first Board member who ever visited classrooms in the schools. It was a revelation. Some of the teachers were simply marking time and accomplishing nothing, while others were excellent. I remember one day visiting three different kindergarten classes in different schools. In each room the students were on the exact same page in their letter books. I soon learned that they were the most rigid of all teachers, uniformly throughout the district. We worked to change that. We encouraged innovation and local initiative rather than uniformity. Each school began to develop its own personality and its own style.

Under my prodding, for the first time in its history, the district undertook a long-range planning project that looked at curriculum, facilities, and resources. While most of the recommendations were not immediately enacted, they formed the basis for future planning.

The most controversial issue was the Human Growth and Development (sex education) program. Under directives from the State Department of Public Instruction, each district was to form a committed of parents, educators and community members to evaluate and advise on a Human Growth and Development Program. The state stopped short of saying that the districts had to implement such a program, which was their intent, but they lacked the courage to antagonize the conservatives who were opposed to it.

The committee was a good cross section, with clergymen, teachers, parents and health care professionals. Almost from the beginning they were under fire from several conservative elements whose criticism was irrational and brutal. Sex education was the lightning rod that attracted the religious right's criticism of public education. One of the groups seemed to be centered in one of the activist evangelical churches in the area, but they dragged in conservative Catholics and Lutherans as well. They were fearful that the course would teach abortion as an alternative, and that birth control would be a part of the curriculum and that it would promote per-marital sex among our students.

To add to the controversy, the Minister who was on the advisory committee was charged with having numerous affairs with women from his congregation and was dismissed from his church when the affairs were known.

The extensive program was integrated into the curriculum from kindergarten through high school, with parts taught in health education, parts in science, guidance, and in the regular classroom instruction. It covered a wide range of items including drug use, relationships, health, hygiene and self-respect. We soon found the critics pouring over the materials on display at the central office in minute detail. They were relentless. Nearly every item was challenged and we had to defend it.

I remember one meeting where one group objected to the use of the proper parts of anatomy in the first and second grade materials.

Yes, we used the words penis and vagina, and there were those who thought this was totally improper. A nurse on the committee countered "What shall we call them, your do do and your wee wee?"

The seventh grade materials contained a section with examples of child abuse. Included in examples was "hard spanking." They came out of the woodwork on this one. I was sitting next to a practicing psychologist on the board during one meeting and leaned over and asked her if she was as frightened by these people as I was. She just nodded, and at a break she confirmed my suspicions: these people felt it was their right to abuse their children in the name of discipline.

At another meeting a speaker objected to the whole treatment of physical and sexual abuse in the elementary curriculum. "This is Brookfield," the speaker stated, "it isn't the inner city and we don't have those problems." One of the teachers on the committee shut her down quickly by stating that already in the school year she had to refer five cases in her class to the police where there was obvious physical abuse. And it was only November.

The opposition seemed to be well-organized and different factions united in their opposition. For some reason they were pushing a sappy program used in some of the Catholic Schools called "Sex Respect" which was a program for a few weeks given in High School. I viewed it and nearly threw up it was so insipid. It was heavily advertised in the conservative talk shows and TV programs, as well as print media targeted at the conservative religious. I wondered how much the advertising dollar influenced some of the people who hawked the program. It reminded me of my seminary training, where we never talked about sex except to say that it was sinful outside of marriage.

The same group brought a busload of high school kids from Sheboygan who had used the program and had the kids giving testimony to how the program was affecting their lives and how they were counseling their peers in the abstinence based program.

There used some weird buzz words such as "secondary virginity" which meant the girl wasn't having sex any more. I can't imagine many kids wanting to tell their classmates that they were no longer virgins, but that they weren't having sex any more. Districts that signed on with that program soon dumped it because it was so badly perceived by the kids and didn't address the problems of unprotected sex and relationships.

What made the group's criticism even more ludicrous is that prior to our developing a comprehensive program, sex education was done by the PTA with a program for the fifth and sixth grades every other year, held in the evening, generally with a physician and a nurse, with a film shown. It was voluntary and parents had to attend with their children. It was a totally inadequate as parts of the information were too late in the lives of the kids and other parts were either not addressed, or far too early for them to comprehend it.

It was an interesting year for School Board meetings, in that we would regularly have a couple hundred people at a meeting and some times we had to hold the meetings in a school gymnasium.

Our opponents on the project were well organized, and all the Board members were flooded with letters and phone calls. At meetings other Board members complained about the dozens of phone calls they were getting each day. I couldn't understand it, but I was getting only a very few. One day I got a call from a woman who lived on the north side of the city. She asked me if I was the Mr. Schmitz on the School Board. I said "yes" and she went on to explain that she was getting my phone calls about sex education. Apparently the opposition group sent out a flyer and asked people to call their Board members. They had my phone number wrong, and some poor little lady was getting all the calls. I got her address and had a florist send her flowers.

At one meeting the group brought a young priest from Elm Grove who spoke about how terrible the whole idea of sex education in school was and that it was probably sinful and this should be the prerogative of the parents to teach their children at home. I had enough and decided to answer the man directly. I ripped him to shreds with arguments from Scripture, from Thomas Aquinas, as well as a host of other Catholic theologians. I demonstrated that the relationship between man and woman was the most sacred human experiences and that we didn't need our local priests to try to attach guilt to every human experience that people could enjoy. The poor guy never showed up again. Most of his supporters disappeared as well. They were the core of the Elm Grove Pro-life activists. They didn't want to challenge me again.

The Board accepted the program on a 6-1 vote and the program was implemented. It was cited by the state as one of the finest Human Growth and Development programs in the state.

Our next great challenge came when Dr. Goedken, the superintendent, asked to take early retirement after many years in the district. We went through a national search for a superintendent, and interviewing candidates was something of a blast. One man appeared quite personable, but seemed to be willing to say anything to get the job. When we met his wife, it was obvious he was not the person we wanted to lead our schools. She did all the talking for him. We finally settled on Dave Cronin from Iowa. He was an agent of change and stayed with the district for four years, when a new board decided on a change. This was after I left the Board. Dave later obtained a superintendent position in a smaller district in Waukesha County, and has been there since.

I remember the two days we spent on a site visit to the district in Iowa where Dave had been superintendent for many years. We spoke with Board members, administrators, and others in the district. A team of us went off to visit one of the elementary schools. Some of us met with teachers, some met with the principal, and one team member who was an elementary principal back in Brookfield wandered off and spoke to the janitors. After our visit we caucused to share our findings. The guy who chatted with the janitors was the one who knew what was going on in the building and the district.

As with every organization, one of the most difficult problems is what to do with that employee who is incompetent but is convinced he/she is doing an outstanding job. We had that with Ruth, who had been in the curriculum office in the district years before. When one of the principals was found to have a scandalous affair with one of his teachers and was relieved of his duties in the middle of the year, Ruth was assigned to fill in as principal for the rest of the year. This was the same year when we closed several schools and had a surplus of principals, so when the school year ended, a man who had more seniority was appointed principal.

Ruth charged discrimination and filed a lawsuit to keep her position. The truth of the matter was that the central office and faculty at the school thought she was incompetent, and didn't want her. However, under threat of a lawsuit, the superintendent, Ron Goedken, made an agreement with her that she would get the next open principal position in the district. It was a horrible mistake and done without a great deal of thought or consultation. But at the time the district did not have a single woman principal. It was an old boys network.

In some of the shuffling, the opening was at the largest elementary school in the district. She was an absolute disaster. Yet each year when it came time to renew contracts she verbally told the administrators that she was going to retire. But when the deadline passed for notification of non-renewal, she changed her mind, or she was absent from the building so that the proper notification would not be delivered to her.

Finally, I called Dave Cronin and advised him that the Board was in agreement on non-renewal, and that she was not to be trusted to keep her word to take retirement. He delivered her notice personally several days before the deadline.

Of course, Ruth wasn't about to take this lying down. She rallied support among the parents from the school, and divided the faculty into those who supported her and those who feared her. She filed for a suit asking for a public hearing on the non-renewal. For three Saturdays in a row we filled the largest room at the administration office to hear testimony for and against non-renewal. She had manipulated some of her faculty and some parents into supporting her. I wondered as I listened if the people defending her really knew what was going on or had simply been convinced by Ruth that the administration and board had it in for her because she was a woman.

I had been to several meetings with Ruth in attendance, and one thing I remember is that she was constantly writing on her yellow pad throughout the meeting. I would have liked to sit next to her or behind her to see what she was writing, but that pen was always on the move. The personnel files in the administration office on Ruth filled an entire bookshelf on her refusal to implement district policy or to even cooperate with the administration on staffing, curriculum and fiscal management of her school. One of the weird things she did was to charge onto the playground because of an anonymous complaint of a parent of fighting during recess. She lined up all the Afro-American kids and marched them into the gym where they were made to sit against the wall during recess each day.

Anyway, after all the testimony was heard, I made the motion to non-renew and it carried. We eventually negotiated a settlement, which was less than what she would have received in a retirement package if she had simply retired. And she had to give a large portion of what she got to her lawyer. I heard from someone after the affair was settled that she fully intended to remain as principal until she was at least age seventy.

We worked hard on negotiations with the Teacher's Union while I served on that committee. We approached it not from an adversarial stance, but rather in a cooperative environment that we would work for the best of all concerned, students, tax papers, and teachers. It started with some serious problems: elementary teacher planning time and health insurance for early retirees. The first we settled with a shortened day once a week that could be used for in-service and preparation time. The second issue proved to be a stickler.

We were at an impasse, almost ready to go to arbitration. I insisted that we have one more meeting to see if we could solve that problem. When I asked a couple questions, everybody understood the problem. Teachers who took early retirement often had some health problems that prevented them from obtaining private insurance, and they were years away from Medicare. I simply asked: " Is it a question of the district paying for health care, or simply access to health insurance?" The answer was access. We settled the contract ten minutes later. I knew that since we were self-insured it was an easy thing to continue our retirees as long as they paid the premiums.

My years on the Board were somewhat turbulent, but nothing like the years after I left when a new regime attained control. I was glad I wasn't there during the battles that ensued.

Not that we didn't have fun. After Board meetings we would often settle in one of the nearby bars for a pitcher of beer and conversation.

It was during these sessions that I acquired my reputation among the educators in the district for my memory of limericks. We would trade them back and forth, and I was always the winner. Most of them were even clean, but clever. Some of my favorites:

> There was a lady up in St. Paul
> Who wore a newspaper dress to the ball
> The dress caught on fire
> And burnt her entire
> Editorial, sports page and all

> How about the young Grecian artist named Phydias
> Whose artistry was invidious
> Till he carved Aphrodite
> Without any nightie
> The result was rather fastidious

> A most marvelous bird is the pelican
> His mouth can hold more than his belly can
> He can hold in his beak
> Enough for a week
> But I'd be darned if I know how the hell he can.

One night I think I went on for nearly an hour without repeating myself. One thing that our Board achieved that few others have been able to claim: we were selected as the outstanding school board for the state of Wisconsin. I accepted the plaque in La Crosse where the School Principals had their annual convention.

At the elections for a second term in our area there were three candidates running for two seats. I knew from the agenda that it was going to be a rough few years ahead. A facilities plan was going to require massive building and remodeling. We'd gone just about as far as we could with some of the buildings. We needed to upgrade both high schools and begin implementing some of the strategic planning that had been done the year before.

I was busy at my job and traveling quite a bit, and it was a strain to juggle school business with my job. I really did not have the time or energy to get into an aggressive campaign. I also knew that one of the candidates running against me would probably win, and would be very disruptive on the Board, a premonition that proved accurate. Linda apparently had the backing of the conservatives and the Christian

Coalition group in the area who had their own agenda on disrupting the public schools, and I was the butt of much of the opposition to the opponents of sex education and the non-renewal of the principal.

I did not campaign extensively, and lost the election by a few votes. Actually I think I came out a winner as the other Board members went through a horrendous three years that resulted in two failed referendums, terminating the superintendent, spending nearly $200,000 to buy out the last year of his contract.

After I wrote a letter to the local newspaper reflecting on the election.. It was a great love letter to Jo Ann and all the evenings of absence she contended with while I was on the Board and looking forward to spending more time with her and my family, thanks to the voters of the district. Several months later, Jo Ann was in to see her doctor, Doug Bower. In her file he had a laminated copy of the letter. I guess it was probably the most read love letter of the year in this area. I have included it here.

Public Forum:

"Shocked and disappointed in the election, at age 54 I decided to have an affair. I sought out the companionship of a long-time woman friend.

A cup of decaf coffee at McDonald, hers with cream. She noticed a tear well up in my eye and leave a telltale track down my cheek. Our hands touched across the table. No words were needed, as her gentle touch told me it would be all right.

We went for a walk in the spring evening. I saw a bluebird near the golf course and wondered if it was nesting in one of the boxes put out by people who care about them. We saw a few daffodils and noticed trees budding with the promise of spring. We walked a long time with few words, but with volumes of emotion. I was in love again.

We talked about the future, Tuesday night movies at the cheap seats instead of School Board meetings, weekends for something other than reading volumes of material to prepare for a Tuesday meeting. When the phone rings, its probably someone selling lawn care or soliciting funds for some noble cause, or maybe a friend.

She suggested I might take up painting. Start with the living room, then a bedroom, kitchen and bath: things that were neglected while I was concerned with education.

We talked about sex and I noted that now the Human Growth and Development had brought it into the classrooms, some teachers had undoubtedly found a way to make it boring. There are better ways to learn some things than doing work sheets. But then I have always thought learning should be enjoyable.

Our walk ended with a reassuring and loving hug. Twenty-one years, and I love that woman for every one of them, especially the one ahead.

Thanks to the people of Elmbrook for the privilege of serving them for three years, and thanks to the voters for making this new fling possible. My wife Jo Ann and I intend to enjoy it to the fullest.

John J. Schmitz

Brookfield

On my wall I proudly display plaques and letters of appreciation for my service to the School District of Elmbrook. When I look at the achievements of the district, I know that I had a hand in laying the foundations for much of the good education that has taken place here. I also proudly handed the diplomas to both my children at their high school graduations.

Chapter Eleven

Insurance Business

During thirty years in the insurance business, I worked as an agent, assistant manager, manager, regional vice president, home office director of agencies, educator, consultant, independent agent...and along the way I met some interesting characters.

I was the last person hired by George, a gentleman of a manager for Mutual of New York. The first agency event I attended was his retirement party, but George continued writing life insurance until a few weeks before he died at age 89.

As assistant manager, I hired the first woman agent in the agency. She was young, bright, and attractive, having been one of the finalists in the Miss Wisconsin Pageant a few years before. Shortly after I hired her, George called me to his office one day for a cup of coffee and began relating that he had hired a woman when he was a manager in Oregon, and how after sales calls, she would ask him to tell her how she did on the appointment. First the conversations would take place in the car, but then she invited him into her apartment and made a pot of coffee. Well, George said, he had to let her go because he didn't want to get involved. "Now John, what would you do in a case like this?" he asked.

"Probably the same thing you did" I replied, "but I wouldn't lie about it afterward." He never brought the subject up again. In reality, George was one of the most honorable gentlemen I met in the business.

Jimmy and I shared an office for about six months. He loved to drink and chase women, frequenting some of the seedier bars around town but convincing his wife that he was out on appointments every night until nearly midnight. Jim was also a chain smoker, who never seemed to have matches.

I belonged to the Jaycees in Kenosha and one member in Kenosha delivered Pepsi to the area bars and supplied the Jaycee clubhouse with matchbooks from some of his customers, among them the topless bars in town. One night I filled my pockets with some selected matchbooks. When Jim asked for matches, I tossed him a book and he put them in his pocket. At night he emptied his pockets on the dresser and his wife found them the next morning. He had a lot of explaining to do.

"Skinny," who was the manager during my years with MONY was a work of art. We could tell whenever he went to a class or meeting, he would come back with a catch phrase and that was all we would hear until he went to another meeting. I remember his going to a regional manager's meeting where someone described his management style as a "prick with a smile." I did notice that Skinny smiled a lot more for a while. The rest of it we already knew.

With an antiquated phone system, each agent was charged for his long distance phone calls. We were supposed to keep a log of them, and hand them in to Skinny's secretary at the end of the month. She'd spend a couple days sorting through all the calls and charge each agent who made them. If there were unclaimed calls, she'd send a list around and hope somebody owned up to them. If no one claimed them, she would phone the party and inquire as to who might have made the call. Some times these could be interesting. One of the agents owned a motorcycle and was trying to sell it. He had it parked in the lot next to the building with a "for sale" sign on it and his phone number. I had been in Kenosha a few days before and wrote a policy on a lawyer in town. He gave me his card, and commented that his number was similar to a massage parlor on the state line, and he was getting calls for them. Having lived in the town, I knew the state line area had a 694 prefix, while the lawyer's was 654. When I saw Jim's cycle for sale, I put a little note on it and said I was interested, leaving the phone number of the massage parlor. Apparently Jim made a call to that number, but since it was a joke, he never wanted to claim it. The sheet of unclaimed phone calls made its way around, and nobody claimed it. So Marian picked up the phone in her office, which was just around the corner from mine, and called the number to find out who might have placed the call. I only heard half the conversation, but it was hilarious.

"Well, one of our agents called this number. Is there anyone there who might have been contacted by one of our agents? Can you tell me the names of the people who work for you, maybe that would help?" She just couldn't let this one go. No one ever claimed the call, and Skinny ended up paying perhaps a quarter for the call.

Skinny would use a green felt tip pen to sign memos and write personal notes to the agents. Usually if an agent got a green note, it was something Skinny wrote without thinking. Dan was a good agent, but spent of time at the hospital with his father who was dying of cancer. His dad passed away, and the funeral was on Saturday.

Monday, Dan came back to the office, and the first thing he found in his mail box was a "green note" from Skinny, telling him it was about time he got off his ass and started working. Dan left the agency, never writing another piece of business for the company.

Reading the applications of agents was always a trip, particularly if they didn't know how to spell. I remember Dan's applications on women. He never failed to mention that the woman had had a "Pabst smear." I never corrected that. I thought the underwriters deserved a good laugh now and then.

We had an interesting assortment of agents. Bob had been with the agency for a half dozen years when I came there. He would spend most of the day with a yellow legal pad writing notes to his policy owners or "orphan" policy owners bringing them up to date on their policies. He wrote them out longhand and would then mail them out. He never bothered to call any of them, and his sales were dismal. He used up more yellow legal pads than the rest of the agency combined. In fact, the office staff used to hide them so he couldn't get his hands on them. Finally, after years of futility, he left the agency. I heard from some of his friends that his family was destitute. He was hardly making enough money to put gas in his car. This was a textbook case of the cruelty of allowing an agent to continue when he / she is obviously never going to be successful. I worked on the principal: "When faith turns to hope, financing becomes charity."

Bill was another non-producer. He'd been in business about twenty years and I doubt if he ever made a living at it. He was a devout Christian Scientist, and when he had a heart attack he went to the VA hospital. He was there for a while, and the doctors put him on medication and sent him home.

Bill went to visit his Christian Science practitioner who told him that it was against his faith to take these artificial medications and that he should put his trust in God. Bill did and less than two weeks later he met his God face to face. I wonder if the Lord asked him why he stopped taking his medication.

One other memory of Bill was the annual awards dinner we had at the Milwaukee Athletic Club. There was an open bar beforehand and a fine sit down dinner. It was usually beef Wellington and for dessert we could expect cherries jubilee, flaming as they brought it to the tables. Each year Bill would ask for something to be made special for him since he could not eat what was the entrée for the evening. If we had beef he would ask for chicken, though on another occasion the beef would have been just fine. I guess it was the one time at an agency event that he could exert some semblance of power – having a special order of food.

Skinny thought he was doing me a favor one time when he recruited an agent for me. Actually he was a referral from someone else, and Skinny just signed the papers and handed him over to me.

One of the first things we do in training is to get the person to make phone calls for appointments. We give them a script, do some role play, tape record a few calls, critique, and then put the agent on the phone with a list of names and phone numbers. We'd give them a sheet to keep score of number of dialings, answers, presentations and appointments. If we had some statistical data on activity and results, we could more easily tailor our training. Well Stu sat down at the desk and started dialing numbers. He didn't seem to find anybody at home. I was in my office and noticed the light on the extension go on, and then it would go off again a few minutes later. I finally checked up on him to see how he was doing. He was in a cold sweat, and kept dialing his own home phone number over and over again. He was afraid to talk to anyone on the telephone. No doubt the worst case of call reluctance I had seen.

Stu had been in the home improvements, siding and carpeting business, and apparently had screwed everybody who knew him at one time or another. So much for building trust in an insurance business!

One of Skinny's quirks was that he always wanted "a good Jewish agent." He had known a few very successful agents who happened to be Jewish and thought if he could just get a Jewish agent that would open the heavens and it would rain money. Every attempt he made to hire a Jewish agent was a dismal failure.

Charlie came from another company, was married with two children. At one time he was much over weight, as was his wife at the time. Then Charlie went on a diet, shed the pounds, got a blow dryer and hot comb for his hair, a prescription to GQ and tried to put on a professional image.

It was common for the agents to stop at one of the bars along Mayfair road on Monday nights after they finished making their phone calls for the night, and occasionally on other nights if they were in the area. Of course, with his new "do" and Gentleman's Quarterly clothes, Charlie was on the hunt.

On occasion he would get interested in one of the women he met at the bar, and if they dated, Charlie would find some pretense to get in a tiff with Kathy, his wife, and move out, back to his parents' house, which left him all the freedom he needed to carry on the affair. Of course, when the woman got to know what kind of a jerk he was under the blow dried hair, and told him to get lost, Charlie would make up with Kathy and move back into their apartment. All the while he would bring his laundry over for her to do. He wore at least two clean shirts each day, as it wasn't proper to be seen in a shirt that had a wrinkle in it.

I remember when he took a few days off to go skiing, and one of the women in the office took a few days off at the same time to make some calls out of town. It was interesting when they arrived back at the office within five minutes of each other a few days later. That romance was hot for a while until Charlie started stalking her.

He took a job with another company as manager, a position I recommended him for. The company had approached me to take over an agency for them. I knew there wasn't much there in way of either business or agency force; I didn't like the contract, nor the products. So I told them I thought Charlie might be available. I owed it to Skinny to stick him one more time without him knowing it. They interviewed Charlie and were impressed with his fine haircut and pressed suit, and hired him. Charlie made his first trip to their home office out east and came back with a new romance: the daughter of one of the Vice Presidents of the company whom he eventually married. Job security? Well, Charlie didn't last very long there, and I remember the clerical office manager of his agency telling me that he certainly did not have the qualifications for a general agent. I already knew that. At long last he divorced Kathy and remarried, as did she.

Some things one never quite learns about the people working for him. During my last year at MONY, there was a group representative in the office who had a part time secretary. Tom lived just a few blocks away from the office, and she had a key to his apartment. She worked half days, and in the afternoons she would entertain the agent callers at Tom's apartment. No wonder my agents always had appointments in the afternoon, but never seemed to show any sales from them.

The agency system was built on "broken promises and stolen renewals." Pressure was put on agencies and agents to get peak production at whatever cost with little regard to ethics. This spawned a host of schemes that were seldom in the best interest of the clients. One of them was to take the dividends from one policy to fund another. This was all right as long as the dividends lasted, which they seldom did beyond a few years, and people were stuck with high priced policies and no dividends. When someone went to a workshop to learn how to use a computer program to fund another policy with cash values from the first, it created a nightmare. Phil, one of the agents, would work out his schemes and even went so far as to help fund the first year's premium with his commissions. Slightly illegal, but nobody bothered to check. The problem was that each time he worked one out, which he did using a hand calculator, he used a somewhat different approach. It created a horrendous service problem.

Another scheme the company came up with was to lend money to pay premiums, first with college students, particularly in the professional fields, and then to business owners. In theory it saved people money since the cost of financing whole life insurance was less than paying for over-priced term insurance the company offered. The client would finance the first year or two and then borrow against the cash values to keep the policy in force. The net result was that people ended up with loans and no insurance in a few years. The agent and the manager had to co-sign the note for the loan. When interest rates rose in the late 70's the program fell apart, and the company found they had a lot of loans they could not collect.

The real corker was an agent from Sheboygan who bought a small printing press and actually printed the standard pages of annuity contracts. On his typewriter, he would type out the specifications of the contract. He'd staple this to the policy pages and application copy and presto, there was an annuity contract. He found a bank that would allow him to open an account in the name of the company (illegal) and pocketed the money. When they finally caught up with him, he had taken between two and three million dollars that they could prove. He spent some time as a guest of the state, with three meals a day, and an hour of exercise in a secure, gated facility.

I had a couple of characters working for me at Paul Revere, where I was manager for five years, taking the agency from dead last in the company to the middle of the top third of eighty-two agencies. The craziest one was Steve, who stretched out at just a shade under seven feet fall. Divorced and on the loose, Steve was always on the hunt. He belonged to several computer-dating services. We could always tell when the lists came out each month. Steve would get the phone numbers and profiles for a half dozen women, but his name would be on as many as fifty lists that the women in the service received. The office phone would begin to ring late in the afternoon, and Steve would be busy having coffee and dinner, and if things worked out well, he'd spend the night, and frequently would move in for a few weeks.

He really had problems. He did not have a place of his own and at times would bunk down in the office over night. He was a compulsive gambler and consistent loser. He was not a very successful agent at the time and certainly lacked charm.

One day, after learning that he had not only moved in with a girl he met through a dating service a few days before, but that she also lent him money, Dolores, our collections clerk and mother of ten, shook her head and asked, "I wonder what those women see in him?"

"Well, Dolores," I replied, "You know he's about seven feet tall. Did you ever think that other parts of his body are in the same proportion?" She blushed and never mentioned it again.

Among my friends in the business was Chuck, who managed an agency until his retirement, for Bankers Life. When he retired I helped clean out the conference room in his agency one Saturday morning. There were several bookcases filled with various books on insurance subjects. Looking at them, there was volume after volume with a bookmark some fifteen or twenty pages into the book. If there were notes in the margins, they followed a similar pattern. After some thought, I surmised what had happened. If he went to a meeting and a book was for sale, he would buy it and put it on his agency expense account. Since the company owned the book and he had to provide an annual inventory of property, he didn't know how to get rid of it, even though he would read only the first chapter or two. So he just stacked them up in the conference room.

I did some training work for an agency called the Defender Agency. Their selection of agents left a lot to be desired. I used to say that they had the statue of liberty in the entrance" "Bring me your poor, your downtrodden, your huddled masses wanting to be insurance agents..." They had one guy who probably hadn't had a shower since the last time he got caught in the rain. Despite all the training, this guy wasn't going to be anybody's insurance agent.

One of the craziest hires was "Wild Bill." When Bill came in for his interview, they hired him on the spot, but one of the owners took him to a barber shop for a hair cut, and stopped at a department store to buy him a belt to hold his pants up. The guy was all mouth and set to argue with anyone at any time. Because of his shoddy business practices there were soon claims filed against the agency's errors and omissions (E & O) insurance. Wild Bill soon became known as "E & O Bill." A few years later the owners of the agency discovered he was gay, and sent him packing.

The agency itself was a work of art. With about fifteen agents, they had several companies to place business with, but their loss ratios and lack of production was such that they would lose companies almost as fast as they could get contracts.

This was a time of high interest rates, and the agency made a practice of all initial checks payable to the Defender Agency rather than to the company. They would then put the funds in a money-market account until the last possible day to pay the companies, and pocket the interest, and sometimes "robbing Peter to pay Paul."

They were evicted from their office building on Greenfield Avenue because they weren't paying the rent. So they moved to Park Place, a new high-rise office building where the landlords gave them six months free rent. They never paid after that either.

The boys ran into trouble when they started offering certificates of deposit to investors who would lend them money to finance commercial insurance accounts. There were several problems: first of all, they had few if any commercial accounts that needed financing; secondly, the state required a license for financing premiums; and third, they spent the money either on agency expenses or for their own accounts and while people were getting their interest, it came not from insurance clients, but rather from additional people who were duped into the scheme. When the scheme fell apart, the two partners were indicted and convicted of fraud. Last I heard they were selling used cars.

Of course, being in a business where you meet a lot of people, you're bound to come across some interesting situations and memorable characters as clients and prospects. I remember whenever Skinny would get a phone call from someone wanting to buy insurance, he would come to one of the agents and think he was doing them a great favor by giving them a lead for a good prospect. We also sold health insurance at the time, and I remember he gave me a lead on some people who wanted to buy health insurance. My first question when I called the man was "When did you find out that your wife was pregnant?"

On another occasion he gave me a lead on someone who lived in the inner city. I set the appointment for about 9:00 AM and when I arrived, I found about twenty or more people lying on the floor all through the house. It was the gathering of relatives from all over the country. Grandma was dying, and they wanted to buy some life insurance. What they really wanted was someone to pay for her funeral.

For a few years I was getting the names of everyone who was leaving the military in the southeastern part of the state. This was when the Viet Nam war was winding down, so there were dozens of them each week. I bought the names from some guy in New York who I found out later was paying someone to steal the names off the military computer. I usually got the name and address of the person before they even arrived home. I did quite a volume of business converting their GI insurance to personal policies. However in many cases these people were still looking for work. As the war wound down, we were also in a recession that would last for a couple years.

I sold some of the names to other agents to make a bit of spending money. On weekends I would look up the phone numbers on mine, and on one occasion I included some of the names with phone numbers on those I sold to one of the agents. A week later Joe came to me and asked if I had more names. He only wanted those with phone numbers. He was too lazy to look them up himself.

I remember going to Green Bay with an agent who needed help putting together some business insurance. The two partners wanted a buy-sell agreement so that if one of them died the other would have the money to buy the business. We were to meet the two men at a home along the Bay. When we arrived, I noticed some frilly lace underwear hanging on the line in the yard. One of the partners was a male stripper. The other I soon discovered had owned a strip joint in Racine years before and left Racine when one of his gay partners embezzled a ton of money and he lost the bar. They told me they had an entertainment-booking agency. I knew that Teddy the stripper's business partner, had been in that business after losing the bar, working in Milwaukee. The main act that they booked was David, the male stripper.

We took the applications, with Teddy weighing in at about 275, I knew that policy would be rated. In a week I had it in my hands and we delivered it. With David's application we had trouble getting the underwriter to issue it. The company tried to give every excuse in the book. I guess from their inspection report they learned his real occupation and suspected that he was gay, which was the truth. I called the underwriter and asked what the problem was and got a pile of garbage run-around. I asked the underwriter point blank if he wanted a blood test. He mumbled something. I then said that at the time in Wisconsin the law did not allow for blood testing for AIDS and that what he was doing was illegal since the State law prohibited discrimination on the basis of race, color, creed, or sexual preference. I then said that I would have to inform my prospect that the company was engaging in illegal discrimination based on sexual preference and that he had a right to sue the company. Three days later the policy was on my desk.

I delivered the policies and several months later I read in the paper that Teddy had been arrested. It seemed that they were also running a string of massage parlors throughout the Fox Valley and that their main business was adult bookstores and prostitution through the massage parlors. Teddy did a stint in prison but the policies stayed in force.

On another occasion I met with a dentist who replied to a mailing about disability insurance. He gave me the creeps as soon as I met him. We never did make the sale. A couple years later I read that he was convicted of molesting his patients, particularly small boys, whom he would sedate in his back office. He did some time in prison also.

I also called on a young attorney to try to sell some disability insurance. I made my presentation and compared our policy with the one that was offered by the State Bar Association, which he had. We ended the conversation about twenty minutes later without a sale. I left a proposal with him including my comparisons. A few days later I received a bill in the mail from the attorney for "consultation about disability insurance." I sent it back to him with a nasty note, copy to the State Bar of Wisconsin. Never heard from him again.

On another occasion I had called on a lawyer at least a half dozen times. His secretary would take my card back to her boss in the back of the office. Each time the answer would come back that he was in conference, or could not see me at the time and I should come back later.

One day I was in the area, and tried a different tack. I knew the secretary by name at this time, so I told her that I was completely out of business cards, and I knew that her boss must have at least a dozen of them on his desk. Could she please see if I could get some of them back? She disappeared and returned a few minutes later with her boss who was just chuckling at the ruse. He hadn't heard that approach before. He became a client that day.

I called on an acquaintance, a former nun, who lived in an apartment on Milwaukee's east side. We were filling out an application for insurance when there was a knock on the door of the apartment next to hers. She quietly told me to shut up and listen. Things would get interesting.

We heard some giggling as the door closed. A few minutes we heard a squeak, squeak, squeak as apparently there was a roll out bed. Within minutes we heard more squeaking and then the grunts and screams of orgasm. She told me this goes on several times each day. I wondered what kind of shock this had to be to a woman who had recently left the convent.

Another person I had as a client taught a Catholic school in Kenosha. He was the only male on the faculty and very popular with the kids and their parents. I found him to be quite a creative person interested in the kids. When he left the school at the end of the year and moved to Milwaukee, I wondered what happened. A few months later I saw him on the news. He was the local spokesman for the gay community on some issue or the other. I wonder how the people who had kids in the parish school reacted to that news.

One of the companies I worked for had a program for people in the military. I met some interesting characters through that program. I called a lead I got one day, and the guy told me I should come down to the ship which was in the harbor that day. I got directions and when I arrived, I had to be "piped aboard," which meant identifying myself and the person I was to see, permission was given and I was escorted aboard. I didn't know that the person I was seeing was the captain of the Westwind, an ice cutter that was stationed in the Great Lakes during the winter. I wrote the policy in a few minutes, and then the Captain gave me a tour of the icebreaker. It was an interesting ship to say the least. I learned that the ice breakers have a complex system of pumps that move water around the ship to keep it pitching front to back and side to side so that it is always in motion when in ice floes.

With most insurance agencies, sales contests are a big part of the routine. I remember an agency for Mutual of Omaha had a new manager who got the idea to have each of his agents tell him what prize they wanted from the contest and they'd negotiate the production he or she would need to get that prize. One of the young agents told him he'd like to spend an evening with a hooker. They agreed on the terms. The agent met his quota for the contest and the manager somehow found a girl for the night for the agent. The only problem was that everybody knew about it. The manager was gone within a week.

One of my agents once worked for another company in Chicago. They had a December contest each year in which each agent would pledge the amount of business they would write for the month. If they met their quota, management would deliver the policies for them. One of the agents who was a mediocre producer at best came in with a pledge of more business than he had written all year, over a million dollars of life insurance. Every day the manager would look for the applications, and saw none. Finally, just before the agency closed on New Year's Eve, the agent showed up with a stack of applications for life insurance along with the checks for the premium. The manager took one look at the applications and told the agent they could not accept these applications. The men were all members of the Chicago Mafia. The agent looked at the manager and replied, "If you can't get them issued, then you tell them," and walked out. It was the last December contest in the agency.

In another agency, the female office manager was providing some additional services to some of the agents, particularly the big producers. The agency got a new manager, and the woman offered him the same fringe benefits. Rick liked that so much that he moved in with her. Well, that removed a nice fringe benefit from the agents and they simply stopped writing business for the agency, placing their business elsewhere. Six months later he was gone.

You always find a few characters who have to learn the hard way. One of the young agents in the office drove a Buick Riviera, one of the first cars to feature the chrome plated spoke hubcaps. They went for about $75.00 each. The manufacturers had not yet made the inter-locks standard, and he lost one of his. On Sunday he went to the "Seven Mile Fair," a flea market south of Milwaukee, and found someone selling hubcaps. He asked if they had one for a 1970 Buick Riviera with the spokes. The man in the booth looked over his display and said he didn't have one here, but if he could come back in about an hour or so, he would send someone back to the warehouse to get one for him. Two hour later the agent went back to the booth and paid the man $25 for a spoke hubcap. When he got back to his car, he noticed that he had only two hubcaps. I guess he learned where the warehouse was located.

For two or three years we had an annual over-night golf outing at Fox Hills near Manitowoc. We'd have a cocktail party and dinner at night, play a round of golf the next morning and come back home. It was a chance for the agents and their wives to get a night away. It was a good motivator for the agency.

Mike, who would drink a washtub if it was free, had more than his share the night before. He was there with his girl friend of the week, since he seemed to change often at that time. We had an eight o'clock tee time. All of us in the foursome had golfed with Mike before and knew that he had a tendency to under-count his scores on a consistent basis, so we were watching him. He was a good golfer if you let him keep score, but only so-so if he had to count every stroke.

The first hole was a par four, and he took a double bogey. He tried to tell us he had a par. The second hole was a par 3 and he again under counted. The booze from the night before was still keeping him in a hangover haze, and his language with each missed shot was purple.

On the third hole we teed off over water. Mike topped his first shot and it went in the water. Of course he used his favorite Anglo-Saxon word for intercourse and teed up another ball. A mighty swing brought the same results. The same F—— word with a bit more emphasis. He put another ball on the tee, and promptly hooked that one into the woods to the left. Again the F—— word.

Danny, who was also in the foursome, just puffed on his cigar and said "Judy and I did that last night too."

Mike put his driver back in the bag and walked off the course.

Mike's cheating didn't end on the golf course, but extended into a few other areas of his life as well. Skinny supervised him directly and prided himself that Mike was doing so well, better than the rest of the younger agents in the group. Then the complaints began surfacing. Policies had not been delivered, people not even knowing they had applied for insurance, dividends and cash values missing from old policies, wholesale misrepresentation and what not. If Mike wasn't around, they directed the phone calls to me. I kept a careful log, and when I had enough of it I went to Skinny and told him either Mike goes now or I go to the Insurance Commissioner and the District Attorney. Well I got a big lecture that this was not a proper thing to discuss with the rest of the agency since this was going to put him on the spot to do something.

"Precisely" I replied "It's about time."

Mike was history and Skinny sent out a letter to every one of his clients stating that Mike had left the agency and that I was assigned to service their accounts. Within days my phone began ringing. I managed to meet with most of the people and straighten out the messes that Mike had made. There were people who had no intention of applying for insurance but had replied to some questions Mike asked to "just see if you would qualify if we should decide you need additional insurance." He had all the information he needed, completed the application, forged a signature on the bottom, and took the money for premium from the client's old policy.

Skinny and the Home Office were upset that I wasn't "saving" all these policies. How could I? Mike was a crook, Skinny swept everything

281

under the carpet for a couple years, and now they wanted me to convince the people they should go along with his scams. Besides, if I saved the policy, I didn't get a dime for it. But if we returned their money, Skinny would have to eat the charge-back of commissions that had been paid to Mike.

When I began teaching continuing education classes for agents, I got acquainted with a lot of people who knew Mike and many of the others that I worked with. Mike's reputation spread far beyond our agency, as he did the same wherever he worked after that.

When I started in the insurance business, underwriting was very tight, requiring a medical exam by a doctor for just about everything. I remember one doctor we used in Milwaukee who had his office in the Marine Bank Building downtown. Just about everyone we sent to him came back with elevated blood pressure, meaning either a rated policy or a decline. We even went so far as to have his instruments checked and they were accurate.

I had an occasion to take a client to his office one day. He was on about the seventeenth floor, and the examining room was a small niche that looked out through the glass walls. There was a nice view of the lake, but also a nasty look down at the street and rooftops below. Anyone with the least fear of heights would have problems. I never used him again.

We had another doctor in Kenosha as an examiner. About the only thing to recommend him was that we could get someone in to see him just about any time. There was good reason. His office was a disaster, the doctor unkempt and we had people come back to us worried that they caught something just by being in his filthy office.

As assistant manager of the agency, I was responsible for hiring, training and supervising the agents in my unit, which numbered as high as fifteen at one time. During my years with Skinny we'd have our annual awards banquet at the Athletic Club, and he'd hand out awards for everyone who did anything during the year. It was always a fun night, with an open bar, good food and a chance to get out with the spouses of the agents and staff. I know it must have cost a bundle but this was all expensed back to the company. During all these events, I never did receive a word of thanks or recognition from him. It hurt.

During six years as assistant manager of the agency, my unit was always in the top five of some fifty assistant manager units in the region. Not only were my agents good producers, but the business they wrote stayed on the books. The persistency of my units business led the company each year, even ahead of the agency in general.

Someone asked me once why my unit was never number one. I replied that I wasn't willing to do what it took to be number one, namely compromise my ethics. Quite frequently the agents and assistant managers who showed up first on the list were gone shortly after, usually because of some ethical problems. I was never willing to do that.

In the spring of 1978 I attended the regional conference for Assistant managers in Illinois. There I received the first and probably the only, "Grand Slam" award for meeting my quota in new hires, production from new hires, over all unit production and persistency of the business. I came back to the agency on Friday and showed off my plaque and hung it on my wall.

Skinny called me into his office and told me that I "spend too much time reading my own press releases" and that he was going to reassign my top producer out of my unit. I knew his contract and I knew mine. This meant that my income would decrease quite a bit and his would increase.

I argued a bit, but knew that it wasn't worth the effort. He complained that I hadn't hired enough new agents (I had three in pre-contract at that time).

I went home, wrote out a letter of resignation, mailed a copy to the regional office and on the weekend went in and cleaned out my office. I left a copy of my resignation on his desk and another on the desk of the office manager.

The first call I got at home was from Helen, the office manager. She said "I guess this looks like it's final." said "Yes."

She then said I guess you're true to your word. "You always said if Skinny screws with your compensation you'd quit, and you'd do it without warning, and there would be no turning back." She wished me well and offered letters of recommendation if I needed them.

Skinny came in about 10:00 and found my letter on his desk. He spent the rest of his day with his door closed, accepting no calls. Finally at the end of the day he phoned, telling me that he thought my "action was a bit hasty."

I replied that I thought it should have happened long before. He hung up.

Of the fifteen agents I had in my unit at the time, there were three who remained a year later. Soon after Skinny was terminated.

Having worked long hours for at least six days most weeks for the past few years, I was looking forward to a little time before I jumped back into the rat race. Thursday of that week I got a call from the regional director for Paul Revere Insurance. He was coming to town and wanted to meet with me. We met at their office in Bishop's Woods at 11:00, had lunch, and I signed contracts as agency manager, retroactive to the prior Monday, and I was given a plane ticket to Columbus Ohio for the following Monday for orientation.

The agency I inherited at Paul Revere had been without a manager for several months, and was dead last among the eighty-two agencies in the company. When I left there five years later, we were thirteenth out of eighty-two. We marketed disability insurance for professionals, mainly to doctors and people in the medical professions. I left because the company had been acquired by another conglomerate and was consolidating operations. I did not want to be the last rat off the ship. Less than a year after I left, they closed the Milwaukee agency. Paul Revere ceased to exist as a company some time in the early 1990's, being caught up in the corporate acquisitions and mergers that spread through the agency system in insurance. The law protected the public and policy owners, but the ones who paid the price for the corporate horse-trading that went on were the agents and agency managers.

In the early 80's I did some training for an organization that sold limited partnerships in real estate. They would buy apartment houses or office buildings, and they re-sell them as limited partnership shares. The entire set-up was a tax strategy in which investors would put up about 20% of the purchase price of the building, while the rest was borrowed from a bank. The investors would get to write off the depreciation and interest for the entire amount, even though they put up only a portion of the money. I wrote a training program for their representatives and established a life insurance agency for them to go along with the sale of their securities.

I quickly learned that I did not want to invest in any of the schemes. The buildings were often purchased by the principal of the firm, who then sold them to the partnership at an inflated price, and then it was syndicated to investors with as much as 30% going to the person or company who put the partnership together.

Securities laws demanded that there be an inquiry into the suitability of the investment for the person buying it. These were generally fudged or ignored and many people who bought tax shelters had no taxable income to write the deductions off against.

Most of these partnerships generated little or no benefit to the people who bought them. The tax laws on "passive investments" changed in 1982, and people were stuck with shares that would fetch only a small percentage of their original investment. The system was built on greed and promise of tax relief and great profits. The profits came only to the people who put the partnerships together. They paid too much for the properties, anticipating high appreciation rates and hefty tax relief. None of which came true in many cases. Besides, in this case, there was a management company owned by the same people who had a perpetual contract to manage the buildings, including janitorial, maintenance and rental duties. This company seemed to be the only one that profited on an annual basis for the investment.

For a few years I was an instructor for a pre-licensing training school that did "crash courses" for insurance agents to pass the state insurance exams. At the time, applicants were required only to pass an exam to get their licenses. No schooling was required. As a result we often had people in class who had flunked the exam at least once, often several times. It seemed every month for a couple years Roger from southwest Wisconsin would show up in my class. He had failed again. He always knew which question he missed. I tried to convince him that it had to be more than one question. I feared that some day he might be someone's insurance agent.

I remember teaching a course in Green Bay on property and casualty insurance while another instructor did the life and health in another classroom. When we took our first break, about ah hour into the class, one of the students came up and wondered where I was in the book since he was having trouble following me. I looked at his book and saw that he should have been in the life and health class. At noon I had lunch with the other instructor who ribbed me about the fact that a man could be in my class for an hour and not know that he was in the wrong class. The real kicker came when I got back in the room after lunch. I had another student who had the same problem.

Beginning in 1988 I spent four years with Catholic Family Life as superintendent of Agencies. Bill was my boss and probably one of the most inept people in the business. He started as an agent but couldn't cut it there, so he took a job as a brokerage representative for another company. From what I heard, he failed miserably there too. I knew from my first day on the job that I was a threat to him. His management style was strictly inside the box. He took pride in everything being orderly and neat, even if there wasn't much to put in order.

When I came, we had two agents in the entire state of North Dakota, one of whom was yet to produce a single piece of business and the other who had not spoken to Bill for months. Bill showed me a map of the state with lines drawn in to mark out protected territories. He had done the same with Indiana, where he had several non-producers under contract.

There was no system for selection of new agents, no manual for training them, and every new agent hired seemed to be on a different contract. While traveling to agencies around the Midwest, I wrote a General Agent's manual and an agent's training manual in motel rooms at night. We presented them at the meeting for the agents in October. Both of them were landmarks for the company. We had about 15 producers when I arrived. Four years later we had over 120.

I started there in June and learned that there had not been a sales promotion or contest in the five years Bill had been running the show. I surmised since his performance never qualified for a contest prize, so he didn't have much enthusiasm for them. I set out to change that, and ran a theme contest for the month of August, based on the Olympics, which were getting underway. It was a watershed for the agents, renewing their enthusiasm for the company and greatly increased production.

Bill came to me in July and asked me if I could make arrangements for an agents' meeting that he had been trying to get for the past five years. Two hours later I had invitations ready for his signature, a site for the meeting, an agenda for three days and guest speakers lined up. It was a tremendous success.

Our second contest of the year took a new twist. Talking with some of the support staff in the Home Office, they wondered why we gave prizes and stuff to the agents while the people in the Home Office simply got more work to do. I agreed, and we structured the contest differently. Each agent would be paired with someone in the Home Office, and if the agent won a sales prize the Home Office partner won the same. It succeeded beyond expectations. The Home Office people pushed their agent partners so hard that we had the best year end production in the history of the company.

Each contest we ran had a theme, and I would do some research on the theme. Progress reports would include information gathered from my readings, so the people got into the spirit of the contest very easily. We did one on the Olympics, one on football, basketball, baseball, the circus, Kentucky Derby, and a cute one on fireworks. This one started on the Fourth of July, and to announce it I found some red mailing tubes. We cut a short length of cord and made it look like a fuse. The contest materials were mailed inside the tube. Cute and effective. What was normally a dull month turned out to be a bonanza for sales.

With the spring contest, we sent a note around to the staff telling them that we would be providing lunch on a certain day. We brought a couple grills and did a cookout in the parking lot. A few brats and burgers and a pot of baked beans, a few desserts; everyone appreciated it, and had a good time. I never had problems working with other departments. However, it did create a lot of jealousy with my boss Bill.

While Bill appeared on the surface to be a paragon of virtue, he pulled some things that were unconscionable. The Knights of Columbus, as it has been for years, was a strictly captive company, and didn't allow its agents to be contracted with anyone else. Bill solicited many of them and had them contracted and licensed under assumed names. In one case the business went under the name of the Knight of Columbus agent's wife's maiden name. She never saw the insured, had nothing to do with the transaction and the company accepted the business in her name, even knowing that she was not the producer. For some reason Bill thought recruiting Knights of Columbus agents was the answer to all his problems. They were fraternal agents with some experience, licensed and were supposedly trained. In retrospect, they seldom turned out to be producers and in most cases we spent a lot of money on somebody else's problems.

However The Knights of Columbus were not without fault either. One of the agents Bill had contracted wrote a policy on a priest who was chaplain of the local Knights of Columbus Council. The priest had heart problems and was uninsurable. So the general agent took the physical exam for him and the policy was issued. One of the men in the agency got wind of it and complained to the head of the sales department for the Knights. The matter was hushed up quickly. The general agent in question caught the Home Office guy in bed with someone else's wife at a convention the year before. Home office wouldn't dare take any action against him.

A real ethical breach at Catholic Family came from the top producer who would tell a client anything to get her hands on the money. In one case she convinced a couple that they should take out a mortgage on their home with Catholic Family and put the money in a Universal Life Policy. The mortgage would be tax deductible, and the money in the Universal Life would grow income tax free. It sounded good. A 7% mortgage that was tax deductible and 10% interest on the Universal Life policy income tax free. What she didn't tell them was that there was a 6% load charge on the premiums of the life insurance policy and that there were mortality charges. The man wasn't in perfect health, and the mortality charges were more than double what was anticipated. And a few months later the company reduced the rates they were paying on Universal Life policies and they paid only 4% on the first two thousand dollars. When the man got his annual report, he saw that he was losing money instead of making money. He was irate to say the least.

Rather than admit the client had been lied to, and return his money, Bill tried to defend Ida, the agent, for nearly five years as the case dragged on. It finally ended up in a lawsuit that made the headlines in the newspaper and Ida retired on disability. The publicity of the case opened the floodgates and many other cases unraveled as people complained; the company's sales in the area plummeted.

About two years after I left there I happened to see Bill's monthly sales bulletin. He wrote a column on the state of the agency, with some motivation intended. This one began with ominous words. "This is the worst month we've had in five years." Doh!

When the State of Wisconsin started requiring continuing education for its agents, I was contacted by Hondros College to teach classes for them. I have been named their instructor of the year on two occasions, and have conducted the instructor's meetings as well as writing several of the new courses for the school.

The experience put me in contact with a large number of agents around the state, and in a given period every two years, I have had some two thousand or more agents in my classes. There have been some interesting moments.

I had a man fall asleep in class in Eau Claire one year. There were some fifty people in the room, and I continued talking while the guy snored. I instructed the people in the room to get up in small groups of three or four, very quietly and we'd re-convene around the pool area for some small group discussion. I got everyone out of the room and finally walked out, with the man still snoring. About a half hour later he woke up and wondered what had happened. He finally found us around the pool. We all had a good laugh at that one.

I was teaching a class in Madison when a freak February thunderstorm roared through town, knocking down power lines and trees, leaving the hotel in darkness. It was the last day we were having class for the qualification deadline, with a twelve-hour marathon day and we had four hours of class to go. I had about 120 people in the class that day and we were in the basement meeting room. I talked to the manager of the hotel and got a case of candles they used in the dining room. We finished the course by candlelight.

On another occasion I was teaching an evening class to a small group. I noticed a very pregnant woman leave the room for a bathroom trip a couple times the first hour and every few minutes I noticed she squirmed in her chair and became flushed. We took a break and I asked if she was all right. She replied that she was having back pains but she was OK. Back pains hell, she was going into labor.

We called her husband and told him what was happening and I had someone drive home, which was on the way to the hospital. She had the baby about two hours later. I don't know what I would have done if her had water broken during the class.

Of course, I was not above a practical joke now and then. One of the best was my April Fools' joke that I repeated a few times at various places. I printed up a sign for each of the rest rooms. "Temporary Ladies" went over the men's room, and "Temporary Men's" went over the ladies sign. It was interesting to see the confused look on people's faces as they headed for the rest rooms, turned around and walked away. It only worked well when the doors were not visible from each other.

Another of my favorites is to send a series of twelve letters roughly mimicking the twelve days of Christmas to someone who is totally unaware of who might be sending them. I sent them in red envelopes so they were sure to get noticed and read. The partridge in the pear tree is a little bird found in the plant in the lobby… the five golden rings all have "Dutch Master" printed on them, all the way to the entire drum and bugle corps showing up for the last day. I remember doing this to a good friend who had no idea where they were coming from. I showed up at the office one day and Judy pulled me by the tie into her office.

"You're the one who's been sending these," she pulled out all the red envelopes. "I checked out everybody else I knew, and only you would be creative enough to do this."

I had to admit it and we had a great laugh.

On another occasion I was invited to give an entire two-day workshop for the Fraternal Insurance Agents of California for their annual convention. The first day was for the management people, and the second day included all the agents as well. I started the day with a bit of warm up humor.

"You all know the story of Demosthenes, the Greek orator. He was born with a speech impediment: he stuttered. Every time he tried to talk to people they laughed at him. In his despair and frustration he walked along the seashore, his mind filled with thoughts of how society could be better run. He picked up a handful of pebbles and put them in his mouth and began to speak to the waves. When he finished he threw a pebble into the sea and put the rest in his toga and returned to town. The next day he did the same, and each day after that until they were all gone. When he tossed his last pebble away, his stutter was gone, and he had polished his oratory skills to such an extent that when he went back into Athens he attracted large crowds, and his ideas became the foundation for democracy not only in Athens but also in the western world.

Well, when an agent comes into the insurance business we give them a mouth full of marbles, and each time he sells a policy he can throw away one of the marbles. And when he's lost all his marbles, they make him a manager.

When I came into the business I used to collect business cards from other agents, who were all too willing to give them to me. Some read "agent" and others were "special agents." Others had "district agent" on their cards. One that always intrigued me was the term "general agent." I thought that meant something like a general contractor, a person who could sell all kinds of insurance for all companies.

When I was elected to the School Board, at one of the first meetings we were discussing revisions in the Math curriculum. There was algebra, geometry, trig, calculus, statistics and a course called general mathematics. I asked the superintendent if the General Math course was one that encompassed all the disciplines of math and was meant for the most advanced and gifted students. He looked at me over his "half glasses" with that condescending look that only educators can give and replied "No John, that's the course for the kids who can't make it in the other courses." Now I know what a general agent is. The entire day was a success. The officers of the California fraternal group said it was the finest day of conferences they had ever had.

One of the things that insurance agents have been trained to do for generations is to get referrals from their clients. Generally they are good sources of business, but there is a danger. They tend to replicate themselves. So if you have low-life clients, the referrals will tend to be no better. But even then there are surprises.

I got a referral for health insurance from a client who was working for a car-rental agency at the time. He rented a car to the couple and they asked if he knew anyone who could get health insurance for them. He gave them my name and number.

I made the appointment and asked a few questions before I presented the proposal. I asked about their occupation and they told me they were self-employed. I said I would need them to be a bit more specific than that. The woman replied: "Let me show you what we do."

She led me into their basement, which contained an assortment of whips and bondage equipment hanging on the walls, along with a couple racks for torture. I said no thanks, I don't think the company will issue a health insurance policy and left. About two years later, watching the news, I saw a woman taken into a police van when the cops raided a dungeon on the north side of town. It was the same couple, busted at last. I called the guy who gave me the name and asked him if he remembered these people.

On another occasion I called on a couple, who were policy owners of the company. The man was being a complete jerk. He didn't have the courtesy to listen to me, but kept pacing around the room. I was sitting on the couch in the living room when I smelled something. I looked down at my feet and noticed I must have stepped in some dog shit on the sidewalk. I knew there wasn't going to be a sale, so I quietly moved my shoe back and forth under the coffee table ahead of me. I was able to wipe all the shit off my shoe in a place where they wouldn't find it for a while. I didn't make the sale but I sure felt good.

In the thirty some years I spent in the insurance industry, there have been a lot of changes. When I started, most of the agents worked for a company that supplied them with office space, fringe benefits, training and assistance. My agent's contract with MONY was titled "Lifetime Contract." It was expected that an agent who joined the company could spend his entire career with that company and indeed many of the richer benefits of working for that company were deferred for many years and heavily favored the most productive agents. As companies merged, were acquired, consolidated and whatever, the ones who suffered the most were the agents in the field. The contracts under which they produced insurance business for their companies simply changed and they had no say in the matter, unless they wanted to quit their jobs. Many companies declared their agents "independent contractors" which meant they paid Social Security taxes as a self-employed business and the company saved their part of the payroll taxes. Yet many of these same companies maintained "captive agent" contracts that did not allow their agents to place business with other companies. Other companies did away with their agency system entirely. A few companies have gone direct marketing, either through advertising on radio and TV or on the Internet.

One of the reasons for curtailing or eliminating the distribution system is the fact that it costs a company more than $1.00 to put a dollar's new premium on the books, when you consider the cost of the underwriting process, agents commissions, and the like. A company actually does not make money on a policy for the first few years. So if that company stops writing new business, it will show a better profit picture in the short run. It's like the storekeeper who doesn't replace his inventory. This particularly happened when companies were acquired by another insurance company, or the current owners wanted to improve the balance sheet to prop up the value of their stock.

During the 1970's companies began assuming higher interest rates for legal reserves which guaranteed that the company would have the money to pay claims when they occurred. There were several factors involved. The higher the interest rate assumed, the lower the premiums

293

would be. Companies traditionally were using anywhere from 2% to 3% interest rates to set their premiums. This kept the premiums higher than needed. If the company paid dividends, some of this excess would be returned to the policy owners. The other factors, such as mortality and company expenses did not change much.

I remember being at a meeting when the company announced that it had reduced premiums on their life insurance policies by about 40%. The agents were dancing on the tables. I told them they had to be crazy. They'd just taken a 40% pay cut and were celebrating.

During the 1970's consumer advocates began publishing comparisons of life insurance and annuity policies. Everybody wanted to look good by comparison. Some companies merely manipulated their math a bit and showed up very good at ten years, but they may have been horrible in nine or eleven years. One didn't have to be a genius to know that. The other ploy was to make outlandish projections for future earnings on the policy's cash values, some even as high as 12% or even 15%, something they knew could not be maintained for a long period of time. The rule was simply this: "We'll promise you anything you want, as long as we can break our promises."

As the competitive climate got hotter, some companies engaged in practices that proved to be the un-doing of their companies. On the one hand, they made investments that were not wise or were even downright stupid. While insurance regulations limited the percentage of a company's assets that could be invested in the stock market, they were free to invest in " fixed assets" such as mortgages and bonds. This included the "high yield bonds" (junk bonds) that were used to finance leveraged buy-outs. While these bonds may have had a higher yield, they entailed much high-er risk. The thinking was that if one or two of these bonds defaulted they would still be safe. What they did not envision was that as some of the bonds defaulted, the rest of the junk bonds were devalued as well, and this put a great deal of pressure on their statutory reserves.

Many of the real estate limited partnerships in the late 70's and early 80's were heavily financed by insurance companies. When the tax law eliminated the income tax deduction for most of these arrangements in 1982, these partnerships were in trouble as investors defaulted on the payments they were expected to make each year. This precipitated crisis not only with insurance companies that heavily invested in these real estate loans, but also had a great deal to do with the collapse of many of the savings and loans around the country. A number of insurance companies in danger of default were acquired by a stronger company, in many cases a company overseas.

In their greed to acquire assets under management, a few companies looked to pension funds as a source of money to manage. To entice a pension they gave guaranteed investment certificates (GIC's) that guaranteed a set rate of interest for a set number of years, generally ten years. Some went to far as to even guarantee that rate for money added to the fund during the term. When interest rates were double digit high, things were fine, but during the mid 1980's interest rates suddenly fell to half of what they were at their peak in the early 80's, and some of these companies were forced to pay the high interest rates on the investment contracts, even though their own earnings were substantially lower.

Another problem was with underwriting. I jokingly referred to the underwriting department as the "sale prevention department." There was a period of a few years when companies were re-evaluating their underwriting practices and taking some risks that they would not have before. One of the tools they used was the contracts with companies that would re-insure the risks. I remember being at a company meeting at which the vice-president of underwriting explained that they had a treaty with a re-insurer that allowed them to bind the re-insurer up to a half million dollars on a policy without the re-insurer having a part of the decision. He went on to say that if anyone had an impaired risk, he could give a standard issue in most cases up to a half million dollars. He'd simply pass the risk off to the re-insurer. They soon lost their re-insurers and went out of business, with another company buying the business.

In the early seventies, the life insurance companies were awash with cash. Changes in policies and distribution systems meant tighter profit margins, and the competitive climate fueled by consumerism lured companies to risky financial practices with the promise of high returns. A quarter century later and some of the proudest names in the industry were subsidiaries of a foreign conglomerate, while others had vanished from the scene completely, their policies serviced by another insurer.

Looking back over the years as agent, assistant manager of an agency, running my own agency for two different companies, working as a regional vice president for another, as superintendent of agencies in the home office, as consultant, trainer, teacher, I guess I have done just about everything in the life insurance business. Yet, just when I want to say nothing will surprise me, someone comes up with a new wrinkle that catches me off guard. I have earned the respect of many in the business. I have hired and trained somewhere around 500 agents for various companies. I have had perhaps ten thousand or more in continuing education classes that I conducted. I like to end these classes with the words that Don Clifton from Nebraska who spent years trying to figure out what it was that made a good agent good. As a platform speaker he was excellent and he began and ended each talk with a little poem.

> Isn't Strange
> That Princes and Kings
> And clowns that caper
> In sawdust rings
> And ordinary folks
> Like you and me
> And builders for eternity
>
> To each is given a
> bagof tools
> A shapeless mass
> A book of rules
> And each must build
> Ere light has shone
> A stumblin block
> Or a stepping stone

Epilogue

When we return from a trip, we sit down and sort through the photos and try to relive the memories of the experience. With a little luck we get the film developed and the pictures sorted in time to get the second wave of memories before the credit card bills arrive. I hope I have shared some snapshots of my life. What was it like?

You really had to be there. Like photos of a landscape they hardly do justice to the emotion of the experience. Has it colored my values and beliefs? Obviously.

I once met an atheist who explained that an atheist is not one who does not believe in a supreme being but rather one who rejects the concept of God that the "theist" believes. I pondered that thought long and hard. I am certain that I no longer accept the "God" that many "theists" believe exists, or the God taught in the Catholic schools of my youth or even the seminary. The concept of God is formed by our experience and values. Are we much better than the ancients who believed that their gods rode chariots across the heavens or threw lightning bolts from the sky in anger? Perhaps, but our concept is still bound by the limits of our own minds and experience.

What exactly do I believe? What exactly do any of us believe? It is far to simplistic to accept what others have said without question. Some of the great tragedies of history have been perpetrated by those who blindly followed the prodding of religious teachers. To sift through the credo of family background, seminary training, service to the Church as a priest and life after leaving the active ministry and say that I do not carry remnants of that experience would be dishonest to say the least.

I recall the training under the nuns in grade school and the priests in the seminary on the subject, that God is the supreme bookkeeper who keeps track of our every action, even our most intimate and fleeting thoughts and judges whether we have sinned or given him glory. Given the immensity of the known universe, to say nothing of what lies beyond the reach of our most powerful telescopes, beyond time and space, it is hardly conceivable that what I do or think or the words I pray at a moment in time will be of great consequence to the power that brought that universe into being.

Is our God one who is moved by our reciting the exact words of certain prayers, or who will reward those who mouth the words of belief or contrition? Is God going to select a small "remnant" from the multitude of the human race to reward with eternal bliss while the remaining humans are untouched by the largess of the divinity? I hardly think so. How does this relate to the concept of a loving Father-God?

Are we to take each single word and verse of the Bible as the infallible and inspired word of God? Even the most ardent "Bible thumpers" pick and choose what they will accept. Most of them eat pork and work on the Sabbath (Saturday) and do not forgive the debts owed them each seven years. These are all Biblical. The Bible was written by believers and for believers, reflecting the culture, beliefs and times of both the writers and the audience to provide a religious framework for the believers of its time. It is also tinted by the language and literary styles when the books were written and every translation seems to have difficulty capturing the subtle nuances that may have been evident to the original readers. Yet it does form a body of solid moral concepts that have universal application. But are we to believe that the development of religious and moral thought ended with the death of the last apostle? Who determined which books would be included in the Scripture? There's some disagreement between Catholics who contend there are 72 books and the Protestants who recognize only 56. There were many more once considered. Our seminary training was founded on the premise that little happened in the development of theology or religious thought since the thirteenth century, or at least since the Council of Trent's restatement of acceptable belief following the Reformation.

What about the Church? Or should we say Churches? The early Christians were not burdened with buildings and mortgages. From the earliest recorded human history men have built elegant structures for their worship of the deity and as cultures change and religions wane most of these ancient structures have fallen into ruin. The question remains as to whether the onus of supporting physical structures has diverted energies from the mission of religion or have the structures become a diversion and eventually leading to the hollowing out of religious conviction among adherents who inherit the problems of supporting a monument to the past? The electronic age has brought a new dimension to religion: the television preacher, against a background of a robed choir and orchestra, with Bible in hand, presuming to speak for the Lord from the Holy Book. It is interesting that seldom do they talk about the real issues in the lives of people, things like poverty, racism, white-collar crime, and corporate greed. One message that is always clear: they need money, lots of money, to continue their ministry - tax deductible money, for which there is little or no accountability once it is received.

It is interesting that God required only Ten Commandments but the body of laws enacted in His name by religious bodies fill volumes, most bearing sanctions of guilt and sin that God is presumed to enforce on the guilty at the behest of Church lawgivers. Catholic tradition has taken one line from the Gospels: "Whose sins you shall forgive they are forgiven and whose sins you shall retain, they are retained" as divine authorization to enact an entire body of rules and regulations, all of which bear the sanction of eternal hellfire. Most of these regulations are an accommodation to the current practice of religious leaders at one time. For example the Lenten fast in its origins was needed to extend sparse food supplies. Celibacy originally was enacted to maintain control of Church lands and titles in noble families in the feudal system of the Middle Ages. It was more about succession of Church lands and titles than about theology or Biblical roots. It continues today to maintain control by the hierarchy and the Vatican, despite the shortage of available and high quality candidates willing to pledge to a life of celibacy as the price of admission to Orders.

It would be naïve to hold that religion and the church is without flaw, just as our own lives by definition are often filled with failures. In our personal lives we have not often institutionalized the arrogance that is typical of religious bodies. Is the world a better place because of the Judeo Christian tradition that has been a part of my life and culture? The answer is a resounding "Yes." Have the religious influences been an important part in the formation of my values and ideals that have shaped my life? Again a firm "Yes."

I have tried to live my life according to high personal standards that recognize the consequences of my actions on those whose lives have touched mine in time and space. When I have finally drawn my last few liters of breath, I hope that my epitaph might be that lives of those I met are better that our paths have crossed, and that my God will be pleased with my efforts.

Poems of a Courtship

1969-70

In the midst of a foggy dusk
I walked along the shore
—alone
The waves smiled in turn
As they angled by and vanished on the sand
—in rhythmic whispers
The distant buzz of traffic,
The groan of a fog horn,
A piercing blast from a passing train,
The bark of a dog,
Shrill laughter of children at play
—broke in upon my mist-veiled world.
And I wanted to fill the world with my cry
And bring a silent peace
To my thoughtful solitude.
But I did not.
A light glowed faintly:
I knew the fog would go
And the sun would warm a new day.
But darkness had come

11 NOVEMBER 1969

The Glow of autumn sun
Drifts lazily through grey-blue clouds
Now and then a flash of warmth
Sets ablaze the multi-colored fall
—but always the chill returns.
The woods annoys me
As it counts my every step
And sends a rustle
Whispering far and wide
I remember how I longed to hear my footsteps
In the tender blades of spring.

CHRISTMAS EVE

—alone
Snowflakes fluffed the blanket of white
in gentle silence
Carols in stereo
couldn't muffle the sounds
of an empty house
Presents beneath the tree
—torn wrappings rolled in untidy balls
and scattered on the floor
An empty glass
another partly filled—
Santas had come and gone
Somehow a miracle happened
there was peace
and joy
I was not alone I knew that somewhere
you were alone too
and wanted to be with me

I share your misery
playing this little game
how I wish we were free
the pain is easier knowing that we will
funny how we try to arrange to see each other
and not have to explain to anyone
and when we're together in a group
we pretend each other isn't even there
and hope no one notices the warm glow of joy
when our eyes meet
when we're able to steal a few minutes together
alone
we're almost afraid of each other
or is it that we know the game must go on
so we go our separate ways
filled with beautiful presence
and wear our separate masks
and wait in pain
until we can be alone again
the little notes, the phone calls just knowing that you care
but there are so many chains to break
we've so many miles to go
and so many tomorrows to prepare for
now there is a crowd wanting to see a game
damn—some day we'll not play this again

17 January, 1970

I see a crowd
and look for you
pretending you're there
—even when I know you're not
because I want so much to have you near.
But when you are
we play this cursed game,
two marionettes on tangled strings
pulled by ever so many puppeteers.
The lines, the gestures,
all in the script we dare not change,
—it would ruin the act
for those who came to see the show.
How I wish the lines would break,
or someone cut them.
We'd be together, you and I
but we're tied still
and the act goes on.
Damn the strings, the puppeteer,
he'll never say the line I want,
he'll never say "I love you."

17 JANUARY, 1969

Monday
Monday —I used to dread the thought
again I would hear the echo
solitary footsteps in the misty darkness
on a road to nowhere
I listened to the distant passing sounds
to know someone was there
somewhere...but where?
And each Monday was like the last
or the next
Another line on a calendar that measured nothing
and if it did
   who cared?
Monday?
Monday! The sun always shines
with the promise of tomorrow
will she call this week?
or send a note signed "love"
will we see each other...
—steal an hour of ecstasy
your lips touch mine
soft and gentle and warm
—strong
Monday! Tomorrow is nearer
Our love stronger
I cannot wait till Monday!

8 FEBRUARY, 1970

Snowflakes wind –driven
Like pellets stung my face.
Gone
The promise of Spring
Cold is more biting
Now the sun
Has warmed with hope
The expected tomorrow
So far way
So uncertain

WINTER, 1970

Michigan Avenue
Six o'clock – snowing
White, then black, adulterated,
Sloshing to the curb under taxi wheels.
People waiting, people rushing.
Neon glows warm
In the cavern of darkness.
The wind cold and cruel
Swirls snow around the corners of my world.
I clutched my coat to my chin
And buried a stinging hand deep in a pocket.
I felt a bead—a handful—
That had been around your neck
Suddenly, I was warm again

19 FEBRUARY 1970

A flower of spring
my love
long unawakened
coaxed
to venture tender shoots
by a sun how here then gone
to return with kinder warmth
a flower of spring
gently brought to life
to grow
in the freshness of warm-chill
and tease
the morning sun
with buds as yet
unopened until
some silent morn
to greet the blushing dawn
with full-fresh bloom
it's spring

SPRING, 1970

Spring
Rays of sunlight
brighten my morning window
Redwing blackbirds
silhouetted
against the dawn-blue sky
cheer
the still freshness.
A robin chirps
playfully
on naked branches.
Day wears on
Clouds steal in
to shroud the sky
And chill returns.
I miss you.

I took a walk
in sun-filled Spring
birds sang in chorus
and hopped and scratched
White-crested waves softly kissed the pebbled shore
remnants of winter's brown and litter
bestrewed the matted grass
—a sprout of green
tulip maybe?
or dandelion? it didn't matter yet
It was life
straining to clutch the sun-warmth
to come to be
to live
to grow
The breeze was pure
and fresh and ever so gentle
I wanted to shout my bubbling joy
and watch all day
this miracle
But then my eye began to blur
and moist
I wanted so
to share it all
with you
A cloud came and I hurried back
to get my coat

23 APRIL, 1970

I saw a bluebird today
—almost in my hand
She sang a lyric cher-wee
And winged away
In graceful flight.
I know not where
But she'll be back
Because it's spring
And not fall

24 APRIL, 1970

A little tear
melts through all bravery
to warm a lonely cheek
And streams its way
in the quiet of the night
as if there were no one
to wipe it away with gentle love
before it is wasted away
in the solitude
of darkness

29 April, 1970

You cut these lilacs
two red
one white
to grace my table
and then you took them
away
And I was happy
for the moment
and the memory
But I missed them

24 MAY, 1970

We laughed about the waves
smiling as they spread upon the sand
and playfully splashed the rows of ice
that outlined white along the shore.
I tried to put together a few words
to make some sense
—and didn't!
You being there
—so warm and close
quiet-relaxed

you said a lot—but few words
they didn't matter
Your lips met mine
—a moment too brief
so filled with desire
that was tender and gentle
but strong
I love you
The groundhog
 didn't see his shadow
—But it is still
 a long time till Spring.

2 FEBRUARY, 1970

Today
I touched a leaf-bud
it was hard
protective
preparing yet for spring
I thought to pick it
but did not
spring will come
it will unfold
its beauty
in time
I will wait